LINCOLN AND THE ILLINOIS SUPREME COURT

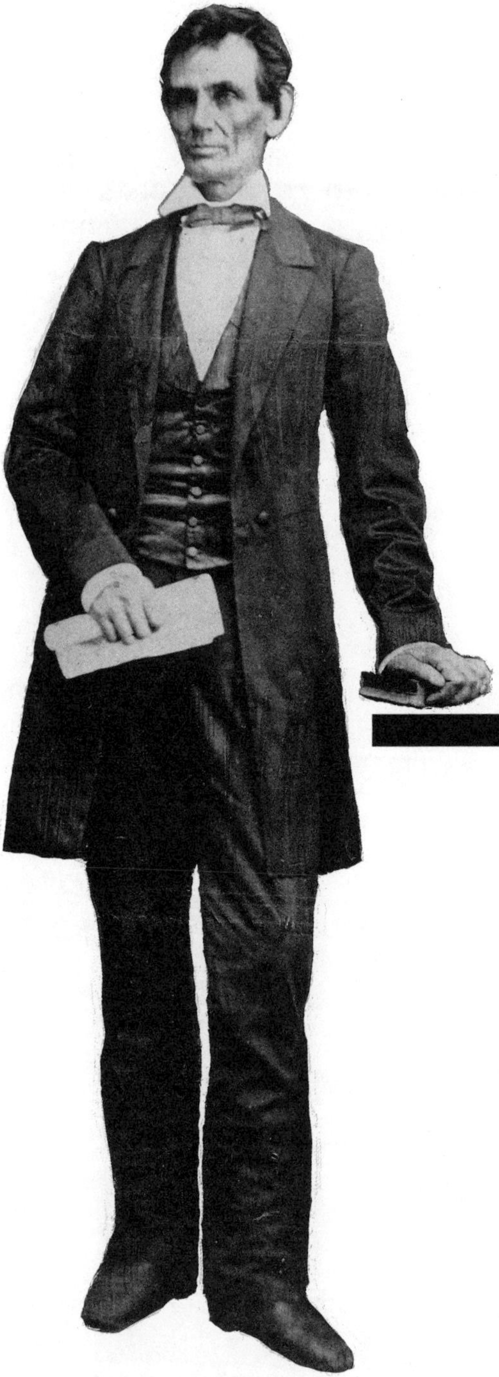

LINCOLN AND THE ILLINOIS SUPREME COURT

Dan W. Bannister

Edited by
Barbara Hughett

1995
Springfield, Illinois

Frontispiece: Lincoln photo from the Lloyd Ostendorf Collection.
The three original Illinois Supreme Court justices, from old engravings (left to right): John Dean Caton, Lyman Trumbull, Samuel Hubbel Treat.

Also by Dan W. Bannister:
Lincoln and the Common Law (1992). Human Services Press, P.O. Box 2423, Springfield, Illinois 62705

© Copyright 1994 by Dan W. Bannister

Published by Dan W. Bannister, 22 West Washington Place, Springfield, Illinois 62702. All rights reserved. No part of this book may be reproduced, stored in a retrieval system, or transmitted in any form or by any means, electronic, mechanical, photocopying, recording, or otherwise, without the permission of Dan W. Bannister.

ISBN: 0-9644649-0-X

Library of Congress Card Number: 94-96808

Bannister, Dan W.
Lincoln and the Illinois Supreme Court (first edition)
Includes bibliography and indices

Printed in the United States of America
This book is printed on acid-free paper.

First edition

10   9   8   7   6   5   4   3   2   1

For my wife Audrey,
who has given me her unstinting love, loyalty,
and understanding for two score and seven,
plus three, years of married life.

Contents

Preface *ix*

Part I 1
Chapter One The Common Law 3
Chapter Two Lincoln, the Lawyer 12
Chapter Three The Antebellum Supreme Court 15
Chapter Four Lincoln's Fellow Lawyers in his Appellate Practice 33

Part II 43
Chapter Five Public Entities and Officials 45
Chapter Six Animals 65
Chapter Seven Railroads 72
Chapter Eight Agency 95
Chapter Nine Family Relations Law 98
Chapter Ten Torts 104
Chapter Eleven Wagering 121
Chapter Twelve One of a Kind 124

Part III 149
Chapter Thirteen Court Procedures 151
Chapter Fourteen January Term 1860 165

Appendices 173
Bibliography 175
Glossary 177
Index of Illinois Supreme Court Opinions 179
Index of State Officials, Jurists, Judges, and Attorneys 183

Preface

IN LINCOLN LITERATURE, relatively little has been written about Abraham Lincoln's legal career. The biographies mention his circuit trial court travels and travails. They detail how he endured numerous personal inconveniences as he was visiting small undeveloped towns to win cases for appreciative clients by means of his quick wit and legal skill. There is not much of substance, however, written about his law practice, especially his practice in the arena which affords a lawyer perhaps the truest test of his intellect, reasoning ability, and persuasiveness—the appellate courts. For Lincoln, this arena was the Illinois Supreme Court. His great success here is recognized by comments of perceptive scholars and in the reading of the opinions in the cases in which Lincoln participated. *Lincoln and the Illinois Supreme Court* focuses on a cross-section of his performances before that tribunal.

There has been a veritable mother lode of Lincoln material available for use by scholars to judge his competence and importance as a lawyer for at least 134 years—the official *Illinois Reports* of the cases in which Lincoln was involved, which were decided by the Illinois Supreme Court. These cases have been available in law libraries and lawyers' offices since the first report of such a case in 1838. Between 1838 and 1861, there were at least 333 Illinois Supreme Court cases involving Lincoln in which written opinions by that court afford us an opportunity to measure Lincoln's competence as a lawyer. I submit that this lode is by far the best natural resource by which objective opinions as to his prowess as a lawyer can be measured.

The case reports are objective; there is no recognizable effort on the part of the justices writing the opinions to propagandize Lincoln as a superior lawyer. One must read the cases, or objective summaries of the cases, attempt to discern Lincoln's specific role in each case and, as objectively as possible, measure the quality of that input. This is difficult to do, especially given the very limited information that is written in many of these reports. One starts with a bias that he was a superior lawyer. The case reports are, on one hand, tedious and at times confusingly inadequate but, on the other hand, they are nuggets from which one can recognize the deft hand of a master lawyer.

This writer literally stumbled upon this lode when introduced to the subject as a legally trained volunteer with the Lincoln Legal Papers project—assigned to brief each of Lincoln's cases before the Illinois Supreme Court. The objective of the Lincoln Legal Papers project is to collect, organize and publish all available material pertaining to Lincoln's legal practice, and to mine the courthouses where Lincoln practiced law to find new materials pertaining to that practice—sources where the materials are at least 134 years old and still available, despite the ravages of time, natural disasters, and discovery (and purloining) by collectors of Lincoln memorabilia over those many years. The talented and ingenious staff members of the project have far surpassed their expectations in the discovery of original Lincoln material. My portion of the project was far easier, since the source documents were readily available and easy to read, as the official Illinois Supreme Court reports have always been printed.

As my work on the project continued, my own recognition of Lincoln as a competent appellate lawyer grew, as did my recognition that these written records also represented a cross section of the essential development of the common law of Illinois, influenced strongly by Lincoln's work. The common law provided necessary protection for the civil rights of Illinois citizens. The written cases parade a treasure trove of superbly literate legal prose.

As an afterthought, while briefing these cases in the specific form needed for their inclusion in the categorized data files, the decision to also summarize each case in the narrative form emerged. These cases were published in 1992 in *Lincoln and the Common Law*. My intention in this earlier work was to share these Lincoln nuggets with anyone interested, and to present them in chronological order as insights into the development of Lincoln as a lawyer and the development of Illinois common law, and to share the enjoyment of the literary efforts of several of the justices. This presentation seemed inadequate, and further searching for a better presentation to prove Lincoln's competence as a lawyer brought me to the format of this book.

Lincoln's role in these cases is not always discernable, and objective measures of success are not easily definable. But history's evaluation of Lincoln as a lawyer depicts him as being very able and successful. This judgment seems always to have been based on his success on the trial circuit —both in the courts and in the camaraderie with his fellow lawyers on the circuit. A few historians have recognized the most objective measuring device, namely his appellate work before the Illinois Supreme Court; but there have been few attempts to translate these Supreme Court opinions into an easier-to-read and more understandable source. Such is the purpose of this book.

Lincoln and the Illinois Supreme Court is organized into three parts, with several chapters within each part. Part I gives the essential background to assist an understanding and appreciation of the essence of the issues involved in the cases cited, and provides general information about Lincoln, the lawyer.

Also included in this first part is some general information about the common law of England, which was adopted by the Illinois legislature in 1819. The panoply of rules and principles contained in that body of law provided the structure for an organized society in which a citizen's personal and property rights could be protected.

Information is included about some of the important people in Lincoln's appellate practice: the Illinois Supreme Court justices and the lawyers he associated with in that practice. The justices who sat on the antebellum Illinois Supreme Court were an interesting assortment of men with varying degrees of ability. These, of course, were the people Lincoln had to convince of the rightness of his cause. Many of these men made important contributions to the state's welfare, not only during their terms as justices, but also before and after their tenures on the court.

Some of the influential lawyers who worked with Lincoln added important ingredients to his success. These included his three successive partners in Springfield, his *ad hoc* partners on the circuit, and attorneys throughout the state who sought his assistance when they brought appeals to the Supreme Court.

Part II includes substantive case reports, organized by topics. The cases presented here involved vital common law rights, which were not only of importance to Lincoln's clients, but also to society, especially when issues were considered for the first time in Illinois and thus set precedents for future comparable issues. Such cases fleshed out the English common law as applicable to the evolving needs of Illinois.

Part III is based on the importance of legal technicalities in the cases appealed to the Supreme Court. An appeal could not be made just because the loser in the lower court didn't like the outcome of a trial. There had to be some perceived material error made at some phase of the pre-trial and/or trial proceedings which had been called to the attention of the trial judge, with the judge ruling against the aggrieved party. This was the crux of the appeal, and all the appellate attorney's arguments had to be addressed to this point.

All the cases in Part II were appealed based on alleged irregularities, which are not emphasized in those case reports since I have included them for other reasons. The Part III cases represent a cross section of alleged mistakes in the technical proceedings, and show a trend in recognition that the true purpose of our judicial system is to serve justice in the protection of a citizen's rights. The sequence of cases in chapter fourteen *(January Term 1860)*, for instance, is indicative of how important Lincoln was to the Lincoln-Herndon partnership. Most of these cases were lost on appeal because of procedural errors in the preliminary phases of the trial. In some cases, Herndon was virtually on his own.

I have presented 144 of Lincoln's Supreme Court cases here. There were 333 cases before that court involving Lincoln in which a formal opinion was written. All of these were summarized in *Lincoln and the Common Law* (1992). I chose what seemed to be the most interesting of these cases to expand upon in this book.

The total body of cases included those in which Lincoln's name was specifically listed as one of the advocates in the opinion. I have also included cases which list one of Lincoln's partners as an advocate during the periods when his various partnerships were active, and have included others in which the Lincoln Legal Papers project's researchers believe Lincoln was involved. For those seeking a definitive number of Lincoln cases, the ensuing CD/ROM compilation from the Lincoln Legal Papers project should provide that information.

My logic in including these extra cases is that in a two-man partnership—which each of Lincoln's was—there is a strong presumption that each partner knew what was going on in each appellate case and made some contribution. The best example of this is his partnership with John Todd Stuart, who was in Washington most of the time during that partnership.

The Lincoln Legal Papers project, based in Springfield, Illinois, has been gathering information about Lincoln's law practice, including his practice before the Illinois Supreme Court, and has endorsed prior opinions that Lincoln was a very able lawyer. Dr. Cullom Davis, director and senior editor of the project, has announced that a CD/ROM publication of about 100,000 documents pertaining to Lincoln's legal practice will be available in 1997. This will be, by far, the largest assemblage of valuable material on Lincoln's entire law practice, and will provide future scholars with the best raw material located in one place that anyone has ever had to study Lincoln's legal career. The project also plans to publish a five-volume series of Lincoln's most important legal work, including detailed analyses of many of his significant cases.

Some scholars have noted that his especial legal talents were most apparent in his work before the Illinois Supreme Court. Several have detailed samples of appellate cases. Albert J. Beveridge, in *Abraham Lincoln, 1809–1858* (1928), called attention to Lincoln's superior skills as an appellate lawyer, citing several cases to support his position. Many of Lincoln's railroad cases are noted in John W. Starr's 1927 book, *Lincoln and the Railroads.* In 1960, John J. Duff *(A. Lincoln, Prairie Lawyer)* offered his opinion that Lincoln did his best legal work before the Illinois Supreme Court, and again provided examples from some of Lincoln's cases before the state's highest court. Lincoln's talents as an appellate attorney were reiterated in 1977 by Stephen B. Oates in *With Malice Toward None: The Life of Abraham Lincoln.*

Duff decried the shortage of definitive information about Lincoln's Illinois Supreme Court cases, saying again that the only dependable sources of information about his appellate practice were the case reports, as follows:

> No review of Lincoln's cases in that court [the Illinois Supreme Court] has ever been made, using the original files, and because of their dispersal it is doubted that such a study could now be conducted. In only a dozen cases do the available files contain anything written by Lincoln, much of the important information having been rifled therefrom; the looting, in fact, has been almost as thorough as in the courts of the Eighth Circuit. These are limitations which no compiler can hope to entirely overcome. Fortunately, the official reports contain, in many instances, rather full recitals of the facts and essentials of the arguments advanced by Lincoln. At all events, a proper critique upon Lincoln's work in the Supreme Court can only be based on a reading of the official *Illinois Reports* of all his cases in that court.

Lincoln and the Illinois Supreme Court was conceived on the premise that Abraham Lincoln was a very successful appellate lawyer, recognizing that the most definitive objective information to support this premise lay in the official reports of the Illinois Supreme Court. These reports are a chronological record of individual cases decided by the state's highest court. The general format of each case report provides basic information about the trial court decision which prompted the appeal, including time and place, and the parties, attorneys, and judges involved. Also set forth are the reasons the appealing party believed error had been made in the proceedings, and the opinion of the Supreme Court, together with the judicial reasoning which supported the court's opinion.

This is the only record about these cases, since there were virtually no detailed official records made in the trial courts. Some additional information will be available when the Lincoln Legal Papers project publishes the results of its research. Even then, we will still be troubled about how to measure effectiveness. One of the difficulties is in identifying the specific input Lincoln had in each case, when there were usually other lawyers working with him. Some of the case opinions do include arguments and supporting cases submitted by the attorneys, including some by Lincoln, which justified the court's decision. I assume Lincoln played a major role in each case in which he was involved but do not have objective proof (with the exception of those heard during the January term 1860, which is the subject of chapter fourteen).

The next difficulty lies in finding an objective standard. Won/lost percentages seem the most appropriate. However, these were greatly influenced by the trial proceedings, and Lincoln had not always been involved in the trials of the cases when he represented one of the parties on the appeal.

Mistakes made at the trial level cannot always be overcome by a great performance by the lawyer for his client in the appellate court. There were also cases where Lincoln represented clients when the legal precedents were against him. It's more difficult to win a case in such instances, but a client is still entitled to representation after these facts are explained. The attorney might believe the precedent is wrong and that the decision could be reversed; or the attorney might believe the facts of the case could not be proven and/ or there were distinguishing facts in this case. In any event, all litigants are entitled to representation if they pay for it, and Lincoln was pragmatic enough to recognize this. Also, even if the won/lost percentage is favorable, there is no standard as to what the percentage should be to qualify the lawyer as "outstanding." I have no comparable won/lost ratios for other lawyers deemed successful during this time—Stephen T. Logan, for example— though this resource material certainly could be used for this purpose.

I submit this book to support history's opinion that Abraham Lincoln was an outstanding appellate lawyer, with the most important evidence of this being a presentation of specific cases. The criteria for selection of cases to appear in this book were objective, without any bias to show only "wins." To the best of my knowledge, each case involved Lincoln. At least one of the following additional criteria had to be present in a case for it to be included in this work: importance of the case in establishing or reinforcing a common law precedent, topical interest, a clear writing style of the opinion, and examples of procedural errors affecting the judicial decisions.

The cases have been summarized with the intention of including enough of the case to satisfy the legal technician and enough prose style to be easily understandable. The linkage of these cases is intended for necessary background information. The cases are part of Illinois history: the precedents they established or reinforced formed an essential basis of the living body of Illinois common law, which provided the underlying structure which produced order in a growing society. Civilization is not possible without a supporting base of rules to protect a citizen's personal and property rights. Lawyers like Lincoln, and the justices and judges of the antebellum judicial system, were absolutely essential in building and rebuilding this common law base.

I submit that Lincoln emerges as an important contributor to this common law development with his predominant role in the Illinois Supreme Court.

My involvement with these cases began with a recommendation by my old friend John R. Chapin, a third-generation lawyer in Springfield and chair of the Lincoln Legal Papers Advisory Committee, to Dr. Cullom Davis, director and senior editor of the project, that I serve as a volunteer legal associate in the project. My assignment was to brief 333 Illinois Supreme Court cases in which Abraham Lincoln was involved. Dr. Davis and his staff are doing a very impressive professional job, and it has been a pleasure and privilege to work with them.

I want to express my appreciation to the Lincoln scholarship community for welcoming a neophyte Lincoln student into their midst. I especially thank James T. Hickey and Frank J. Williams for reading the completed manuscript and offering their very helpful suggestions. I am grateful to John Y. Simon, who read a few chapters from early drafts and provided some useful comments on the focus of the book, and to David Richert, who lent his editorial expertise to the final draft. Many thanks to copyeditors Barbara Ranes and Frank O. Williams for their fine work on the final manuscript.

Major contributions to this book include the editing and advisory participation of Barbara Hughett, a writer and editor with special interest in both the Lincolns—Abraham and Mary—and the American Civil War. She is currently president of The Civil War Round Table of Chicago and the Lincoln Group of Illinois, and serves on the board of directors of the Abraham Lincoln Association. She is editor of three newsletters published by historical associations, and is the author of *The Civil War Round Table: Fifty Years of Scholarship and Fellowship* (1990) and *The Lincoln College Story: 1865–1995* (1995).

Muriel Underwood, a very talented graphic designer, with many years experience in book design, is this book's designer and typographer. She is a member of several professional design organizations and has been for many years a volunteer instructor of a letterpress workshop—approximating the printing equipment used in Lincoln's day, and a far-removed technical step from the computer with which this book has been produced.

The three of us have worked together on this volume. We sincerely hope you enjoy it, and that it enriches your knowledge of Abraham Lincoln, and enhances your knowledge and opinion of his impressive legal credentials.

DAN W. BANNISTER, J.D.
November 1994

Part I

Chapter One

The Common Law

EVERY ORGANIZED SOCIETY needs a body of rules of law to govern the behavior of its citizens in order to protect the personal and property rights of each individual. Laws are classified as criminal or civil. Definitions of criminal acts are established by the legislative body of the particular governmental entity. An action of an individual cannot be deemed criminal unless it violates a specific statute or governmental regulation.

On the other hand, civil rights and obligations are protected by the common law, which includes specific laws enacted by the appropriate legislative body and by decisions of the highest court of appeal for that governmental entity. The English common law had developed over the centuries since the issuance of the *Magna Carta,* in 1215, through a combination of legislative statutes enacted by Parliament, and by legal decisions made by the highest appellate courts in that country.

The American colonies, as they transformed themselves into states, needed a body of rules to protect the personal and property rights of their citizens. Most of the colonies adopted the English common law for this purpose. This was true for all the states except Louisiana, which adopted the Napoleonic Code as its basic body of rules.

Illinois became a state in 1818. The first law enacted by the legislature designated the common law of England, together with all statutes made in aid of the common law which were of a general nature and not "local to the kingdom," as the "rule of decision, and should be considered as of full force, until repealed by legislative authority." The adoption of the common law provided the basis for an orderly society.

The significance of the adoption of the common law—to one anonymous citizen at least—is well-expressed in a letter written to the major Illinois newspaper, *The Intelligencer,* in 1818: "Let us enquire what this common law is. . . . It is in the words of an able judge, the perfection of reason; it has for its foundation the general customs of the kingdom, the law of nature, and the law of God; it is founded upon reason and is said to be the perfection of reason acquired by long study, observation, and experience, and refined by learned men of all ages.... Its continuance, therefore, the warmth with which it has always been supported, and its general adoption throughout the United States is the best evidence of its utility and excellence; it is the birthright of every citizen, the only safeguard he hath for the protection, not only of his property but his family."[1]

Under the constitution of Illinois, the powers of the three bodies of government are separated in the same fashion as they are in the United States Constitution. The legislative branch passes the laws, the executive enforces them, and the judicial interprets them. This basic separation of powers caused some careful deliberation by the Illinois Supreme Court as to what its constitutional limits were in changing the civil law.

When the English common law was agreed upon as the basis of Illinois law, it was recognized that the exigencies of a newly emerging state created conditions and circumstances which were not present in England. Thus different rules were at times required to secure justice for the state's citizens. All agreed that the legislature had the power to enact statutes which superseded any statutes or appellate court decisions, whether from England or Illinois. The question that required the most soul searching by the Illinois Supreme Court involved whether or not it had the constitutional authority to change the common law. There were several cases in which Lincoln was involved wherein the authority of the Supreme Court to allow the trial courts to disregard precedent decreed by earlier decisions in the highest tribunal—in England or Illinois—was the major point of contention.

The first such case was *Field v. The People ex rel. McClernand*,[2] December term 1839. Chief Justice William Wilson, reversing the lower court decision, recited the primacy of Illinois Supreme Court opinions, as follows: "...when the supreme judicial tribunal of a state had declared what the law was on any point, when the same point came again in litigation, all other courts were bound to conform to its decision. A different rule would destroy all the stability and uniformity in the rules of law, which are so essential to the administration of justice and the safety of the citizen. If every judge can decide according to his private sentiments, without regard to precedent and authority, there may be as many rules of decision as there are circuits; and the decision of one day would furnish no rule of decision of the next." Thus he rebuked Sidney Breese, who had been the trial judge, who said in his opinion that he knew about two cases which held the opposite of his ruling, but that since he didn't agree with them, he was going to disregard them. (This case is reported more fully in chapter five.)

Later opinions of the Illinois Supreme Court prompted some additional thoughtful questioning as to whether different conditions in Illinois might indicate a different ruling than was appropriate in England. *Lincoln and the Common Law* (1992) includes all 333 Illinois Supreme Court cases in which Abraham Lincoln was involved. These cases were presented in chronological order, and I observed the thoughtful agonizing of the court as the state increased in population, and in productivity and political activity. These changes influenced the judiciary to seriously question what should be the governing rule in Illinois in given situations. The trends in the questioning of blind adherence to common law precedents grew in pace with other growth.

The next Lincoln case to serve as an example of this trend is the dissenting opinion in *Maus v. Worthing*, December term 1841.[3] Lincoln represented Amos H. Worthing, who had won a judgment against Jacob S. Maus in the Tazewell County Circuit Court. Maus appealed the case to the Illinois Supreme Court. Lincoln noted that the appeal bond (required in appeals to the Supreme Court) had been executed by a person whose authorization to bind the surety was not signed under seal, as the law required. The letter containing the questioned signature was written by W. S. Maus to John A. Jones, as follows: "I hereby authorize you to sign my name to a bond to be given by Jacob S. Maus, in an appeal to the supreme court . . . [signed] W. S. Maus"

The common law was clear that such a document required a seal; a mere signature, even though witnessed, was not adequate. Historically, a seal was a wax-like substance which was placed on a document that was impressed by a unique mark. As the implementation of this rule developed, the actual seal could be replaced by the letters "L. S." (*Locus Sigilli*, "place of the signature") or the word "seal." The contested document in this case had none of these, and the appeal was denied.

Justice Breese objected to this decision, in his opinion, as follows:

> I cannot concur in the opinion just delivered by the court. I acknowledge respectable decisions have been cited to sustain it, and am disposed to give them all the weight to which they are entitled. The rule, as laid down, seems to me to be destitute of any good reason on which to base it, and altogether too technical for this age. How a scrawl made with pen and ink, and affixed to the name of the writer of the letter, which is the authority to execute the appeal bond, could give it any additional validity, I cannot discover. It is conceded, if the writer's name had this magic scrawl affixed to it, it would then be sufficient, and it would then possess all the efficacy of a sealed instrument or deed.
>
> The general tenor of our laws has made great inroads upon many of those technical and refined notions which it was considered at one time heresy to question, and with the improvement made in other respects, it would seem to be time to release such proceedings from the dominion of a rule so arbitrary, so technical, so wholly inapplicable to our condition, and so little calculated to promote justice.
>
> It was once a rule that a bond could only be discharged by something

of as high a nature as the bond itself; yet who will now doubt that a parol [oral] receipt is good against such a bond? The ancient rule is, also, that if there be a subscribing witness to a bond or note, he must be called to prove its execution; proof of the admission of the party that he did execute it, being inadmissible. Yet would this court, if called upon, sanction a rule so absurd? You may hang a man on his own confession, but he shall not pay a debt of twenty dollars evidenced by his note of hand or bond, on the same kind of proof! I cannot consent to yield up my judgment, in any case, because others have decided a point in a particular manner, unless I can see the reason of the decision. Seeing none in this case, and believing that the purposes of justice are not all subserved by an adherence to such antiquated rules and unmeaning technicalities, I dissent from the opinion. I think the letter of request ample authority to sign the appeal bond. Several of my brother judges coincide in the views here expressed, but think the rule is the law, with which they cannot interfere, it being for the legislative power to change it. I think differently. I am of the opinion that the courts are bound to see the propriety and reason of every rule, before it received their sanction and approbation, in cases wherein there are no statutory provisions applicable; in such cases the will of the legislature, as expressed by them, is the law, however unwise or unreasonable it may be, if no constitutional provision is violated. Not so in other cases—we should know the reason why it is, and should be so; and if the alleged reason is absurd, we should not yield our acquiescence.

Breese had decided against judicial precedents at the trial of the Field case. Thus the thoughts in this dissenting opinion are consistent with his beliefs as a judge.

The classic case in the evolution of the English common law as the unqualified law of Illinois is *Seeley v. Peters*,[4] December term 1848, in which the English common law on fencing responsibilities was specifically rejected. William Peters's hogs entered Samuel Seeley's property and ravaged wheat shocks. Under the English common law, an owner of animals had the responsibility to fence in his animals so that they would not trespass on other people's property. Peters said animals had always been allowed to forage at will in this country, and if Seeley wanted to protect his wheat shocks, he should have provided an adequate fence to keep wandering animals out. The majority of the Supreme Court agreed, and ruled that Peters was not liable to pay for damages caused by his animals. Justice John Dean Caton dissented, and the dialogue provided by the two opinions reveals the different views on the primacy of English common law at that time, including where the responsibility for changing the common law resided.

Justice Lyman Trumbull, in writing the majority opinion, agreed that the common law had been adopted in Illinois "so far as the same is applicable and of general nature." He went on to discuss further considerations in the adoption of the common law:

> It must be understood [that the common law has primacy] only where that law is applicable to the habits and conditions of our society and in harmony with the genius, spirit, and objects of our institutions. . . . However well adapted the rule of the common law may be to a densely populated country like England, it is surely but ill adapted to a new country like ours. If this common law rule prevails now, it must have prevailed from the time of the earliest settlements in the State, and can it be supposed that the early settlers of this country located upon the borders of our extensive prairies, that they brought with them and adopted as applicable to their condition a rule of law, requiring each one to fence up his cattle; that they designed the millions of fertile acres stretched out before them to go ungrazed, except as each purchaser from government was able to enclose his part with a fence? This State is unlike any of the eastern states in their early settlement, because from the scarcity of timber, it must be many years yet before our extensive prairies can be fenced, and their luxuriant growth sufficient for thousands of cattle must be suffered to rot and decay where it grows, unless the settlers upon their borders are permitted to turn their cattle upon them.
>
> Perhaps there is no principle of the common law so inapplicable to the condition of our country and people as the one which is sought to be enforced now for the first time since the settlement of the State. It has been the custom in Illinois so long, that the memory of man runneth not to the contrary, for the owners of stock to suffer them to run at large. Settlers have located themselves contiguous to prairies for the very purpose of getting the benefit of the range. The right of all to pasture their cattle upon unenclosed ground is universally conceded. No man has questioned this right, although hundreds of cases must have occurred where the owners of cattle have escaped the payment of damages on account of the insufficiency of the fences through which their stock have broken, and never till now has the common law rule, that the owner of cattle is bound to fence them up been supposed to prevail or be applicable to our condition. The universal understandings of all classes of the community, upon which they have acted in enclosing their crops, and letting their cattle run at large, is entitled to no little consideration in determining what the law is, and we should feel inclined to hold, independent to any statutes upon the subject, on account of the inapplicability of the common law rule to the condition and circumstances of our people, that it does not and never has prevailed in Illinois.

Justice Caton dissented from the majority opinion, which reversed the judgment of the circuit court which had held Peters liable for the damages his hogs caused. Caton had been the trial judge whose judgment was reversed, but we can safely concede this was not why he sought to defend his earlier decision. He admitted in two earlier Supreme Court decisions which reversed his trial court decisions that he had been wrong in his rulings at those trials, and these statements plus some comments on his reasoning in this case can be found in chapter three.

In his dissent, Caton first stated the appropriate statute specifying the adoption of the English common law and then said:

> Let us first inquire whether this admitted principle of the common law was adopted by this statute, for this is questioned by those who disagree with me. That it is 'of a general nature,' is too clear to require argument, and its exclusion, if sustained at all, must be upon the ground that it is not applicable. What did the legislature mean by the use of the word 'applicable'? Applicable to the nature of our political institutions and to the genius of our republican forms of government, and to our constitution, or to our domestic habits, our wants, and our necessities? I think I must ever be of opinion, that nothing but the former was meant, and that to adopt the latter is a clear usurpation of legislative power by the courts. If we adopt the former, but little difficulty will ever be experienced in applying the rule, and the question propounded will always be of a legal character, for legal rules will always determine whether any given portion of the common law is consistent with, or hostile to, the genius of a republic or the principles of our constitution. By this principle, the rule by which any portion is excluded, or adopted, will apply with equal force all over the State. If we adopt the latter, then we are driven to examine, not a question of law and principle, but of convenience and policy. By this latter rule, we might have to hold a principle of the common law in force in some portions of the State and not in others; or in some places it might be well adapted to the genius, and customs, the wants and expectations of the people, while it would be the very reverse in others. We should have to investigate, and decide upon facts, without any legal mode of trying them, and not law. If we say that we will not enforce a principle of the common law, because, in our judgment, a different rule would be better for the general good, or more just in principle, or more conformable to the habits and ways of the people, then it seems to me that we are legislating, and I know not where we should stop in this course of judicial legislation. If the courts may say that this rule or that of the common law is not law because a different rule could be more just, or would suit the people better, then they must admit that their judgments are infallible, and there is no longer any occasion for a legislature to alter the common law, for the courts will happily make all needful alterations. The very statement of such

a proposition, in plain terms, is too startling to find an advocate, and too dangerous to admit of defence, and yet, it seems to me, that we are rapidly verging to that alarming position, if we are not already there.... At least, so long as the court might be mistaken in its notions of convenience, it demonstrates the propriety of leaving that question to the legislature, where it properly belongs.

In another case, Caton stated the need for flexibility in the adoption of the common law and in the powers and responsibilities of the legislature and the courts in determining applicability of the common law. In *St. Louis, Alton and Chicago Railroad Company v. Dalby*,[5] December term 1857, the court ruled on the responsibilities of railroads for wrongful acts done by its employees. There was little ruling law on the responsibilities of corporations at that time because they were few in number and young in age. Commenting on this, Caton said:

Indeed their [corporations] multiplication is astonishing, if not alarming. It may be, and probably is true, that more private corporations were created by our legislature in its last session, than existed in the whole civilized world at the commencement of the present century. The state of things has necessarily led to a more careful study of the whole subject, both by legislators and courts. Experience, that safest teacher to those who will observe and reflect, has enabled our law makers to more accurately judge what powers should be conferred upon a corporation to accomplish a particular object, so that, as far as practicable, capital may be induced to undertake the enterprise, and shall be justly protected; and on the other hand, to protect the rights of the public and individuals against the encroachments and oppression by the corporations. So, too, the courts.... It has become the duty of the courts so to administer the law as to secure them in the evil enjoyment of those powers, and to protect the public and individuals against the abuse of those powers.... It follows, as a necessary legal consequence, that if, by the exercise of those powers either express or implied, which they possess, they commit a particular wrong, they must be held responsible for such wrong, and the courts must necessarily adopt the known and appropriate remedy for the redress of such wrong.

The principle of applying known remedies to the exigencies of the new cases as they arise, is one of the great pillars of strength of the common law, without which, it would have fallen and broken to pieces, by its own rigidity, centuries ago. He who studies the common law only by looking at the decisions which have been made under it, without studying its philosophy, and understanding the reasons which prompted those decisions, can never become fully imbued with its true doctrines. He is compelled to say that where there is no precedent, there is no law. The decisions under the common law are most surely its expounders, but, in order to understand such expositions, we must understand why such decisions were made, and such decisions do not become precedents for the government of any other case where those reasons do not exist; and it may be safely said, as a general rule, that decisions that are only supported by fallacies are not the true exponents of the common law, and such decisions must be often repeated and long acquiesced in, before they become what are considered authorities. In such cases, it may be better, no doubt, for the legislature than for the courts to change them.

Caton believed the legislature was the only body of the state government that could override the Supreme Court precedents as stated in his dissent in the Seeley case. However, in the Dalby case nine years later, he held that the common law must bend or it would shatter. The justice somewhat qualified his opinion that only the legislature could make such changes in his closing line, which stated that in cases where change was necessary, "it may be better, no doubt, for the legislature than for the courts to change them."

The Supreme Court was the most convenient and flexible vehicle for overriding precedents. The legislative action to enact a statute, including the approval process by the executive branch, was much more ponderous and uncertain. It is also difficult, if not impossible, to foresee every issue involving protection of an individual's personal and property rights in advance of need—which would be necessary in order to have a statute ready in advance to solve that need.

Also to be considered is the importance of political party loyalties, which can influence legislative activities as well as judges and justices, as demonstrated in the Field case and its aftermath. A Democratic judge (Breese) ruled in favor of a Democratic governor (Thomas Carlin) at the trial, with the case reversed by a Whig majority on the Supreme Court. Then the Democratic majority in the state legislature decided the four-justice Supreme Court should be increased to nine, with five Democrats elected to these new justice positions.

Mason Brayman was a member of the Illinois bar in 1842 and was also editor of the *Illinois State Journal* newspaper for many years. In 1844, as a private enterprise, he commenced work on revising the statutes of Illinois. In an introduction to this project when it was presented to the legislature, he commented on the origin of the statutes, and the confused state of the law:

> It was to be expected that the early enactment which proceeded first from the territories, then from state governments, would be crude, imperfect, and unharmonious. They were not adopted together, as a distinct body of statute law, nor with any view to their connection or consistency with each other; but hastily produced at different times and

places, in obedience to the ever varying wants and circumstances of an unsettled, scattered, and heterogeneous population.... We may readily conclude that they found but little leisure for the business of legislation and they made their laws as they made their log cabins, their roads and bridges, as they needed them for their shelter and protection.[6]

NOTES

1. Buck, Solon J., *Illinois in 1818*. Urbana:University of Illinois Press, 1967 (second edition, revised and reprinted on the occasion of the Sesquicentennial of the State of Illinois), 255.
2. 3 *Ill.*,* 79; Bannister, Dan W., *Lincoln and the Common Law*.** Springfield: Human Services Press, 1992, 8.
3. *Ibid.*, 26; *Ibid.*, p. 14.
4. 10 *Ill.*, 130; *Ibid.*, p. 127.
5. 19 *Ill.*, 352; *Ibid.*, p. 208.
6. Palmer, John M., *Bench and Bar of Illinois*. Chicago: Lewis Publishing Company, 1899, Vol. 1, 231.

* *Illinois Reports* (sometimes abbreviated Ill. Rep.) are the official reports of the Illinois Supreme Court decisions. Volume 1 was published in 1831. In these notes, the volumes will be referred to as *Ill.*, with the Volume number preceding and the page cited afterward.

** Henceforth, *Lincoln and the Common Law* will be referred to as *LCL*.

Chapter Two

Lincoln, the Lawyer

WITH THE EXCEPTION OF HIS ONE TERM in the House of Representatives (December 1847 until the Spring of 1849), Lincoln practiced law in Springfield, Illinois, from 1837 until he left Springfield in 1861 to become President of the United States. He practiced before all levels of courts—from the justice of peace courts, to the trial courts in the state circuits and the federal district courts, and the supreme courts of both the state and federal government. The popular image of his practice centers on his home-spun yarns and tactics, which—enhanced by his talent for argument—combined to win victories for his clients.

Biographers have agreed that Lincoln enjoyed the life on the circuit, and that he was a popular and successful advocate. His experience in these county courts honed his public speaking talent, and enhanced his ability to make well-reasoned, influential arguments. This experience also gave him name-recognition which helped his political career. He made many friends on the circuit, and earned the respect of citizens and political leaders in the counties in which he practiced. Thus, this part of his life was important preparation for his subsequent political career.

Speaking of Lincoln's life on the circuit, Albert J. Beveridge said:

> Lincoln spent at least six months of every year away from Springfield riding the circuit, and he was the only lawyer that attended the courts in every county seat. His prolonged absences irritated his wife, who often confided to their next door neighbor that 'if her husband stayed at home as he ought to she could love him better.' Court was held in the various counties from the middle of March to the middle of June, and again from early September until the first of December. For more that three years after his Congressional term the Eighth Circuit comprised fourteen counties, Sangamon, Tazewell, Woodford, McLean, Logan, DeWitt, Champaign, Vermillion, Piatt, Edgar, Shelby, Moultrie, Macon, and Christian. It was nearly one hundred miles long by almost one hundred and ten miles broad, nearly one fifth of the entire area of the State. In 1853 the Circuit was

reduced to eight counties, the last six named being transferred to other districts; and four years later Sangamon, Woodford, and Tazewell were attached to the Seventh District.

The Judge of the Eighth Circuit was David Davis, who had been elected to that office in 1848 when he was thirty-three years of age. He continued on the bench by re-election until 1862 when Lincoln appointed him a Justice of the Supreme Court of the United States.[1]

When he wasn't on the circuit, Lincoln devoted much of his time to his practice before the Illinois Supreme Court. As he became experienced and known around the circuit, many appellate cases were referred to him. Historians comment favorably about Lincoln's performance before the state's highest court. Beveridge, for example, wrote about Lincoln's Supreme Court prowess as follows:

> ... Lincoln's best work as a lawyer was in arguments of cases for the [Illinois] Supreme Court. For such arguments he never failed to prepare with utmost thoroughness. He examined available precedents, carefully studied the textbooks; his briefs and addresses to the court were well-reasoned and strongly supported by the authorities; and he was usually successful. All told he had one hundred and seventy-five cases in the Supreme Court, of which he won ninety-six. Lincoln's conduct of cases before the Supreme Bench was, by far, his most distinguished effort at the bar. His arguments covered almost the whole range of the law and included values from a three dollar hog case to a disputed liability on a note for over one hundred and thirty thousand dollars. He appeared for subscribers of railroad stock who refused to pay and for the railroad company to collect stock subscriptions.[2]

Stephen B. Oates has noted that:

> Though Lincoln labored diligently in the federal and state circuit courts, he did his most influential legal work in the prestigious Supreme Court of Illinois. In all he participated in 243 cases before that tribunal and won most of them. It was here he earned his reputation as a lawyer's lawyer, adept at meticulous preparation and cogent argument.[3]

John J. Duff wrote:

> Contrary to popular belief, it was in the Supreme Court, and not in the circuit, that Lincoln had his greatest impact as a lawyer. During the period when the outlines of the state's jurisprudence were being established on an enduring basis, he helped to mold, in a significant way,

doctrines of law laid down by the state's most authoritative court. If the principles involved seem commonplace today, one needs to be reminded that Lincoln had no encyclopedias of law, no digests to go by—only the maxims of the English common law as set forth in *Blackstone* and applied by a few adjudications from the older sister states. It would not be rash to claim for him that, in exploring areas that the Illinois courts had not yet clearly delineated, he hacked out important precedents in the law of that state and, more than any other Illinois lawyer of his generation, made a distinct contribution to law that governs today. Herndon's statement that Lincoln was 'a great lawyer... in the Supreme Court of Illinois' is for once, no exaggeration. He was an uncommonly fine appeals lawyer.[4]

NOTES

1. Beveridge, Albert J., *Abraham Lincoln, 1809–1858*, 2 vols., Vol. 1, 512, 513.
2. *Ibid.*, Vol. 1, 573.
3. Oates, Stephen B., *With Malice Toward None: The Life of Abraham Lincoln.* New York: Harper & Row Publishers, Inc., 1977, 104.
4. Duff, John J., *A. Lincoln, Prairie Lawyer.* New York and Toronto: Rinehart & Company, 1960, 243.

Chapter Three

The Antebellum Supreme Court

THE 1818 ILLINOIS CONSTITUTION PROVIDED for a separation of powers comparable to that of the Constitution of the United States. It established the executive branch, headed by an elected governor; the legislative branch, comprised of two elected houses of representatives of the people; and the judicial branch, initially consisting of four justices, chosen by the legislature, to serve on the Illinois Supreme Court. The major function of this court was to rule on cases appealed to it from the district courts, which were also established by the state constitution.

A secondary function of the court was to assist the governor in approving legislative measures. The governor was not given veto power, but—along with the four Supreme Court justices—served as a Council of Revision, which reviewed all bills passed by the legislature before they became law. If a majority of the council members decided a bill should not become law, it was returned to the branch of the legislature where it had originated. The recommendations of the council were attached to the bill and it was reconsidered. After this reconsideration, the bill could become law by receiving a majority of the votes in each house of the legislature.

The 1818 constitution provided that, in addition to the responsibilities required as members of the Supreme Court and the Council of Revision, the justices would also serve as trial judges in the circuit courts. The state was divided into four judicial districts with a justice to hear trials assigned to each. In 1824, five circuit court judges were elected by the legislature, and the Illinois Supreme Court justices were relieved of the trial court work. However, the legislature of 1826–27 turned the newly appointed circuit court judges out of office and required Supreme Court judges to once again act as circuit court judges.

Because of a growing population, in 1829 the legislature established a fifth district to cover northern Illinois, and added the position of another circuit court judge to serve the new area. In 1835, to lighten the work load

GENEALOGY OF JUDGES
OF THE ANTEBELLUM ILLINOIS SUPREME COURT

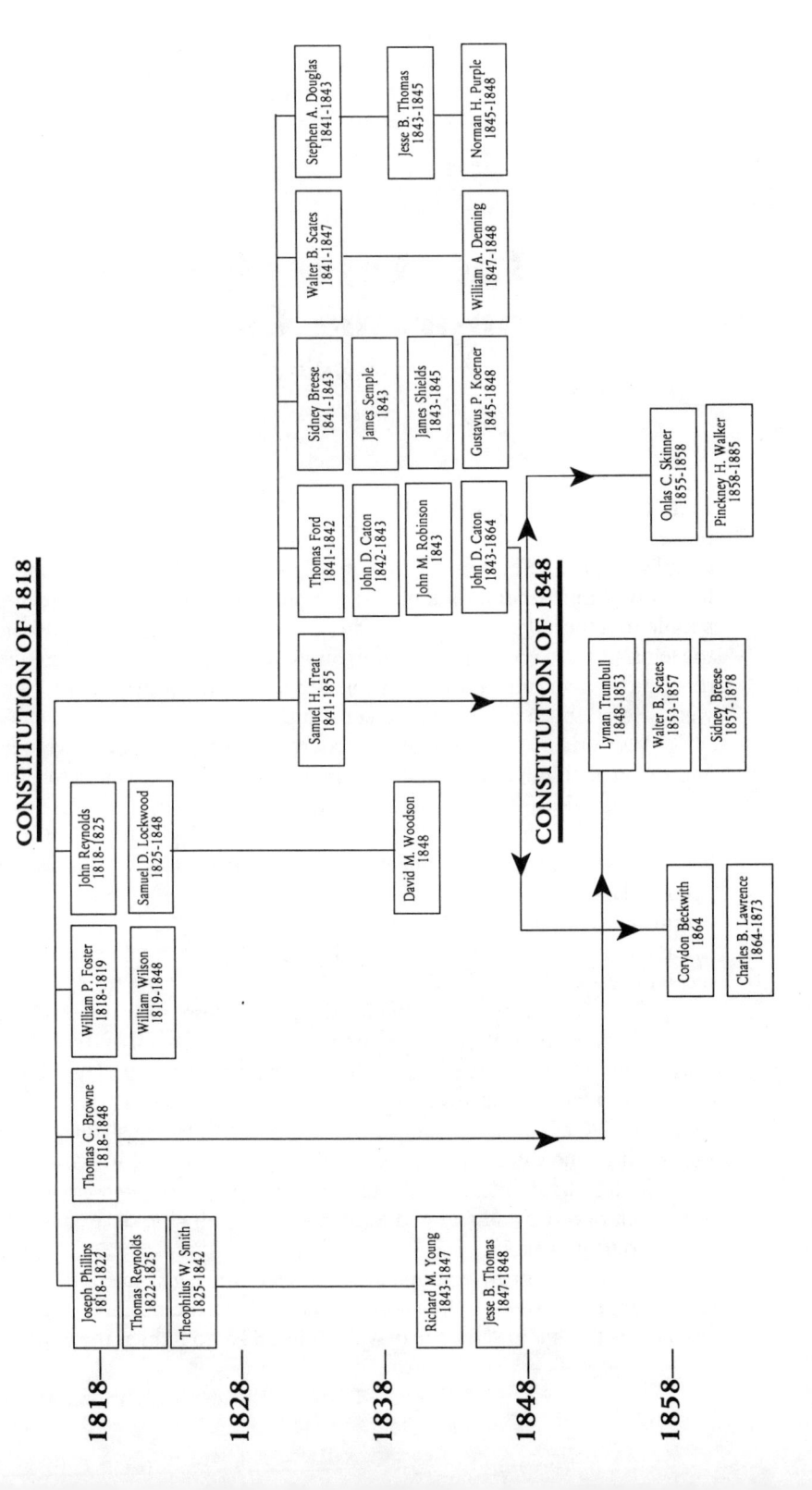

CONSTITUTION OF 1818

- Joseph Phillips 1818-1822
- Thomas Reynolds 1822-1825
- Theophilus W. Smith 1825-1842
- Thomas C. Browne 1818-1848
- William P. Foster 1818-1819
- William Wilson 1819-1848
- John Reynolds 1818-1825
- Samuel D. Lockwood 1825-1848
- David M. Woodson 1848
- Richard M. Young 1843-1847
- Jesse B. Thomas 1847-1848
- Samuel H. Treat 1841-1855
- Thomas Ford 1841-1842
- John D. Caton 1842-1843
- John M. Robinson 1843
- John D. Caton 1843-1864
- Sidney Breese 1841-1843
- James Semple 1843
- James Shields 1843-1845
- Gustavus P. Koerner 1845-1848
- Walter B. Scates 1841-1847
- William A. Denning 1847-1848
- Stephen A. Douglas 1841-1843
- Jesse B. Thomas 1843-1845
- Norman H. Purple 1845-1848

CONSTITUTION OF 1848

- Lyman Trumbull 1848-1853
- Walter B. Scates 1853-1857
- Sidney Breese 1857-1878
- Onias C. Skinner 1855-1858
- Pinckney H. Walker 1858-1885
- Corydon Beckwith 1864
- Charles B. Lawrence 1864-1873

1818—
1828—
1838—
1848—
1858—

of the existing justices and the one circuit court judge, five additional circuits were carved out of the existing five circuits. The legislature then elected five judges to fill those slots.

The last legislative act changing the responsibilities of the Supreme Court justices and circuit court judges occurred in 1840. At that time, five additional justices were added, circuit court judges were again eliminated, and the nine justices again served as circuit court judges. The addition of these five justices was the response of the Democratic legislature to "pack the court" after Governor Thomas Carlin, a Democrat, was thwarted by the Illinois Supreme Court. Carlin tried to remove from the office of secretary of state, Alexander P. Field, a Whig incumbent in place when Carlin was elected. (This case is detailed in chapter five.) This alignment of the Illinois court system remained in place until a new state constitution was established in 1848.

The political nature of the legislative choices of the justices is well demonstrated by the selections of the Democratic majority legislature. This legislature elected five Democrat party men as the additional justices in 1840. However, those five, along with Justice Caton who replaced Justice Thomas Ford when he became governor in 1842, were outstanding appellate judges of the antebellum period.

The selection of the original four justices in 1818 was obviously difficult, as measured by their subsequent performance. One was a charlatan at best, another served the longest term of any of the antebellum justices while contributing little to the work of the court, and the other two served only for short periods of time. There was a dearth of possible candidates at that time. Most of the attorneys were recent migrants to Illinois, who had received their training and experience in other states. Fortunately, the attorneys who had migrated to Illinois had served in earlier-established states which had also adopted the English Common Law as their model. Thus, they did have experience in the basic background law of Illinois. In the first twelve years of the court's service, there were 353 cases heard, with most of these occurring after 1825, so the volume of appellate work did not challenge the justices. They spent most of their working time as judges presiding over trials in the district courts.

The antebellum period of the Illinois Supreme Court can be divided into three sections: 1818–1840, 1841–1847, and 1848–1861. Lincoln's practice in the first phase was very limited. The first case in which he could have been involved was in 1837, when his then-partner, John Todd Stuart, was listed as the attorney for one of the parties. Between 1837 and 1840, there were eight cases in which Lincoln was probably involved.

The second phase, commencing after the court had been expanded by adding the five justices, found Lincoln very active. He averaged twenty-five cases before the state's highest court each year until he began his term in the United States House of Representatives in 1847. In the third phase, his case workload, while influenced by the extent of his political activities, continued at a high level and with cases of greater magnitude.

1818-1840

The first four justices elected by the legislature in 1818 were: Joseph Phillips (1818–1822); Thomas C. Browne (1818–1848); William P. Foster (1818–1819); and John Reynolds (1818–1825).

John M. Palmer describes the organization of this first court as follows: "The legislature had but little difficulty in selecting a chief justice, for on the first ballot Joseph Phillips received thirty-four of the forty ballots cast; for associate justices William P. Foster and Thomas C. Browne were chosen, and finally John Reynolds was selected, having received twenty-two of the whole number of forty votes."[1] He goes on to say that all writers agree that Phillips was an admirable choice, being a lawyer of fine intellectual endowments. He held the office for nearly four years when he resigned to become a candidate for governor. An objective opinion of his work by reading the cases during his tenure is impossible, because he only presided over seventeen cases during this time. These cases take up only the first fourteen pages of Volume I of the *Illinois Reports* (1819–1831).

Thomas C. Browne, an associate justice of this first court, was admitted to the bar in Kentucky, came to Illinois in 1812, and served in the house of the territorial legislature in 1814. Although he served until 1848, when the new constitution reduced the number of justices to three, he was not chosen to be one of them.

Frederic B. Crossley said:

> Judge Browne was a man of integrity and apparently discharged the duties of his office to the best of his ability. He was not a man of great attainments, or a profound lawyer, and although occupying a position in the supreme tribunal of the state during a period when nearly all the leaders in different branches of the government were engaged in laying the foundations of the future of the great state, and thus placing posterity under lasting obligation for their labors, he did not seem to have participated prominently in any of the work of such leaders. He did not deliver an opinion of weight upon any subject during the entire period of his service as a judge and although a member of the Council of Revision, he did not take any prominent part in progressive legislation or development of the statutory law. He maintained himself in office through his political influence with members of the legislature and was at no time popular with the people. . . . His fame as a member of the Supreme Court rests chiefly upon the fact that the attempt to impeach him for general incompetency was the first attempt to impeach a justice of the Supreme Court.[2]

John Reynolds was born in Pennsylvania, moved to Illinois in 1800, and was admitted to the bar in 1812. Although he was a candidate, he was not re-elected to the court by the legislature in 1825. Palmer said he was better known as a politician, and was an undistinguished lawyer. He was elected governor of Illinois in 1830.

William P. Foster was the fourth member selected by the legislature for this first court. He was neither a member of the bar, nor did he practice law. According to Thomas Ford, in *History of Illinois* (1854), as quoted by Crossley:

> Foster, who was one of the judges, was almost a total stranger in the country. He was a great rascal, but no one knew it then, he having been a citizen of the state only for about three weeks before he was elected. He was no lawyer, never having studied or practiced law, but he was a man of winning, polished manners, was withal a very gentlemanly swindler, from some part of Virginia. It might be said of him as it was of Lambro, 'he was the mildest mannered man that ever scuttled a ship or cut a throat, with such true breeding of a gentleman that you could never divine his real thoughts'.... He was assigned to hold courts in the circuit on the Wabash, but being fearful of exposing his utter incompetency, he never went near any one of them. In the course of one year, he resigned his high office, but took first to pocket his salary, and then removed out of the state. He afterwards became a noted swindler, moving from city to city swindling strangers and prostituting his daughter, who was very beautiful.[3]

The Illinois Supreme Court apparently wants to ignore the deplorable Foster incident. It does not include his name with the other justices who have served on the court in the list proudly displayed in a prominent spot in the Illinois Supreme Court building.

Foster was the first one of the original four to be replaced. The legislature chose William Wilson (1819–1848), a native Virginian who studied law in that state. He came to Illinois in 1817, and in 1818 was proposed for election to the Illinois Supreme Court. However, on the ballot he was six votes short of being elected. He was elected in 1819 and, like Browne, served until he was replaced under the reorganization of the court under the 1848 constitution. Crossley said, "During the long period of his occupancy of a seat in the Supreme Court he commanded the respect and confidence of the people and while there are few decisions written by him of unusual distinction, his was the sort of solid, substantial service needed during the days of construction, perhaps more than the kind offered by more brilliant but less consistent minds."[4] Palmer wrote that Wilson "was a judge, and nothing else; in no sense was he a politician."[5] One measure of his recognition as an important member of the court was his reelection as chief justice for four consecutive terms until he retired in 1848.

Phillips was the next one of the original group to be replaced. His replacement, Thomas Reynolds (1822–1825), had commenced the practice of law in Illinois in 1812, and was elected to the court in 1822. He moved to Missouri where he became a member of that state's legislature and a circuit court judge. He was elected governor in 1840. (He was not related to Justice John Reynolds.)

Thomas Reynolds was replaced by Theophilus W. Smith (1825–1842). Governor Ford said about him: "Judge Smith was an active, bustling, ambitious, and turbulent member of the democratic party. He had for a long time aimed to be elected to the United States Senate; his devices and intrigues to this end had been innumerable. In fact he never lacked a plot to advance himself or to blow up others. He was a laborious and ingenious schemer in politics."[6] His chief claim to fame on the Illinois Supreme Court was his escape from impeachment trial in 1833 by a narrow margin. He continued to hold office until he resigned in 1842.

John Reynolds was replaced in 1825 by Samuel D. Lockwood (1825–1848), who was licensed to practice law in New York in 1811, and in Illinois in 1818. Crossley said, "The career of Judge Lockwood indicates he was one of the most popular and forceful men of his time, in that he was apparently never an office seeker, he held positions of trust and honor in the state for more than fifty years, to most of which he was elevated by administrations with whom he was not in political sympathy."[7] In 1851, he was appointed by the legislature to be trustee of the land department of the Illinois Central Railroad, a position he held until his death in 1865.

1841-1847

Of the four justices on the court when the case of *Field v. People ex rel. McClernand* was heard in 1839, three were Whigs (Browne, Wilson, and Lockwood) and one was a Democrat (Smith). The five additional justices were all Democrats—Treat, Ford, Breese, Walter Scates, and Stephen Arnold Douglas.

Even though the 1841 appointments were politically motivated, the five people chosen were all highly qualified. Justice Caton, who succeeded Ford in 1842, was definitely one of the best. The additions, plus Lockwood and Wilson of the old court, formed a very competent court.

Samuel Hubbel Treat (1841–1855) settled in Springfield in 1834 and entered in the practice of law. He was appointed circuit court judge in 1839 to fill a vacancy and was elected to the circuit court judgeship in 1840. He was elected to the Illinois Supreme Court in 1841, and served until 1855, when he resigned to accept the position of judge of the District Court of the United States for the Southern District of Illinois. While Treat was serving on the state circuit court, Lincoln appeared before him many times. Treat most frequently presided in Sangamon County, with Springfield as the county seat.

Thomas Ford (1841–1842), a native Pennsylvanian, moved to Illinois and was admitted to the bar in 1829. He was appointed a prosecuting attorney by Governor Ninian Edwards in 1829, and was reappointed in 1837 by Governor Reynolds. Thereafter he was elected a judge four times by the legislature—twice as circuit court judge, once as judge of Chicago, and to the Illinois Supreme Court in 1841. He was nominated and elected governor of the state in 1842. After retiring as governor in 1846, he practiced law in Peoria.

Sidney Breese (1841–1843; 1857–1878) was the editor of the first volume of *Illinois Reports,* which included Supreme Court cases from the first organization of the court in 1819 through the end of the December term, 1831. (The volume was referenced as *1 Breese* as well as *1 Illinois.*) He was elected a judge of the Second District Circuit Court of Illinois in 1835, and served until his election to the Illinois Supreme Court. Breese was elected to the United States Senate in 1842, but was defeated for a second term by James Shields. He practiced law until his election to the state legislature in 1850, and was elected speaker of the house. In 1855 he was again elected a circuit court judge, and in 1857 was reelected to the Illinois Supreme Court. Breese was one of the most able jurists on that court. His interest in and support of the Illinois Central Railroad is covered later in the chapter.

Walter B. Scates (1841–1847; 1853–1857) was admitted to the bar in 1833. He was a circuit court judge before his election to the Illinois Supreme Court in 1841. He resigned in 1847 to resume his private law practice. Scates was again elected to the Supreme Court in 1853, and served until 1857, when he once more resigned. Crossley comments, "He was not a brilliant jurist, but his decisions are expressed with unusual clearness and are most noticeable for their conservatism and tendency to follow existing authorities...."[8]

Stephen Arnold Douglas (1841–1843), a native of Vermont, studied law in New York and moved to Illinois in 1833. He was admitted to the Illinois bar that same year. In 1835, he was elected state's attorney by the Illinois legislature. In 1840, he was appointed secretary of state when Alexander P. Field resigned after Illinois Governor Carlin unsuccessfully tried to appoint McClernand to that position. Douglas was elected to the Illinois Supreme Court in 1841, and remained there until he was elected to the United States House of Representatives in 1842. He was reelected two years later. Douglas was elected to the United States Senate in 1846, and reelected in 1852. The "Little Giant" is probably best known for his debates with Abraham Lincoln during the campaign for the United States Senate in the election of 1858, which Douglas won. Two years later he was defeated by Lincoln for the office of President of the United States. He died in June 1861, after a grueling tour of the southern states for the Lincoln administration, in an attempt to hold the country together and avert the Civil War.

This court of nine members heard 149 cases in which Lincoln was involved between 1841 and 1848, when the 1848 constitution reduced the Supreme Court to three members. These five new justices had a significant impact on the Court. They wrote 140 of these 149 opinions during that seven-year period.

The most active justice in the replacement group of justices, from 1842 to 1848, was John Dean Caton (1842–1843; 1843–1864). Caton was born in New York and practiced law there before moving to Chicago in 1833. He was appointed to the court in 1842, when he was twenty-nine years old, to fill the balance of the term of Thomas Ford, who had been elected governor. Ford's term expired at the end of 1842, and the legislature elected John M. Robinson, who became a justice on January 14, 1843. Robinson died on April 27 of that year, and Caton was again appointed as a replacement. Caton was a very effective justice. His observations about how the justices arrived at their decision in one important case are included later in this chapter.

Caton commented on his concept of his responsibilities as a jurist as follows:

> This state of things impressed upon me the idea of great responsibility. The jurisprudence of the state was then in its infancy. We were then laying down rules which were to be followed by those who would come after us, and it was of the greatest importance, not only to ourselves, personally, but to the profession generally, that these rules should be such as to bear the test of time and of the closest scrutiny, and I intend to spare no labor or pains to accomplish this result.[9]

There were eight other justices who served various terms during the interval before 1848. Only Gustavus P. Koerner, Norman H. Purple, James Shields, and Richard M. Young wrote opinions in cases involving Lincoln. These justices, listed chronologically by appointment date, are:

James Semple (1843), a native of Kentucky, moved to Illinois in 1818, and was licensed to practice law in Missouri in 1824, before returning to Illinois in 1828. He was elected to the Illinois Supreme Court in 1843, and resigned that same year to accept a seat in the United States Senate.

James Shields (1843–1845) was born in Ireland and came to America after being shipwrecked in Scotland. He emigrated to Illinois in 1826, began the practice of law in 1832, and was elected to the state legislature in 1836. He served as state auditor in 1839, and came to the Illinois Supreme Court in 1843. Shields served two terms in the United States Senate, and was a general in the Mexican War and the Civil War. (It was with Shields that Lincoln almost fought a duel in 1842.)

Jesse B. Thomas (1843–1845; 1847–1848), who was born in Ohio, served two short appointed terms on the Illinois Supreme Court. When serving on circuit court duty, he was the presiding judge at the trial of Joseph Smith, founder of the Mormon Church.

Richard M. Young (1843–1847), a native of Kentucky, was admitted to the Illinois bar in 1817, served as circuit court judge in 1825, and as a United States senator from 1837–1843. He resigned from the Supreme Court in 1847 to become commissioner of the General Land Office in Washington, D. C. Crossley said, "The close of his life was disastrously clouded by insanity."[10]

Norman H. Purple (1845–1848) was born in New York and practiced law in Pennsylvania for several years. In 1837, he moved to Illinois where he became a very successful practitioner of the law. He was appointed to the Supreme Court in 1845 and elected in 1846.

Gustavus P. Koerner (1845–1848), born in Frankfurt am Main in Germany in 1809, was graduated from Heidelberg University in 1832. He became a lawyer and participated in a revolt in 1833. He was wounded and fled to America, settling in Belleville, Illinois. General Usher D. Lindner wrote in his book, *Reminiscences* (1879), "When [Koerner] was appointed Judge of the [Illinois] Supreme Court, [Governor] Ford did it in deference to the German Democrats of St. Clair County, as he told me himself."[11] Koerner became a Republican in 1856, because of his opposition to the Kansas-Nebraska Act. After his service on the Supreme Court, he was lieutenant governor of Illinois, from 1852 through 1856, and was chairman of the state's Republican convention of 1858, which nominated Abraham Lincoln for the United States Senate. Koerner was Lincoln's second ambassador to Spain (1862–1864). Dissatisfaction with the Ulysses S. Grant administration led Koerner to the Liberal Republicans in 1872, and back to the Democrats by 1876.

William A. Denning (1847–1848) replaced Scates when he left the bench to practice law. Denning was from Franklin County, served as judge for the Third District, and returned to that position from 1848 through 1853.

1848-1861

Of the nine incumbent justices in 1848, two were retained by the people in the election prescribed by the new state constitution. Caton and Treat, with the third justice elected, Lyman Trumbull (1848–1853), constituted the new court. Trumbull began the practice of law in Illinois in 1837. He was born in Connecticut in 1818 and practiced law in Georgia before relocating to Belleville, Illinois, in 1837. He was elected to the lower house of the Illinois General Assembly, as a Democrat, in 1840. A year later, he had charge of the bill increasing the size of the Illinois Supreme Court, which was opposed by Lincoln.

Lincoln and Trumbull moved in the same social circles, however, and

Mary Lincoln served as Julia Jayne's bridal attendant when she married Lyman Trumbull in 1843. Trumbull served as Illinois Secretary of State from 1841–1843.

Twice elected to the Illinois Supreme Court, he resigned his seat in 1853 to resume his law practice. However, opposition to the Kansas-Nebraska Act drew him back into politics. He went back to the Illinois House in 1854, and became the most prominent Anti-Nebraska Democrat from southern Illinois. He defeated Lincoln and James Shields in a bid for the United States Senate in 1856. He became a member of the new Republican Party and a close ally of Abraham Lincoln. He was a powerful senator—chairman of the Judiciary Committee during the Civil War and a major postwar architect of Reconstruction.[12]

The general provisions of the 1848 state constitution did several things which affected the Illinois court system. It abolished the Council of Revision and divided the state into three grand divisions of the Supreme Court, with the people of each to elect one justice to serve for nine years. The constitution established nine judicial circuits, with the people in each circuit to elect a judge to serve for six years. Circuit court judges were required to hold two or more terms annually in each county in his circuit. It also added county courts.

Lincoln practiced before Caton, Treat, and Trumbull until 1853, when Scates replaced Trumbull. Scates served until 1857, when he in turn was replaced by Sidney Breese, who also had prior service on the old court. Treat was replaced by Onias C. Skinner (1855–1858), and he was replaced by Pinckney H. Walker (1858–1885).

Onias C. Skinner (1855–1858) practiced law in Carthage and served as a circuit court judge from 1851–1854, and was elected to the Illinois Supreme Court, where he served from June 4, 1855, until April 19, 1858, when he resigned.

Pinckney H. Walker (1858-1885) was a native of Kentucky, and moved with his father to McDonough County, Illinois. They were among its first settlers. "His early educational advantages were necessarily limited by the environments of time and place, but a strong determination, added to pronounced intellectual powers and good health, carried him over all the educational wants of the times and gave him a fair position as a scholar."[13] He served on the circuit court bench in Pike County, prior to April 1858, when he was appointed to succeed Skinner on the Illinois Supreme Court. In the succeeding year, he was elected for the full term, and was reelected, dying on February 18, 1885, only four months prior to the expiration of his third term.

So, from 1858 to 1861, the three Supreme Court justices were Caton, Breese, and Walker. Lincoln was involved in 174 cases from 1849 to 1861, with final decisions on a few of these rendered after he had left for

Washington to assume the office of President of the United States.

Caton offered some interesting comments about how a chief justice was selected:

> For this court (the new supreme court of three justices established with the adoption of the Constitution of 1848) Treat, Trumbull and myself were elected.... The constitution provided that we should cast lots at that term (December 1848), as to which should hold the office for nine years, which for six years, and which for three years. This we did very quietly and by ourselves in our room. Treat drew the longest straw, and so became chief justice of the court; I drew the second and Trumbull the third. Before Trumbull's term expired he was elected a senator to Congress, and Scates was elected to fill his vacancy. Before my term of six years expired Treat was appointed United States District Judge for the Southern District of Illinois, when I became chief justice for nearly six months, or from January to June, inclusive.[14]

The Constitution stated that the justices elected in December 1848 would stand for reelection in June 1849, but the legislature provided these three would continue as justices for their respective terms commencing June 1849. Caton goes on to comment on this:

> At the expiration of my term thus extended, I was elected to succeed myself for the nine year term, in June 1855. At the same time, Judge Skinner was elected to fill the vacancy caused by the resignation of Judge Treat, who was appointed United States District Judge, when Scates, who had been elected in the Third Grand Division to succeed Judge Trumbull, became chief justice by virtue of his holding the oldest commission.
>
> As before stated, at the June election in 1855, both Skinner and myself were elected, and on this I received my fifth commission as judge of the Supreme Court of Illinois.
>
> As the Constitution provided that the judge holding the oldest commission should be the chief justice, the governor, perceiving that embarrassment might arise from the omission of the constitution to determine who should become chief justice when two of the judges should hold commissions bearing the same date, issued my commission one day earlier than that of Skinner. When we met at Mount Vernon for the November term, 1857 of that court, Skinner claimed that the governor had no right thus to determine who should be chief justice, and that a fair way to settle the question was by casting lots for it. Of course the decision of this question fell upon Judge Breese, who had been elected to succeed Judge Scates in June 1857. Judge Breese decided that as I actually held the oldest commission, the constitution declared that I should be the chief

justice, and then I took my seat as presiding officer of that court for the second time, and held that office until I resigned, in 1864.[15]

After the justices heard a case argued, they would review it in private, and one of the justices would be assigned to write the opinion of the court. Justice Caton was author of many of the cases Lincoln argued. Justice Breese also wrote lucid opinions. Since these two justices were especially interesting and influential men, I have included short essays on special aspects of their careers as part of this chapter.

JOHN DEAN CATON

Prior to the revised Illinois State constitution of 1848, Illinois Supreme Court justices had responsibilities to hold trials in the various county seats of the judicial circuit to which they were assigned. When judgments from one of these circuit court trials were appealed, the judge who handled the trial was usually also serving as a justice, and had to participate in the decision as to whether or not he had made a mistake or two at the trial. And sometimes when this occurred, this same person had the privilege of writing the opinion overruling his judgment in the circuit court. On some of these occasions, the justice spoke of the trial judge as if he had been some uninformed stranger who didn't know any better, when it had been his own decision that was overruled. But not Justice John D. Caton, who in at least three cases found himself in that position. Two of these follow and the third, *Seeley v. Peters*,[16] is included both in chapter two and chapter twelve. In the Seeley case, Caton was overruled; still believing he had been right in the circuit court rulings, he wrote a thoughtful dissenting opinion.

Both attorneys and judges in the circuit court practice of those times had little time to prepare for many of their cases. The attorneys and a judge traveled from county seat to county seat in a continuous expedition until all the counties had been visited during that particular term of the court. The entourage arrived on Sunday, and the attorneys met with new clients to discuss and prepare for trial cases that started on the following day. The only law books the attorneys and judges had were those they could carry on horseback. It was the attorney's responsibility to present at the trial the legal precedents he relied upon to win the case for his client. The judge presided at each trial for one or more days, depending on how long it took to hear all those presented at that term in each particular place. He justifiably relied on the adversarial attorneys to provide the pertinent legal precedents to support his rulings.

The first case we mention here is *Favor et al. v. Marlett*,[17] December term 1844, which was an appeal from a trial in the Kane County Circuit Court, before Judge John D. Caton. In an opinion written by Justice Caton, the court reversed the decision. Lincoln and T. L. Dickey represented the appellant (Favor) in the Supreme Court. O. Peters represented Marlett.

Kimball Favor owned a shop in Aurora, Illinois, and F. M. Grant was his tenant. The rent was overdue, and Favor seized certain furniture belonging to Grant, and had it sold to pay the rent. However, Isaac Marlett was owed money by Grant, and had taken an assignment on the same property as security for that debt. Marlett sued Favor, and recovered $92. Grant was allowed to testify as to the value of the furniture. Favor objected to his testimony on the grounds that Grant was interested in enhancing the value of the damages. The court overruled this objection, and this is the basis of the appeal.

Caton started his opinion as follows: "In this case I have no doubt but I improperly admitted Grant, as a witness to testify as to the value of the property, for the taking of which this suit was brought." Grant had a greater interest in having Marlett prevail, because he would have received any balance left after the furniture was sold and Marlett paid off. Favor took the property, sold it, and kept the balance. Caton said he relied on a New York case, *Alexander v. Mahon*,[18] which held that a person in a comparable situation had interests in each side that were equally balanced. However, Lincoln submitted a case in arguing the appeal, also from New York *(Graves v. Delaplaine)*,[19] which held that a witness is incompetent to create or enhance a fund from which he is to be benefited, either by receiving money or having his own debts paid. Caton said this case controlled because Grant did not have balanced interests for either side, and thus his evidence should not have been received.

Obviously the Graves case was not submitted in the trial, as Caton stated he would have ruled differently if it had been. The logical explanation is that Lincoln did not go to Aurora to try the case but was involved in the appeal to the Supreme Court. He submitted the ruling case there, and his client prevailed.

Kimball v. Cook,[20] December term 1844, was another case where Judge Caton's rulings at the trial were deemed erroneous by the Supreme Court. In this case Amos Cook filed his bill in the La Salle County Circuit Court, under the act of 1839, for the purpose of enforcing a mechanic's lien. Cook had a contract with Lovell Kimball by which Cook was to do millwright work at a flouring mill, for which he would be paid $4800 in two installments of $2400, the first during the work and the last when work was completed. Kimball paid the first installment only, and Cook sued him for the balance to enforce a mechanic's lien. The trial was before Judge Caton and a jury, and Cook was awarded $2400. Several exceptions were taken during the trial, and the court ruled against Kimball. These rulings were the basis of the appeal.

Lincoln, O. Peters, and T. L. Dickey represented Cook on the appeal.

Justice Caton wrote the opinion reversing the judgment for the Supreme Court. Lincoln was able to support all Judge Caton's rulings on behalf of his client, except one, and this error in ruling was sufficient to cause the court to reverse the judgment. That particular ruling was the refusal of Judge Caton to allow Kimball to read, as evidence to the jury, that portion of his answer which was responsive to the bill of complaint. In a court of law a defendant's answer was not admissible as evidence, but in a court of equity it could be. Caton examined the enabling statute of the law of 1839 establishing mechanic's liens, and concluded that the language prescribing the procedures necessary to perfect the mechanic's lien were much more consistent with the principles of equity than of law. Thus he concluded on this point: "I have no doubt but I decided wrong in the court below, and that the answer of the defendant, so far as it was responsive to the bill, should have been read to the jury as evidence."

Caton's dissenting opinion in *Seeley v. Peters*,[21] December term 1848, is commented upon by him in his autobiography, *Early Bench and Bar in Illinois* (1893). His observations give valuable insights into Caton's relationships with his fellow justices, the respect he had for his duties, and his reasoning on why it was so important to him to write the dissenting opinion. He also alludes to his thought process regarding whether or not he had made the proper ruling in *Kimball v. Cook,* reported above:

> The next case to which I am inclined to refer is that of *Seeley v. Peters,* 5 Gilm. 130. The only question arising in that case was whether the common law of England, which required that the owner of domestic animals should restrain them from going on uninclosed premises of another, was in force in this State or not. The case was tried before me at the Peoria Circuit in 1847. I had previously bestowed great labor and care in examining the question and thought I understood it thoroughly, and upon the trial I instructed the jury that the common law of England prevailed here, and that the owners of stock were liable for damages if permitted to stray on the uninclosed lands of another.
>
> After the case had been argued and submitted, we retired to the conference room with the record, [and] we all expressed our opinions of the case. No assignment of the record was made to any one to write the opinion, nor was any vote taken as to what the decision should be, but I at least supposed that it would be considered at a future conference, when each member of the court would have an opportunity of assigning his reasons for the conclusion at which he arrived; and so the case was passed, and the conference proceeded to consider other cases.
>
> For several days this case was not again referred to. Finally an opinion was read reversing the judgment, which was approved by a majority of the court, holding that the common law had been repealed by

the first section of the law of 1819, and also that it was not applicable to our condition in life, as existing here, and that our people had always supposed that the law required every man to inclose his own premises to keep off the stock of others roaming at large.

To say that I felt chagrined and mortified at being thus ignored by what had been considered by them outside the conference, and it was manifest that they had studiously avoided any intercourse with me on the subject. I was a member of the court with as many rights and duties in connection with it as either of the other members, and to practically expel me from it bespoke some cogent reason, which they did not care to explain to me. To assume that I would unduly endeavor to secure a decision affirming my ruling on the circuit, as might naturally be implied from being thus excluded from the conference on the case, I felt sure was not justified by my past action as a member of the court. They certainly knew that I had never shown any sensitiveness at having my own decisions reversed, but had always shown an ardent desire to obtain correct decisions, whether they might affirm or reverse my circuit rulings. The case of *Kimball v. Cook,* 1 Gilm. 423, had been heard before the nine judges, and while I had heard the argument I declined to vote upon it, because I was in great doubt whether my decision upon the circuit was right or not, and I saw it would require a most laborious examination of the statute to satisfy myself on that point; but when the vote was taken it was found that four members of the court voted for affirming and four for reversing. While that would affirm my judgment by an equal division of the court, I was by no means satisfied that the decision would be right, and so consented to take the record and write out an opinion which would decide the case, whichever way I might conclude the law to be. I did so, and after a very careful examination of the statute I was entirely satisfied that I had committed an error in the court below, and so wrote out an opinion reversing my own judgment, and when I read it in conference three of the four who had voted for affirmance appeared to be convinced with me that the judgment should be reversed, and so it was done, and my opinion was adopted as the opinion of the court, excepting Judge [Richard M.] Young, who wrote a dissenting opinion.

Indeed, I thought my associates should have appreciated that my only desire was to have cases decided according to the law, without the least regard as to whether I, or some other judge, had made the decision in the lower court, which was under review at the time. I know I was just as anxious to reverse my own decisions, when satisfied of the error, as if they had been made by another judge. My only desire, and my ambition, was to lay down the law in the Supreme Court so that it would stand the test of time and scrutiny, rather than to perpetuate an error upon the records of the court from a false pride of opinion, which would afterward be found to be erroneous. I felt that lasting fame could only be secured by right decisions at the last, and that by affirming an error I could only weaken what reputation I might otherwise acquire. It is no reflection upon the capacity or integrity of a judge that his decisions at *nisi prius* should be reversed on appeal. There he must decide cases upon first impression, without that thorough examination which would enable him to form a matured judgment. Chancellor Walworth was taken from the circuit bench and made chancellor of the State of New York, and yet, whoever will have the curiosity to examine, will see that proportionally more of his decisions as circuit judge were reversed, than were those of any other judge who ever sat upon a circuit bench of that State; still his great reputation as a jurist was never impaired by that circumstance.

If I know myself, I know that I never had the least sensibility about having my judgments rendered on the circuit reversed in the Supreme Court, and I never admitted the idea that it was for that reason that I was excluded from the conference in the consideration of this case.

Perhaps it was because the other judges did not care to bear the infliction of hearing me argue the question in conference, which had been so well argued at the bar, and upon which their minds were conclusively made up; but for all that I did feel it keenly, and at once resolved to write a dissenting opinion, in which I thought I could demonstrate that the decision had not been the law before, although it must become the law afterward, at least for a time, and I did my best to do so. I certainly showed that the first section of the act of 1819, which was strongly relied upon, had been repealed and never afterward re-enacted; that many decisions of as respectable courts as any in the Union, and exactly in point, sustained a ruling of the court below, and that whether it was contrary to the genius of our institutions, and of the habits and notions of our people, were questions for the Legislature, and not for the court to determine. I understand that the Legislature has since that time enacted several laws modifying or changing the rule laid down by the court in that case, but I have not taken the trouble to examine them.

In looking over the report of that case after the lapse of so many years, I see that my dissenting opinion was unpardonably long, and that some of its expressions were more pungent than I wish they had been, but I am still satisfied that I was right in my conclusions as to what the law was. It is evident that when I wrote that opinion, I could not but feel the sting which had been provoked by what seemed to me to be a discourtesy; in this I am now satisfied that I was wrong, for I am entirely convinced that no discourtesy was intended. I am happy now to remember that the event never produced a shadow of coolness or ill-feeling between us; the same harmony and personal friendship always afterward existed as it had done before.[22]

SIDNEY BREESE

Breese served in the United States Senate from 1843-1849, and as a member of the Illinois General Assembly in 1851-1852. As a member of these two legislatures he was able to advance his dream of a major railroad running north and south through Illinois. An article in *Politics and Politicians of Illinois* lists the details of his life and includes his major accomplishments. This article, quoting an elaborate memorial address by Melville W. Fuller, of Chicago, before the Illinois Bar Association at Springfield in January 1879, on the life and services of Justice Breese, states that Justice Breese believed he was fully justified in receiving credit for "projecting" the Illinois Central Railroad. In October 1835, he "called attention of the public to the importance of a direct connection of the Illinois and Michigan Canal, then in course of construction, with the lower Mississippi at Cairo, by a railroad," going on to describe with more specificity the route of a proposed railroad, and he "labored steadily to bring it about, opposing, however, the act of February, 1837, for a general system of internal improvements."[23] In 1844, as a United States senator, he introduced legislation that was passed, establishing a naval depot and dockyard at the confluence of the Ohio and Mississippi Rivers, and granting to Illinois alternate sections of land to aid in construction of a railroad—the Illinois Central Railroad—from the point of termination of the Illinois and Michigan Canal to the Ohio/Mississippi junction. In 1851 when he was Speaker of the House of the General Assembly,

> ... the act was passed incorporating the Illinois Central Railroad Company, and giving it the benefit of the grant, and Judge Breese thus witnessed the close of his long labors in this direction ... and it was in that year that he published a letter in which he says: 'I claim to have first projected this great road in my letter of 1835, and in the judgment of impartial and disinterested men my claim will be allowed. I have said and written more in favor of it than any other. It has been my highest ambition to accomplish it, and when my last resting place shall be marked by the cold marble which gratitude or affection may erect, I desire for it no other inscription than this, that he who sleeps beneath it projected the Central Railroad.'[24]

NOTES

1. Palmer, John N., *The Bench and Bar of Illinois.* Chicago: The Lewis Publishing Company, 1899, 13.
2. Crossley, Frederic B., *Courts and Lawyers of Illinois.* Chicago: The American Historical Society, 1916, 185.
3. *Ibid.,* 164, 165.
4. *Ibid.,* 232.
5. Palmer, 32.

6. Crossley, 226.
7. *Ibid.,* 208.
8. *Ibid.,* 320.
9. Caton, John Dean, *Early Bench and Bar of Illinois.* Chicago: Chicago Legal News Company, 1893, 83.
10. Crossley, 232.
11. Linder, General Usher D., *Reminiscences.* Chicago: Chicago Legal News Company, 1879, 189–91
12. Neeley, Mark E., Jr., *The Abraham Lincoln Encyclopedia.* New York: Da Capo, 1983, 313–15.
13. Palmer, 55.
14. Caton, 93.
15. *Ibid.,* 94.
16. 10 *Ill.,* 130; *LCL,* 127.
17. 6 *Ill.,* 385; *Ibid.,* 70.
18. 11 Johns 185
19. 14 Johns 148, 160.
20. 6 *Ill.,* 423; *LCL,* 73.
21. See note number 16.
22. Caton, 181–84. References to *5 Gilm. 423* are identified as 10 *Ill.,* 130 and, *1 Gilm. 423* as 6 *Ill.,* 423 in the *Illinois Reports.* The earliest *Illinois Reports* were identified by the particular editor, as well as chronologically. For example, Sidney Breese was editor of the first volume of *Illinois Reports,* which is identified alternately as *1 Breese* or *1 Illinois.* Johnathan Y. Scammon was the second editor, and *2 Illinois* is also cited as *1 Scammon. Gilm.* is an abbreviation for Gilman, who was the third editor, with five editions of *Illinois Reports* with his name.
23. Lusk, D. W., *Eighty Years of Illinois: Politics and Politicans, 1809–1889.* Springfield, Illinois: printed by H. W. Roakker, 266–67.
24. *Ibid.,* 268.

Chapter Four

Lincoln's Fellow Lawyers in His Appellate Practice

ABRAHAM LINCOLN HAD THREE SUCCESSIVE PARTNERS during his entire legal practice in Springfield, from 1837 to 1861, as well as at least one partnership in another city, several *ad hoc* partnerships, and additional associates in many of his Illinois Supreme Court cases. In his first two Springfield partnerships, he was the junior partner; in the third, he was senior partner.

His first Springfield partnership was with John Todd Stuart, who served with Lincoln in the Illinois legislature and had served with him in the Black Hawk War. Stuart had encouraged the young Lincoln to study law. Almost immediately after Lincoln moved to Springfield in 1837, the firm of Stuart & Lincoln was formed. John Todd Stuart—a cousin of the woman Lincoln would marry—had graduated from Centre College, in Danville, Kentucky, in 1826; was licensed as a lawyer in 1827; and moved to Springfield in 1828. He soon became a leader in the Whig party in Illinois.

Stuart served in the state legislature from 1832-36. He sought election to Congress in 1836, but was defeated by the Democratic incumbent, William L. May. He was actively practicing law as he began his partnership with Lincoln. However, Stuart ran for Congress again in 1838—this time against Stephen A. Douglas—and was elected. He was reelected in 1840. Lincoln, therefore, was running their law office while Stuart was in Washington, and thus learned the practice of law at an accelerated pace with no experienced lawyer to ease the process. The partnership thrived, and Lincoln's better qualities—including patience, intelligence, and practical sense—served him (and Stuart) well. Lincoln left the firm in 1841 to join Stephen T. Logan. He and Stuart remained friends, and he appeared many times with Stuart before the Illinois Supreme Court—sometimes as an adversary and other times as co-counsel.

Stephen T. Logan was a well-established lawyer with a broad-based practice, and a skilled politician. He was a native of Kentucky, was educated

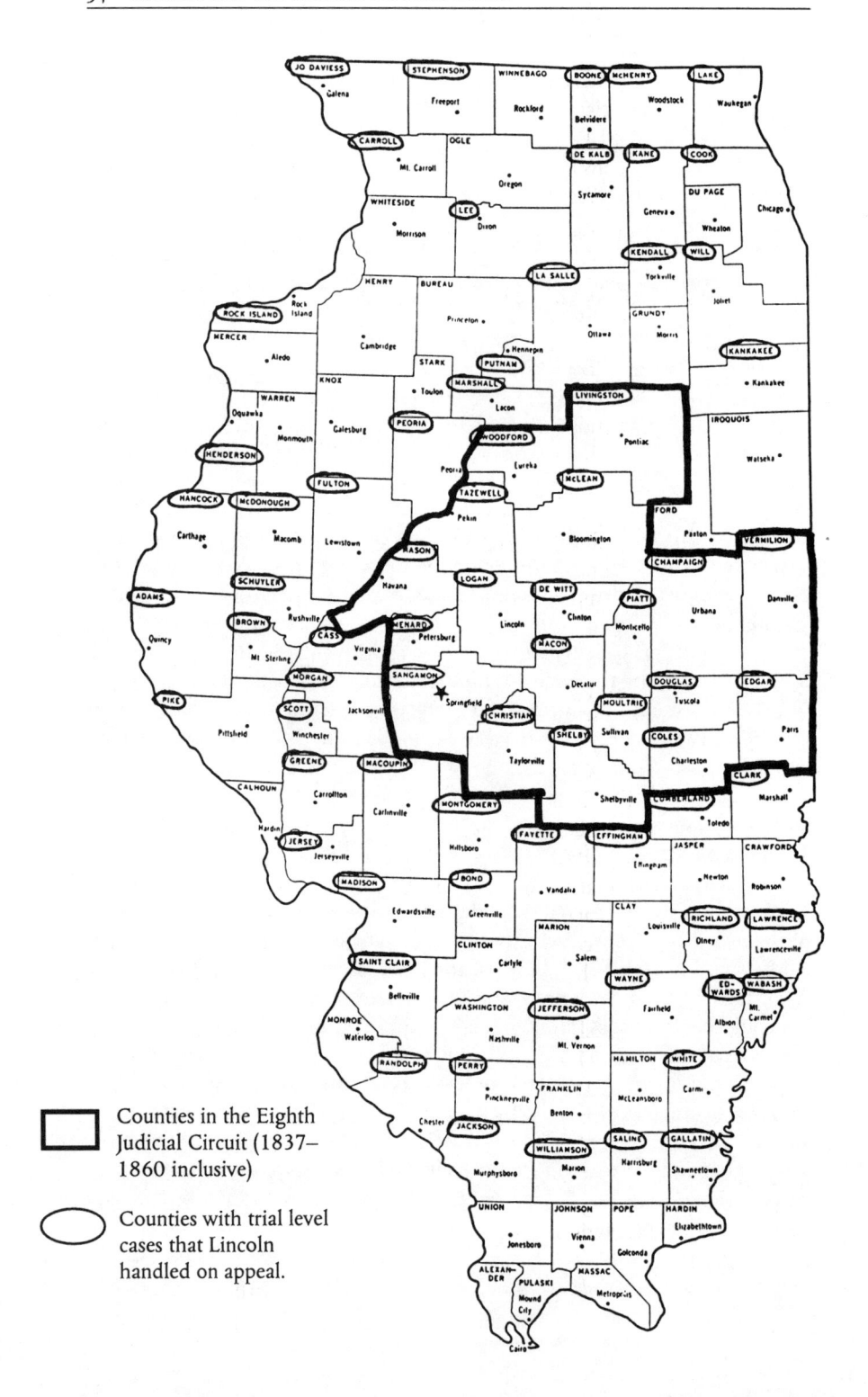

34 LINCOLN AND THE ILLINOIS SUPREME COURT

☐ Counties in the Eighth Judicial Circuit (1837–1860 inclusive)

◯ Counties with trial level cases that Lincoln handled on appeal.

at Frankfurt, and had been admitted to the bar in Kentucky before attaining his majority. He practiced law there until he moved to Springfield, Illinois, in 1832. Lincoln and Logan were close political associates in the 1840s. Logan served four terms in the Illinois legislature (1844–48, 1854–58). *The Dictionary of American Biography* (1933) states that soon after commencing his practice in Springfield, Logan "became one of the foremost lawyers in the state.... Lincoln owed much to his senior partner, for it was during the period of this partnership that Lincoln's serious practice of the law began."[1] The partnership continued until 1844, when Lincoln activated the partnership of Lincoln & Herndon.

William Henry "Billy" Herndon was born in Kentucky in 1818, and moved with his family to Illinois in 1820. The family settled in Springfield in 1823. Herndon attended Illinois College in Jacksonville for a year and then studied law. He worked as a clerk in Joshua Speed's store in Springfield where he became acquainted with Abraham Lincoln. Herndon was admitted to the bar in 1844, and became Lincoln's partner the same year. This partnership would continue until Lincoln's death. Herndon was very loyal to Lincoln and brought important complementary talents which strengthened the partnership. Herndon, for example, managed the office and did much of the research of looking up precedents, as well as arguing some cases in court. Lincoln's last request to Herndon, as he left Springfield for Washington to assume the Presidency, was to keep the old "Lincoln & Herndon" sign on their office, so that when he returned it could be "business as usual."

It was during the years of this partnership that Lincoln's most significant Illinois Supreme Court cases were argued. Lincoln's and Herndon's capabilities as successful Supreme Court advocates became well-known throughout the state, and appellate work was sent to them from trial lawyers and their clients from all over Illinois. Lincoln was involved in appellate cases that had been tried in at least seventy-two Illinois counties. These counties are identified on the state map on the opposite page.

In addition to his conventional partnerships in Springfield, Lincoln had *ad hoc* partner relationships with lawyers on the circuit. These were established for work on trial court business and also for appellate work. The best known of such relationships was with Ward Hill Lamon of Danville, Illinois, in Vermilion County. This is frequently noted in biographies of Lincoln in reference to his cases on the circuit, but there is no record in Illinois Supreme Court Reports of Lincoln and Lamon working together on an appellate case.

It is recorded that Lincoln participated with attorneys from forty counties in appeals from trials in those particular counties; these attorneys are listed in the opinions as being associated with him in the representation of one of the parties. Documentation of these cases includes Lincoln's name along with that of another attorney(s) other than one of his three formal partners. We can see the extent of these *ad hoc* partner relationships by listing the counties from which appeals were taken, the county seat, and the year of the appellate decision. The attorneys' names are identified in the following list as they appeared in the case reports. In some instances, the attorneys are noted only by surnames. Additional information is included about some of these men.

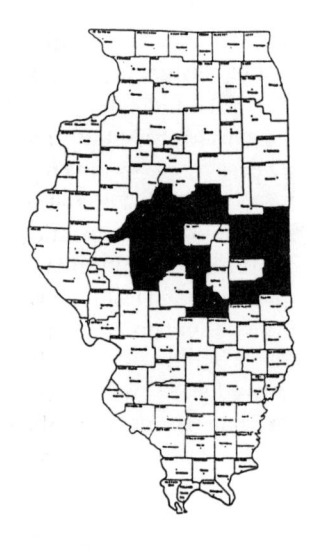

THE EIGHTH JUDICIAL CIRCUIT was the one most traveled by Lincoln. Comprising this circuit, from 1837 to 1860, were the following counties from which Lincoln assisted in at least one appeal.

SANGAMON COUNTY—SPRINGFIELD: E. D. Baker (1844), Baker and Bledsoe (1842), O. W. Browning & Bushnell (1850, 1851), W. J. Conkling (1851, 1857), Benjamin S. Edwards (1851), William I. Ferguson (1845, 1851), D. A. Smith (1854), S. Strong (1841), W. Thomas (1845), and J. B. White (1859).

Edward D. Baker was born in England in 1811, and moved with his family to the United States in 1816. He studied law in Carrollton, Illinois, and came to Springfield in 1835. He served two terms in the Illinois legislature, and in the Illinois Senate from 1840 to 1844. Baker became a very close friend of Abraham Lincoln; the Lincolns named their second son for him.

Lincoln's friend and neighbor James C. Conkling was born in New York City in 1816, graduated from Princeton in 1835, and moved to Springfield, where he began practicing law in 1838. He married Mercy Levering, a good friend of Mary Todd. Conkling was elected mayor of Springfield in 1844, and to the Illinois legislature in 1851.

Benjamin S. Edwards was the son of Illinois Territorial Governor Ninian Edwards, and the brother of Ninian Wert Edwards who married Mary Todd Lincoln's sister Elizabeth. Born in 1818, he attended Yale University, completed his study of the law with Stephen T. Logan, and began his practice in 1840. Edwards formed a partnership with John Todd Stuart in 1843; their partnership continued for forty years.

Orville H. Browning was born in Kentucky and practiced law in Quincy and Springfield. Lincoln represented him in an action he brought against Springfield when he broke his leg in the city streets. (This case is detailed in chapter five.) He was appointed to the United States Senate to fill a vacancy caused by the death of Senator Stephen A. Douglas.

LOGAN COUNTY—LINCOLN: Benjamin S. Edwards (1855—two cases), C. Emerson (1859), Milton Hay (1860—two cases), Logan & Hay (1860),

S. C. Parks (1859), Stuart & Edwards (1855—two cases).

Edwards, Hay, Logan, Parks, Stuart, Edwards all practiced law in Springfield.

In his brief biography of Samuel C. Parks, Palmer says: "In fact, Logan County was seemingly regarded as an out-post of Springfield and Bloomington lawyers, who claimed it as part of its bailiwick and monopolized or 'gobbled-up' all the paying practice."[2] Parks was later appointed by President Lincoln to be a federal judge in the Wyoming Territory.

Milton Hay, who was born in 1817 in Kentucky, moved to Springfield in 1832, and became a student of law in the offices of Stuart & Lincoln in 1838. He was admitted to the bar in 1840 and that same year formed a partnership with Edward D. Baker. In 1861, he became a partner of Stephen T. Logan. Hay was the uncle of John Hay, who later became one of President Lincoln's private secretaries, a biographer of Lincoln (with John G. Nicolay), and secretary of state under Presidents William McKinley and Theodore Roosevelt.

MENARD COUNTY—PETERSBURG: J. D. Urquhart (1846), T. L. Harris (1845).

Urquhart was a native of Virginia who moved to Springfield about 1832. According to Palmer, "He was well-read in the law and in the general literature of the day. He was a gentleman of the old school, with too much refinement to adapt himself to western methods, and therefore achieved no success as a lawyer at the bar of Sangamon County."[3] Urquhart became a partner of Stephen T. Logan in 1837.

TAZEWELL COUNTY—PEKIN: M. Brayman & W. H. Leonard (1843), Milton Hay (1855), H. C. Merriman (1846), Stuart & Edwards (1851), J. B. Thomas (1841).

Jesse B. Thomas later practiced in Cook County, and was appointed to the Supreme Court in 1847 for a one-year term. H. C. Merriman also practiced in Peoria, Peoria County, which is just across the Illinois River from Pekin, and worked on a case with Lincoln in 1845. Palmer said, "I have no recollection of having ever seen Halsey C. Merriman. He was a very popular lawyer, and had been attorney for the town of Peoria when it obtained its charter as a city, which was largely the work of his hands."[4]

SHELBY COUNTY—SHELBYVILLE: Samuel W. Moulton (1853).

Palmer stated that "Mr. Moulton became one of the best lawyers in the state.... [S]addle-bag lawyers from other counties soon learned that it was not worthwhile to visit Shelby County."[5]

MACON COUNTY—DECATUR: C. Emerson (1841).

MCLEAN COUNTY—BLOOMINGTON: M. Brayman & J. F. Joy (1855). This case was the famous *Illinois Central Railroad v. County of McLean,* which is included in chapter seven.

T. Mason Brayman was the first solicitor for the Illinois Central Railroad, and from 1852–1861 was in charge of its legal department.

CHAMPAIGN COUNTY—URBANA: H. C. Whitney (1857).
This is the Henry Clay Whitney who wrote *Life on the Circuit with Lincoln* (1892).

EDGAR COUNTY—PARIS: J. J. Hardin (1845).

John J. Hardin was a cousin of Mary Todd Lincoln and a friend and Whig rival of Abraham Lincoln in the Seventh Congressional District of Illinois. He was born in Frankfurt, Kentucky, the son of a United States senator. Hardin graduated from Transylvania University, and was admitted to the Kentucky bar in 1831. That same year, he moved to Jacksonville, Illinois, and established a law practice there. He served three terms in the Illinois legislature and one term in the United States House of Representatives. When the Mexican War began, Hardin became a colonel of the First Illinois Regiment of Volunteers. He was killed in combat at the Battle of Buena Vista on February 23, 1847. He also practiced in Jo Daviess, Madison, Scott, and Winchester counties.

VERMILION COUNTY—DANVILLE: Baker (1844, 1845), O. L. Davis & D. E. Harman (1858).

COLES COUNTY—CHARLESTON: M. F. Linder (1857), O. B. Ficklin & H. C. Whitney (1857).

MASON COUNTY—HAVANA: Murray McConnel (1845).

The following counties are located west of Springfield, and while Lincoln did most of his trial court practice in the Eighth Judicial District, he also had significant trial work in several of these counties.

MORGAN COUNTY—JACKSONVILLE: David A. Smith (1855—two cases), D. A. Smith and Murray McConnel (1854), William Thomas (1843, 1857), William W. Brown (1840), T. L. Harris (1845).

David A. Smith began practicing law in Jacksonville in 1835. Palmer said his motto was "thorough work and thorough pay."[6] His thorough work included appeals from Sangamon, Scott, Madison, Morgan, Edgar, Cass, and Jo Davies counties—one must presume the "thorough pay" went along with this.

Murray McConnel was born in New York and settled in the Jacksonville area in 1820, before Morgan County was organized, and resided there for forty-five years. William Thomas moved to Jacksonville from Kentucky in 1826. Palmer calls him the "Lord Readsdale of the bar; carried his court papers in the old-style green-baize bag, and even wrote with a goose quill."[7] According to Palmer, William W. Brown was "one of the most distinguished jurists and successful practitioners at the bar."[8]

CASS COUNTY—VIRGINIA: D. A. Smith and H. E. Dummer (1857), J. S. Bailey (1856).

Henry E. Dummer was an early partner of John Todd Stuart, and then practiced in Beardstown.

ADAMS COUNTY—QUINCY: A. Williams (1849), W. Marshall and A. Williams (1845), E. B. Herndon (1860).

Archibald Williams moved to Quincy from Kentucky in 1825 and began his law practice there that year. He was later appointed by his friend President Lincoln to be a judge of the United States District Court in Kansas.

PIKE COUNTY—PITTSFIELD: A. Williams & W. Thomas (1852, 1853).

SCOTT COUNTY—WINCHESTER: J. J. Hardin & D. A. Smith (1844).

The following counties are southwest of Springfield. Lincoln was involved in appeals from seven counties in this area, but with local counsel in only two of these—Madison and Jersey.

MADISON COUNTY—EDWARDSVILLE: D. A. Smith (1851), Joseph Gillespie & Smith (1840), J. W. Chickering (1844), J. W. Chickering, J. J. Hardin & D. A. Smith (1842), N. D. Strong (1844, 1846), N. D. Strong & Junius Hall (1842), Lyman Trumbull & J. B. Thomas (1845), J. M. Krum (1844).

Joseph Gillespie was born in New York state, and came to Edwardsville in 1809. He was involved in many important cases and issues as a lawyer, a judge, and a legislator. Palmer said of Gillespie: "Like Lincoln, of whom he was a warm personal friend, his youth was one of poverty, but in the school of experience they learned the lessons which fitted one for duties that made one the deliverer and preserver of his nation, and the other a most important factor in framing the policy of his state."[9]

JERSEY COUNTY—JERSEYVILLE: R. S. Blackwell (1852).

There were six counties in the near northwest section of Illinois in which Lincoln was involved in cases appealed to the Supreme Court. In three of these counties local lawyers were also involved.

HANCOCK COUNTY—CARTHAGE: Williams (1845).

HENDERSON COUNTY—OQUAKA: Williams & Lawrence (1850)

PEORIA COUNTY—PEORIA: H. O. Merriman (1845), E. N. Powell (1845), Powell & W. F. Bryan (1845).

Palmer said: "Elihu N. Powell came from Ohio at a very early age. He had not the advantage of a thorough education in early life, yet, through indomitable industry and perserverance in his studies, he became a very able lawyer. He had as a partner for some years William F. Bryan. The firm of Powell & Bryan had developed a very extensive and lucrative practice by the time of his death in 1871. Judge Powell was considered the senior member of the Peoria bar. He had the rare facility of being able to cite from memory, giving book and page, any reported case he had ever read."[10]

Lincoln also participated in appellate cases from the southern part of the state, which included Shawneetown, one of the earliest settlements in Illinois.

FAYETTE COUNTY—VANDALIA: C. Walker, J. Butterfield, H. P. Field, L. Davis (1840).

CLARK COUNTY—MARSHALL: J. T. Cooper (1859), Young (1847).

GALLATIN COUNTY—SHAWNEETOWN: Henry Eddy (1844).

Henry Eddy was born in Vermont and studied law in Pennsylvania. He obtained a printing press and in 1818 sailed down the Ohio River to Shawneetown, where he became the editor of the second newspaper to be published in Illinois, the *Illinois Emigrant.*

SALINE COUNTY—HARRISBURG: R. Wingate (1851).

WHITE COUNTY—CARMI: S. D. Marshall (1852).

Though Samuel Davies Marshall was born in Indiana, he moved with his family to Shawneetown shortly thereafter. He went to prep school in New Haven, Connecticut, and graduated from Yale University in 1833.

Marshall practiced law in Shawneetown for the rest of his life.

JEFFERSON COUNTY—MT. VERNON: Walter B. Scates (1853).

Walter B. Scates began his second term as an Illinois Supreme Court justice in 1853. He was a very successful practicing attorney when he wasn't serving on the Supreme Court.

RICHLAND COUNTY—OLNEY: C. H. Constable (1844), A. Shaw (1842).

EDWARDS COUNTY—ALBION: Webb and Constable (1846), Constable (1846).

Lincoln was active in appellate work from the northern part of Illinois in 1844–46, with cases from thirteen counties then and later. In ten of the counties local lawyers were involved with him on the appeals. The most active attorney working with Lincoln on these cases was T. L. Dickey, who practiced in four of the counties.

COOK COUNTY—CHICAGO: J. B. Thomas (1845), J. B. Thomas & B. C. Morris (1845), M. Skinner & G. A. O. Beaumont (1844).

Jesse B. Thomas began practicing law in Chicago in 1845. He had practiced earlier in Springfield. Mark Skinner was admitted to the bar in New York, and in 1836 moved to Chicago, where he formed a partnership with George Anson Oliver Beaumont.

LAKE COUNTY—WAUKEGAN: G. Spring & G. Goodrich (1846).

Grant Goodrich practiced law in New York before moving to Cook County in 1834, where he practiced law and also served as a judge.

KANE COUNTY—GENEVA: G. Goodrich (1855), T. L. Dickey (1844), J. B. Thomas (1845).

Theophilus Lyle Dickey was born in Kentucky, moved to Illinois in 1834, and was admitted to the bar in 1835. In 1836 he moved to Ottawa, where he soon built up a large and lucrative practice. Palmer said that Dickey's "name is prominently connected with the history of Illinois as a lawyer, jurist, and a soldier."[10]

KENDALL COUNTY—YORKVILLE: T. L. Dickey (1844), B. F. Fridley (1846).

Benjamin F. Fridley was the first lawyer to locate in Kane County. He served as the sheriff of Kane County and later as prosecuting attorney for twelve counties.

LA SALLE COUNTY—OTTAWA: T. L. Dickey (1844).

PUTNAM COUNTY—HENNEPIN: T. L. Dickey (1845).
MCHENRY COUNTY—WOODSTOCK: I. G. Wilson (1846).
BOONE COUNTY—BELVIDERE: J. L. Loop (1840)

The case in Boone County, *Scammon v. Cline,* was the first in which Lincoln was designated by name as one of the attorneys on an appeal. Boone County, on the northern border near Wisconsin, is as far from Springfield as any county in Illinois.

JO DAVIESS COUNTY—GALENA: J. W. Chickering (1845), J. J. Hardin & D. A. Smith (1847).

STEPHENSON COUNTY—FREEPORT: T. Campbell & M. Y. Johnson (1846).

NOTES

1. *The Dictionary of America Biography,* Volume 6. New York: Charles Scribner's Sons, 1933, 365–366.
2. Palmer, John M., *Bench and Bar of Illinois,* Volume II. Chicago: Lewis Publishing Company, 1899, 1010.
3. *Ibid.,* 180.
4. *Ibid.,* 294.
5. *Ibid.,* 459.
6. *Ibid.,* 339.
7. *Ibid.,* 337.
8. *Ibid.,* 338.
9. *Ibid.,* 684–5.
10. *Ibid.,* 61.

Part II

Chapter Five

Public Entities and Officials

THE ILLINOIS TERRITORY, which had been organized in 1809, was reconstituted as a state in 1818, and a state constitution was adopted. The fifteen counties in the territory automatically became counties in the new state. The first election of state and county officers took place on September 17–19, 1818, as provided for in the new constitution. Shadrach Bond was elected governor and Pierre Menard lieutenant governor at the first general assembly, which convened at Illinois' first capital, Kaskaskia, on Monday, October 5, 1818.

The new state officials were sworn in on October 6. The state senate confirmed Governor Bond's appointment of Elias Kent Kane to the office of Secretary of State. On October 8, the legislature met in joint session to elect justices of the Illinois Supreme Court; on the following day, the attorney general, auditor, treasurer, and public printers were elected.

No laws were passed in the first session of the legislature because Illinois was not accepted as a state of the union until the United States Senate resolution of December 1, 1818. The second General Assembly of Illinois convened in January 1919. From that point on, the assembly passed legislation establishing the rights, privileges, powers, and obligations of the various governmental entities—including itself—and those of the elected and appointed officials of each political entity.

The interpretation of the Constitution and legislation pertaining to public entities and officials was provided by the Illinois Supreme Court. Lincoln was involved in at least twenty-five of such cases, which will be presented in this section. My intent is to combine them in some meaningful way in an attempt to enhance understanding of the importance of these cases—not only because of the problem(s) resolved in each instance, but for the precedents established.

Many of these cases were brought by and against individuals in their official capacities. Others were brought by a public official at the behest of a private party. The latter are called *ex relatione (ex rel.)*, defined by *Black's Law Dictionary* as:

...upon relation or information. Legal proceedings which are instituted by the attorney general (or other proper person) in the name and behalf of the state, but on the information and instigation of an individual who has a private interest in the matter, are said to be taken "on the relation" *(ex relatione)* of such person, who is called the "relator."

State Officials

The first major case in this category—*Field v. People ex rel., McClernand*,[1] December term 1839—involved an incumbent secretary of state (Alexander P. Field, a Whig) whom Thomas Carlin, a Democrat who was elected governor in 1839, attempted to fire. He sought to fill the post with a fellow-Democrat, John A. McClernand. Nine lawyers were listed in the over one-hundred-page opinion; Lincoln was not listed in the formal court report, but Harry E. Pratt has identified him as representing Field.[2] Lincoln's political orientation was the same as Field's.

The case is an appeal from an action of *quo warranto*—in common law, a claim against an incumbent office holder to inquire by what authority he supports his claim to office. The action was brought in the Fayette County Circuit Court before Judge Breese, by The People upon the instigation of McClernand against Field, to ask by what authority he held the office of secretary of state.

Field was appointed secretary of state in 1829, and remained in office in 1838, when Carlin was elected governor. In 1839 Carlin, by virtue of his authority as governor, appointed McClernand to replace Field. Field refused to leave office, and brought this action in the Fayette County Circuit Court with Sidney Breese as the judge. Judge Breese (who did not become a justice of the Illinois Supreme Court until 1841) held for McClernand. Cyrus Walker, Justin Butterfield, A. P. Field, and Levi Davis were listed in the opinion as representing Field, and J. B. Thomas, S. A. Douglass, James Shields, John A. McClernand, and the attorney general Wickliffe Kitchell represented The People.

The Illinois Supreme Court ruled to reverse the judgment. Chief Justice William Wilson wrote the majority opinion (forty-four pages); Justice Theophilus Smith wrote a dissenting opinion (twenty-seven pages); and Justice Samuel D. Lockwood wrote an opinion which concurred with that of the chief justice (forty-four pages). Each opinion was based on interpretations of the logic of the Illinois constitution. There were many points made at the trial and on appeal that had to be agreed with or contravened by logical argument. There was little case law on this subject in Illinois at the time.

Justice Wilson's opinion stated that neither the executive nor the judiciary could execute any authority or power, except such as is clearly granted by the constitution. Under the Illinois constitution, the appointing power does not have automatic power to remove an incumbent from office. The secretary of state is a constitutional officer whose role and powers are specified in the constitution, and his tenure is undefined and unlimited. The legislature has the power to limit the term of this office, but until it does so, the secretary can hold office.

Justice Wilson cited two Illinois cases, both of which he claimed were indistinguishable from this one, which held that incumbents in government offices could not be removed from office at the will or pleasure of their superior officers. The circuit court judge (Breese) said that he knew about these cases, but since he didn't agree with them, he wasn't going to comply with them. Wilson rebuked Breese when he stated what he thought was very clear: when the Supreme Court has declared what the law is on a given point, in instances of that same point coming up again in litigation, all other courts in the state are bound to conform to the law. Wilson wrote:

> A different rule would destroy all the stability and uniformity in the rules of law, which is so essential to the administration of justice, and the safety of the citizens. If every judge can decide according to his private sentiments, without regard to precedent or authority, there may be as many rules of decisions as there are circuits, and the decision of one day would furnish no rule for the decision of the next.

Justice Smith, in his dissenting opinion, noted that under the United States Constitution, the president could dismiss the national secretary of state. The Illinois constitution, he emphasized, was patterned after the nation's Constitution, and "as the state constitution was adopted in the year 1818, thirty-one years after that of the United States, it is a fair legal inference, that by the adoption, it was intended to adopt the construction given to that from which it was taken, and to which it is in so many essential parts entirely analogous." Thus, Smith held that Field could be dismissed by the new governor.

Justice Lockwood, in agreeing with the majority, pointed out the essential differences in the two offices. The United States secretary of state assists the president in the management of peace and war, negotiation of treaties with foreign nations, and in the regulation of commerce. There must be a confidential relationship between the two, and the president must be able to control the secretary. The power to remove a secretary of state is mandatory for a president. The secretary of state in Illinois has duties specified in the constitution, rendered to both the governor and the legislature. The secretary has no confidential role with the governor, and is not under the governor's control. The settled doctrine is that construction for the purpose of conferring power should be resorted to with great caution, and only for the most persuasive reasons. Such reasons were not present in this case.

Robert Howard, in *Illinois: A History of the Prairie State,* published in 1972, provides some of the political background of this case as follows:

> Carlin in 1838 won the governorship by less than one thousand votes over Cyrus Edwards, who was the former governor's younger brother and had declared for internal improvements. The Democrats, who had held their first convention the preceding year, wanted a candidate from the North. They nominated James W. Stephenson, receiver of the land office at Galena, but learned just in time his accounts with the federal government were short by more than forty thousand dollars. Carlin, who took his place on the ticket, embroiled the Supreme Court in politics by attempting to remove from office Secretary of State Alexander P. Field, a Whig whose lifetime appointment dated back to the Edwards administration. The senate refused to affirm Carlin's appointment of John A. McClernand, an active Democrat for several decades. The Whig majority of the Supreme Court held that the governor could only appoint when a vacancy existed. Democrats made the court an issue in a campaign in which they gained control of the legislature. Field then resigned, and Douglas became secretary of state briefly as he moved quickly up the political ladder.[3]

Lincoln represented Field in another constitutional case, *Field et al. v. Rawlings,*[4] December term 1844, in which Alexander A. Field, as secretary of state, presented to Moses M. Rawlings, as fund commissioner, an account claiming seventy-five cents per bond for affixing the seal of state to one-thousand state bonds. Rawlings paid the bill and took a bond executed by Field as principal, and his sureties, on the condition that Field should return the money with interest, in case it should be decided by the legislature or the Supreme Court that the fees were not legally chargeable. Rawlings brought an action for debt in the Gallatin County Circuit Court, before Judge Scates, contending that Field had an obligation to have the matter decided by the Supreme Court or the legislature, but he had not done so. Even so, the legislature, by the Senate, had decided the fees were not legally chargeable. A judgment was rendered in the amount of $1040.25 for Rawlings.

Lincoln and H. Eddy represented Field and the sureties, and Trumbull and J. A. McDougall represented Rawlings. Justice Shields wrote the opinion reversing the judgment. Firstly, the stipulation in the bond that a decision must be made by the legislature or Supreme Court is expressed, and the guarantors are not chargeable unless either happens, and Fields did not have an obligation to seek either one. The sureties did not stipulate that Field obtain a decision. The court could not add additional stipulation by implication. Lincoln cited *Miller v. Stewart,*[5] and the court agreed it was decisive on this point: "Nothing can be clearer, both upon principle and authority, than the doctrine that the liability of the surety, is not to be extended by implication, beyond the terms of the contract." Secondly, a decision by only one branch of the legislature could not be considered sufficient. Field was liable to repay the money, with interest, if he received the money without authority of law, but his sureties stood on an entirely different footing, and were only liable according to the strict terms of their bond. Thus the judgment was reversed, and the cause remanded, with leave to amend the proceedings.

Another case involving the office of secretary of state was *Trumbull v. Campbell*,[6] December term 1846. Lincoln represented Lyman Trumbull, who had been appointed secretary of state February 27, 1841, and continued to hold office until March 4, 1843, when he was superseded by the appointment of Thompson Campbell. The legislature, on March 3, 1843, appropriated "to the secretary of state, for making the index to the journals of the senate and house of representatives and laws, for copying laws, and making marginal notes and index to laws, the sum of six hundred dollars." The next day, which was Trumbull's last day in office, Trumbull estimated he had done two-thirds of the work, asked for, and was paid $400. Campbell subsequently performed the rest of the services and, alleging Trumbull had been overpaid, brought this action of *assumpsit* in the Sangamon County Circuit Court to recover the alleged overpayment to Trumbull. The court awarded $200 to Campbell. Campbell was represented by Stephen Logan and A. T. Bledsoe.

The Supreme Court, with Justice Treat writing the opinion, reversed the judgment of the lower court, saying: "The only point in this case is, whether the action as between the parties can be maintained. The question was discussed at the bar with much ability, and some embarrassment has been felt in determining it." Treat went on to say that no action could be brought by Campbell. If Trumbull was overpaid, the state could sue to recover it. If Campbell did some of this work, he should be paid by the state, even if Trumbull had been paid for the same work.

Lincoln cited six common law cases and treatises as authorities, and prevailed. Apparently the embarrassment mentioned by Treat was because of the political nature of the trial. The circuit court judge was not identified in the opinion. Treat did serve as judge in many Sangamon County Circuit Court cases during this period.

Lincoln represented George M. Billings who was seeking specific action from Governor William H. Bissell in *People ex rel. Billings v. Bissell*,[7] December term 1857, and brought this application of *mandamus* directly to the Supreme Court which would require Governor Bissell to perform certain acts. Billings owned two $1000 state bonds on which there remained $1860 unpaid interest. Billings wanted the governor to issue him new bonds for the arrearage. He contended that the governor was required to do so under a legislative act entitled, "An act to fund the arrears of interest accrued and unpaid on the public debt of the State of Illinois," which was approved on February 18, 1857. The governor did not concur. Billings was represented by Stuart & Edwards and Lincoln & Herndon. Logan represented the governor.

The Supreme Court, in an opinion written by Justice Caton, denied the application. Caton ruled that the court did not have the constitutional authority to order the governor to perform any public duty. The justice answered a basic argument of Lincoln and his colleagues as follows: "It is urged upon us, that in a government of laws there must be an adequate remedy for every wrong, and that where a clear right exists, there must be some mode of enforcing that right. While human society is governed by so imperfect a being as man, this can be true only in theory. If we were to compel the governor or the legislature to right every wrong which may arise from the omission of duty, then surely they must, in order to make this utopian system perfect, have the power to compel us to do right in every case." Then, "In the formation of the government, equal confidence was rightfully reposed in each department, to which appropriate and independent duties were assigned. If we unintentionally err, and do a party never so great a wrong, there is, and from the nature of our institutions, can be no remedy. If we perversely or corruptly do an intentional wrong, the constitution has provided the only remedy, which is by impeachment; and so of the executive. When acting within the limits assigned to each, neither can control or dictate to the other."

Lincoln represented another secretary of state in *People ex rel. Lanphier & Walker v. Hatch*,[8] December term 1857, which tested whether an act of the governor constituted approval of a legislative bill. The legislature passed an "Act to create senatorial and representative districts, and apportion the representation in the General Assembly of this state." It was properly signed by the leader of each house, and sent to the governor for his action. He inadvertently signed it, thinking it was another matter. He had intended to veto it. His secretary sent the signed bill back to the House of Representatives as was the informal custom. As soon as it was announced in the House that he had signed it, the governor sent a message of disapproval. This action was brought by the authorized printers of the approved legislative acts in the form of a writ of *mandamus* to require the secretary of state to release a copy of the bill, directly to the printer. Lincoln and J. Grimshaw represented the secretary of state. W. C. Goudy, John A. McClernand, and R. S. Blackwell represented The People.

The Supreme Court, in an opinion written by Justice Caton, said the governor may sign and erase his signature. The fact that his secretary reported it as passed was not binding on the governor. It had been the practice of the secretary to report his signature, but this was merely a courtesy, and not binding on the governor. Justice Breese wrote a separate opinion, concurring with the majority. He said, "A power to rectify an error at the proper time, exists with all departments of the government, for they are all liable to err. It is an infirmity of our nature, from which a governor cannot claim exemption."

Lincoln represented The People in an attempt to force discharged trustees of the State Bank of Illinois to turn over their records to newly appointed trustees. In *People ex rel. Koerner & Yates v. State Bank by Ridgley et al.*,[9] January term 1859, Nicholas Ridgley, Uri Manly, and John Calhoun had been appointed by the governor in 1847 to be trustees of the State Bank of Illinois, which "closed its affairs" in that year. The three men continued in that capacity until 1857, when the governor, with the advice and consent of the Illinois Senate, removed Ridgley *et al.* and appointed Gustavus Koerner, George T. Brown, and Richard Yates in their place. However, Ridgley *et al.* continued to hold the books and to operate as trustees. The People, on behalf of Koerner, brought an application for a *quo warranto* (a common law writ asking "by what authority, etc.") directly to the Supreme Court to compel Ridgley *et al.* to turn over the books and responsibilities in the Sangamon County Circuit Court. By agreement, the matter was taken to the Supreme Court. The People were represented by J. B. White, the state's attorney, and Lincoln. S. T. Logan, Hay, and McClernand represented Ridgley *et al.*

The Supreme Court, in an opinion written by Justice Breese, denied the application. *Quo warranto* pertains to a criminal proceedings, and was not the proper form of action in this case. It was contended that the incumbents were "officers" rather than trustees, and that the governor had the power to remove public officers. However, such appointees are truly trustees—their duty is to the creditors of the bank and its stockholders. If any proceeding is brought against them for not properly discharging their duties, it must be brought by a bill in chancery, and by a creditor or stockholder of the bank.

The Illinois Legislature

The powers of the legislature as well as those of the governor and secretary of state were properly tested in the Illinois Supreme Court. In *People ex rel. Stephenson v. Marshall*,[10] June term 1851, such a test was made. The People, represented by Lincoln and R. Wingate, brought this application for a *mandamus* (requiring an official to act) directly to the Supreme Court, to require Judge Samuel S. Marshall to hold court at Raleigh, Illinois. A. G. Caldwell and H. B. Montgomery represented Marshall.

In 1847 the legislature divided Gallatin County; and Saline County was organized, with Raleigh established as the county seat. Thereafter, courts were held in Raleigh at regular times. In 1851 the legislature passed an act combining Gallatin and Saline counties, with a new county seat at Equality. There was no vote of the people authorizing this. Judge Marshall held court in the new county seat pursuant to the act, and would not hold court at

Raleigh. Hence this petition for *mandamus* to order him to do so. The facts are not disputed. The major issue relates to the authority of the legislature to make the changes in the counties and the county seats without the affirmative vote of the people.

The Supreme Court, in an opinion written by Justice Caton, granted the *mandamus*. An affirmative vote of the people is required under the constitution to do any of the things the legislature did here. Justice Caton stated:

> If the constitution is still to be regarded as an instrument of that social character which has hitherto always been attributed to all American constitutions—if it is still to be considered as a law to the law makers, as well as to the citizens, a law which cannot be compassed or provisions are not frittered away, by establishing a rule which will, in every instance, allow its provisions to be disregarded, which will permit the legislature to do the precise and identical thing which the constitution in most express and unequivocal terms, has declared shall not be done, without the vote of the people interested.

Another challenge to the legislative body was a case challenging whether specific legislation had been passed in the proper manner. Lincoln represented Logan County in such a case, *Turley et al. v. County of Logan*,[11] December term 1855. In 1853 the General Assembly passed an act for the removal of the seat of justice for Logan County, by the vote of the people. Later the vote was taken, and resulted in favor of removal. George W. Turley *et al.* filed a bill to restrain the county officers from erecting buildings at the new location on the grounds that, according to the legislative journal, the act for removal had not been read in the House of Representatives the full number of times required by the constitution, and so was not law. The injunction was allowed. In 1854 the same legislature met, and according to the recollection of the members, the manuscript minutes of the clerk, amended the journal, so that it showed the bill had been read the requisite number of times. Logan County submitted this to the Logan County Circuit Court before Judge Davis; the bill was dismissed and the injunction was dissolved. Stuart represented Turley.

In an opinion written by Justice Scates, the Supreme Court affirmed the decree. The same legislature may correct its journals. It had also been argued that there was a law that a county seat shall not be changed unless upon a petition of a majority of the voters. However, the court ruled that such an act is merely advisory, and does not deprive the legislature of the right to do so without petition.

Justice Skinner wrote a concurring opinion stating, "I do not deem it necessary upon this record to decide upon the effect upon acts of the General Assembly, duly authenticated by the signatures of the presiding officers of the respective Houses and the approval of the Governor, of the absence of evidence in the journals of their *regular* passage; and upon this point I reserve my opinion."

In *People ex rel. Ballou v. Dubois*,[12] January term 1860, Martin Ballou represented himself, with Lincoln's assistance, and States Attorney J. B. White represented Jesse K. Dubois, the state auditor. Ballou was duly elected as circuit court judge for the County of Bureau in the twenty-third judicial district in 1857, for a constitutional term of six years. In 1859 the legislature passed an act moving the county of Bureau out of the twenty-third judicial district, and Mark Bangs was elected circuit court judge. Ballou reported for duty, but Bangs had taken over the court, leaving Ballou no place to work. Ballou brought an action of *quo warranto* in the circuit court to recover his office, but lost. While that appeal was pending. Ballou demanded his salary from State Auditor Dubois, who refused to pay him. This action was brought directly to the supreme court for a writ of peremptory *mandamus* directing Dubois to pay Ballou's salary.

The Supreme Court, in an opinion written by Justice Caton, granted the *mandamus*. It is the intention of the legislature to place the judges above and beyond the legislative control or interference, except by impeachment. It is the constitution and not the legislature, which creates the office of circuit judges.

In *Jones v. The People*,[13] December term 1852, Herndon represented The People in a test of the authority of the legislature to regulate retail sale of spirituous liquors. Samuel B. Jones was indicted for selling spirituous liquor in quantities less than one quart, in violation of the statute prohibiting retailing intoxicating drinks, which had been approved on February 1, 1851. He contended the act was unconstitutional. The verdict and judgment in the Morgan County Circuit Court before Judge Woodson was for The People, and Jones was fined $25. Murray McConnel represented Jones.

The Supreme Court, in an opinion written by Justice Trumbull, affirmed the judgment and held that the statute was constitutional.

Trumbull said:

> The powers of the several States to regulate or even prohibit the retail of spirituous liquors within their limits, is expressly sanctioned by the Supreme Court of the United States, in the license cases[14] and there is nothing in the constitution of Illinois to prevent the exercise of this power. By virtue of its police power, every State must have the right to enact such laws as may be necessary for the restraint and punishment of crime, and for the preservation of the public peace, health and morals of its citizens. It is upon this principle that the sale of lottery tickets, and of cards, and other instruments of gaming is prohibited; and who ever questioned the constitutionality or validity of such laws? A government that did not

possess the power to protect itself against such and similar evils, would scarcely be worth preserving.

There were two companion cases testing the power of the legislature to change county seats and affecting the consequences of such changes. They are presented together as Lincoln represented different sides on the same question in these cases.

One of the interesting anomalies of Lincoln's law practice was this willingness of his to represent different sides in cases which involved the same general set of facts. In at least three situations, he represented a party in a case which he won, with the Supreme Court's opinion establishing a rule of law for that peculiar situation. Then later he represented a party on the exact opposite side in a similar situation and lost, with the court citing the previous case as the authority for its decision.

One such set of circumstances involved situations where land in a particular town was donated to the state when the legislature designated that town as a county seat; and subsequently, in each instance, the county seat was moved to another town and the original donors sought to have returned the donated land or its value. In the first case Lincoln represented the county and won; in the second he represented the donor and lost.

Lincoln & Herndon represented Logan County in *Adams et al. v. County of Logan*,[15] December term 1849, and Logan and Stuart & Edwards represented Adams *et al.* The Illinois legislature established Logan County in 1839, and Lucien Adams and others proposed that if the county seat was established in Postville, they would give land and erect a building for the county seat. In 1841 the legislature chose Postville as the county seat, and Adams and his associates did as they promised. Later on, the legislature authorized a move of the county seat to Mount Pulaski and the county sold the courthouse and land; Adams and the others thought it only fair they should receive the benefits of that sale, so they brought this action to recover those proceeds. The Logan County Circuit Court, before Judge Davis, held for Logan County, and this judgment was sustained on appeal. Justice Caton, writing the opinion for the court, said the gifts were not conditional; the donors knew the legislature had a right to remove the county seat to another town, and in any event, the donors had owned much land around that given for the county courthouse and derived benefit from its enhanced value because of this proximity. The county seat of Logan County was later moved to Lincoln, so Mt. Pulaski's was a Pyrrhic victory.

Similar facts existed in the case of *Harris v. Shaw et al.*,[16] December term 1851. Logan and Stuart & Edwards again represented the donors of the land, but this time believed their chances would be enhanced by adding Lincoln to their powerful team, and indeed he participated on the side of the disappointed altruistic citizen who wanted to influence the legislature in designating the most advantageous county seat (to him at least). Here the legislature stipulated that if anyone gave Tazewell County twenty acres of land it would build the courthouse on that property. John H. Harris gave the land in 1835; the county built the courthouse; and Harris sold some of the land adjacent to the courthouse at enhanced value while retaining some of the land for future sale. The legislature later moved the county seat to Pekin in 1850 at the behest of altruistic citizens of that community, specifying that the abandoned land and building would be used for educational purposes. Harris lost in the Tazewell County Circuit Court and in the Supreme Court—despite this aggregation of four of the best lawyers of that time—which cited the Adams case as the reason for their decision. N. H. Purple represented Shaw. Lincoln was "hoisted by his own petard!" Again the court stated that the gift was unconditional, that the legislature had the right to remove the county seat, and that the donor had benefited from the sale of land enhanced by the gift. The fact that the abandoned property was to be used for educational purposes was not material enough to change the decision of the otherwise similar, if not identical, facts.

What his representation of clients in these two cases really tells us is that while the rule of law is clear and will be applied to reasonably similar situations in the future, there is still room for parties to disagree as to whether reasonably similar situations exist, and the facts in any case must be proven sufficiently to a judge and jury to prevail in a law suit. This is why we had then, and still have, adversarial litigation in situations which seem identical to the facts in a ruling case. Lincoln's appearance on each side of seemingly similar situations is not a discredit to him, but evidence that as a pragmatic lawyer he recognized there could be two sides to any issue, and that each side was entitled to competent representation.

Municipalities

The following are five cases involving the city of Springfield, Illinois, that Lincoln participated in before the Illinois Supreme Court.

In *Laswell v. Hickox & Hickox*,[17] December term 1843, Thomas Laswell instituted an action, before the mayor of Springfield, against Horace and A. Hickox, and was successful. The defendants appealed to the Sangamon County Circuit Court, before Judge Treat, on the ground the mayor did not have jurisdiction in this case. It was admitted by the parties that the cause did not arise within the city, and that both Hickoxes were served with a summons outside the limits of the city. Judgment was rendered for Hickox *et al.,* who were represented by Logan. S. Strong, J. C. Doremus, and B. S. Edwards represented Laswell.

The Supreme Court, in an opinion written by Justice Treat, affirmed the judgment. The mayor of the city of Springfield is a local officer, and can exercise only such powers as are clearly conferred on him by law. In the exercise of civil jurisdiction, he is confined to cases in which the cause of action arises within the city, and to cases where the parties to be summoned before him are served with process in the city. Neither was present here.

In *Springfield v. Hickox et al.,*[18] December term 1845, Lincoln represented the city. Perhaps these were the same Hickox folks Lincoln had represented in the Laswell case. A person named "Horace Hickox" was a party in each suit. Hickox *et al.* won each case in any event, even though Lincoln deserted them and represented the city against them. This case was originally an action brought before the mayor of the city of Springfield to recover twelve dollars from Hickox *et al.* for a debt incurred as a penalty under an ordinance of the city requiring licenses to be taken out by merchants, etc. The case was taken by appeal into the Sangamon County Circuit Court before Judge Treat. Hickox *et al.* had a city order (an order drawn by the mayor to the treasurer to pay city funds to a named person[s]) for fifty dollars, which was introduced as an offset, and judgment was rendered for Hickox *et al.* for thirty-eight dollars. Lincoln and W. I. Fergason represented the city of Springfield in the appeal to the Supreme Court. They contended the offset was not an effective claim where the lawsuit was concerned, because there had been no demand on the city to pay the order. Hickox *et al.* had made a claim on the city for the fifty dollars after the lawsuit was instituted, but payment was refused, "there being no funds in the treasury, and proved by the city treasurer that there was not then, and had not been for some time previous, any funds in the treasury, either appropriated or otherwise." Lincoln cited two Illinois Supreme Court cases as precedent. J. A. McDougall represented the Hickoxes.

Justice Purple, writing for the court, affirmed the lower court judgment. He distinguished this case from Lincoln's citations, because the city was involved, and the order was a valid obligation without any demand for payment being made. He concluded by saying: "Mutual demands in equity extinguish each other; and unless we hold the doctrine that political corporations of this sort are not liable to be sued upon their contracts and obligations thus issued—unless we allow them the privilege of collecting debts due them, and compel the holder of their papers to await the tardy operation of an assessment and collection of taxes for the payment of his claim, without the privilege of a set off, I can see no just reason why the judgment in this case should not be affirmed."

In *Browning v. City of Springfield,*[19] December term 1855, Lincoln represented Orville W. Browning (an attorney and good friend of Lincoln), who brought an action for damages against the City of Springfield, alleging that it was the duty of the city to keep its streets in repair, which duty had been neglected, in consequence of which thereof he had fallen and broken his leg. The city demurred to this, which was sustained by Judge Davis in the Sangamon County Circuit Court. Browning, represented by Lincoln and Herndon, appealed, and was successful. The judgment was reversed and cause remanded. Stuart & Edwards and W. J. Black represented the City of Springfield.

Justice Scates, in his opinion for the court, pointed out the difference here from ordinary negligent acts. This act was an example of negligence in not doing something, as opposed to an affirmative action. English common law had no remedy against a city for failure to act, even though by specific statute it was required to do certain things, such as street repair. Scates, citing many authorities, summarized erosion of this common law precedent, stating there should be liability if all the following applied: First, the city is under a legal obligation to repair the place in question. Second, the obligation is a matter of so general and public concern that a criminal action would lie against the city for non-repair. Third, the place is out of repair; and finally, the plaintiff sustained damages. He pointed out that the city had the means to make the repairs. It had taxing powers and also, "all public property of the city is vested in the corporation, with power to cause all male inhabitants of twenty-one years to work three days on the streets." In affirming the city had potential liability in this case, Scates concluded: "With such lights for our guide, and such authorities for our sanction, we not only feel authorized but required to afford the protection sought, and more especially as we think the decisions based upon sound sense in accordance with strict morality, and keeping pace with the progress of improvements of the age."

Lincoln & Herndon, and C. S. Zane represented Springfield in *People ex rel. City of Springfield v. Power*,[20] January term 1861, in a case involving the rights of the legislature to resolve a revenue-sharing agreement between a city and county. N. M. Broadwell represented Power. The legislature passed an act declaring that after certain expenditures are allowed the County of Sangamon and the city of Springfield, the surplus of county taxes should be divided between the city and the remainder of the county in proportion to the amount collected from each. The city's portion should be applied to street repair, and building and repairing of bridges. The county judge, William D. Power, refused to make these allocations, and Springfield brought this application directly to the Supreme Court for a *mandamus* to compel Judge Power to act. The county believed the legislature could not control the revenue of a county, such revenue being the property of the counties, and not to be taken away from them without their consent, to be used and appropriated in such manner only as the county courts of the respective counties may direct.

The Supreme Court, in an opinion written by Justice Breese, granted *mandamus*. He wrote: "While private corporations are regarded as contracts which the legislature cannot constitutionally impair, as the trustee of the public interest, it has the exclusive and unrestrained control over public corporations; and as it may create, so it may modify or destroy, as public exigency requires, or the public interests demand. The whole capacities, powers and duties, are denoted from the legislature, and subordinate to that power."

Lincoln & Herndon represented Robert Bryan who brought an action for assault, battery, and imprisonment against the deputy marshall of Springfield in *Bryan v. Bates*,[21] December term 1853, in the Sangamon County Circuit Court before Judge Davis. Bryan was arrested by Marshall Nathaniel S. Bates for being drunk in public. Justice Scates stated the facts in his Supreme Court opinion as follows: "Defendant was marshall of the city of Springfield, and as such it was his duty to preserve the peace and arrest, etc., all offenders for violations of the city ordinances; and that plaintiff was drunk, in violation of a city ordinance; that the plaintiff disturbed the peace by violent, tumultuous and offensive language, calculated to provoke a breach of the peace, and in like violation of the ordinances of the city; all of which were committed in his view. Wherefore he gently laid his hands upon him and imprisoned him until he could take him before the mayor of the city, according to law. . . ." Judgment was rendered for Bates. Herndon represented Bryan. W. J. Black and Stuart & Edwards represented Bates.

The Supreme Court affirmed the judgment. The power of the cities and their ministerial authorities was not changed by the new constitution. The applicable ordinance clearly set out the authority of the marshall to make such an arrest.

The case of *Petersburg, President and Trustees v. Mappin et al.*,[22] December term 1852, involved powers of the trustees of the town of Petersburg. The case was brought in Menard County Circuit Court before Judge Woodson. Mappin and Estel obtained a license from the town of Petersburg to keep a grocery (an establishment for the sale of spirits); and they, with men with the last names of Atchinson and Lanning as sureties, executed a bond to the corporation, in the penalty of five hundred dollars. Conditions stipulated that they would keep an orderly house, and would not keep the same open on Sunday, or permit gaming or riotous conduct therein. One or more of these conditions was apparently breached, because the town recovered a judgment against all the obligers for the amount of the bond and costs. When the obligers were perfecting an appeal, the trustees of the town suggested a compromise in that the citizens of the town would vote to advise what the trustees should do. One hundred fourteen of the 130 voters petitioned the board to release the judgment upon the payment of costs of $38 by the obligors. The obligors were then released. However, eighteen months later, the board changed its mind, and filed this bill in equity against the obligors, alleging there had been no valid consideration for the release, and praying it be set aside, and execution be issued for the collection of the judgment. The court dismissed the bill. Herndon represented Petersburg, and T. L. Harris and Stuart represented Mappin.

The Supreme Court, in an opinion written by Justice Treat, affirmed the decree. The trustees of the town possess only such powers as are specifically conferred by the act of incorporation, or are necessary to carry into effect the powers expressly granted. They have no power to give away the funds of the town. They may sue and be sued, and the power to prosecute suits on behalf of the corporation includes the right to compromise doubtful controversies. This was done here, and was within the power of the trustees. Whether the arrangement was judicious or not is not the question. A mere error of judgment would not vitiate the settlement.

Lincoln & Herndon represented Petersburg in *President & Trustees of Petersburg v. Metzker*,[23] January term 1959, in the Menard County Circuit Court before Judge Harriott. In this case Griggsby Metzker was tried before a police justice in Petersburg for assault, and fined $10. He appealed to the Menard County Circuit Court, which dismissed the sentence because the ordinance establishing the fine was improper. The charter of Petersburg provided that the town could establish punishment for any crime, consistent with any punishment established by the state for like crimes. For this particular crime involving Metzker, the fine established by the city was from $5 to $50. The law of the state fixed the minimum for this crime at $3. Thomas P. Cowan represented Metzker.

The Supreme Court, in a short opinion written by Justice Breese, affirmed the judgment. The corporation, by its charter, can prescribe no greater punishment for an assault and battery committed in the town "limits than is provided by the State for the same offense." The charter controls the exercise of the power by the town corporation. The city should have set the minimum fine at $3.

People ex rel. Davenport v. Brown et al.,[24] June term 1850, deals with the creation of a township. The Illinois constitution provided that a county could adopt township organization if a majority of the citizens of a county voted affirmatively for it. Woodford County had such an election; 153 voted for it, and 107 voted against it, out of a total of more than 600 legal voters in the county. County Judge Welcome B. Brown, and his associate judges, refused to organize the townships. People *ex rel.* William Davenport brought this petition for a *mandamus* to compel the judges to act. The court dismissed the petition. Lincoln represented The People in the Woodford County Circuit Court before Judge Davis, and on the appeal, the only indication in the Supreme Court opinion is that O. Peters represented The People. N. H. Purple represented Brown *et al.*

The Supreme Court, in an opinion written by Justice Treat, affirmed the judgment. The county courts were created and their jurisdiction conferred by the constitution. None of its powers could be taken away except in the mode prescribed in the state constitution. The power of the county court over the business of the county continues until the township organization is adopted by an affirmative vote of a majority of all the legal voters of the county. The language of the state constitution to establish townships is clear and explicit. It does not mean a majority of those casting votes, but a majority of the legal voters in the county. This did not happen here, so the county judges acted properly in denying the petition for a *mandamus*.

Other Public Corporations

School districts were given authority to assess taxes for school purposes. The Supreme Court indicated in two Lincoln cases that the provisions of any school tax law had to be followed carefully, but tempered the strictures with reason. The case of *W. M. Cowgill & Co. v. Long*,[25] December term 1853, exemplifies the requirement of specific compliance. Herndon represented William M. Cowgill. Here the legislative authority had been given to school districts to assess a school tax. Specific details were prescribed as to how this should be done; these details included a requirement that a school tax not be assessed for a given year unless it was reported to the county clerk by July 1. On July 20, 1850, the inhabitants of a school district in Menard County voted a tax of $500 for the purpose of erecting a schoolhouse in the district. Cowgill and Frackelton were charged $28.26 to be paid by May 14, 1851, and filed this bill against the collector to enjoin him on the grounds the assessment was improper. However, while this suit was pending, on January 21, 1853, the legislature passed an act identifying this specific tax and remedying the defects. The Menard County Circuit Court, Judge Woodson presiding, dismissed the bill. T. L. Harris represented Long.

The Supreme Court, in an opinion written by Justice Treat, affirmed the decree. It is essential for the validity of a school tax that the provisions in the law be exactly followed. This was not done here, and if that was all there was to it, Cowgill and Frackelton would not owe this tax. However, the legislature had the power to correct this, and did so. When the act was passed, Cowgill and Frackelton had not paid the tax, and still had time to do so before their property was seized and sold to pay the taxes. "If the property has since been sacrificed to pay the tax, it is the result of their own neglect."

Then follows the case of *Trustee of Schools v. Allen et al.*,[26] January term 1859, when certain irregularities in the taxing procedure did not void the tax. In 1850 the school commissioner of McLean County sold a portion of the school lands to William H. and James Allen, Jr. Eight years later, the school trustees brought this action in equity to find the sale illegal and void, alleging the prerequisites of the law had not been complied with on the sale. The McLean County Circuit Court ruled for the Allens. Lincoln represented the Allens, and Stuart & Edwards and O. T. Reeves represented the school trustees.

The court, in an opinion written by Justice Breese, affirmed the decree. Breese presented the several alleged irregularities offered by the trustees, and said: "This case, as shown by the proofs in the cause, is wholly destitute of any indication of any fraudulent act or intent, in any quarter by any party. The most that can be said about it is, there are omissions to perform certain acts which the statute required; but which not being performed, in the absence of fraud, should not be permitted to "invalidate" the sale. Then: "The testimony shows that full value was paid for the land at the time it was sold. It is only by the wonderful and magnificent improvements that have been made in that beautiful region since 1851, that has so enhanced the value of all the land in that region, that this sale is sought to be disturbed. It may be a misfortune and loss to the county that the sale was made so soon, but being made fairly and not in violation of any law, it must stand."

Another type of public corporation, a state hospital, also derived its authority from the legislature. Lincoln and others represented the People in *People ex rel. Stevenson et al. v. Higgins*,[27] December term 1853, in the Morgan County Circuit Court before Judge Woodson. The act creating the Illinois State Hospital for the Insane provided for the naming of trustees. These trustees were charged with general responsibility to run the hospital, as well as to appoint a medical superintendent. The superintendent, who should be a skillful physician, would be appointed for ten years and could be removed earlier only for infidelity to the trust reposed in him, or on account of incompetency. The hospital trustees, in April 14, 1853, resolved at a board meeting to remove Dr. James M. Higgins, the medical superintendent, because he "does not possess the kind of qualifications which are necessary to the discharge of the duties of said office, etc." The People on behalf of the trustees, brought this action to remove Higgins, and he demurred. This was sustained, and the matter ended until The People appealed. The formal record of the appeal states Stuart & Edwards, and W. Brown represented The People, and D. A. Smith and M. McConnel represented Higgins.

The Supreme Court, in an opinion written by Justice Caton, reversed the judgment and remanded the cause. The statute was silent as to who had the authority to remove the medical superintendent. However, Caton said, "It was the design of the legislature to confer upon the board of trustees the management of this institution and to confer upon them all necessary powers for that management and control, as the most probable way of accomplishing, in the highest degree, the great and benevolent purpose of its creation." This included the power of removal, but only for the two stated causes so that "no change of political parties or other inferior consideration could ever disturb him in his high and responsible position." Also the reasons stated by the board complied with the statute: "The substance is the same, though, perhaps, expressed in more delicate or less offensive terms."

Taxation

There are several cases involving Lincoln and the Supreme Court which addressed the issue of governmental authority to levy taxes under the State constitution and pertinent legislation. One of them, *Illinois Central RR Co. v. McLean County et al.,* is included in chapter seven. There are two others which are included here that refer specifically to the authority of the legislature to levy taxes.

Rhinehart v. Schuyler et al.,[28] December term 1845, was a case in which Robert Schuyler *et al.* brought an action of ejectment against Lewis Rhinehart to recover possession of certain property in which Schuyler acquired title from Stephen B. Munn. He had acquired the title originally by an auditor's deed in 1831, when the land was seized for unpaid taxes in 1830, and sold to satisfy the tax obligation. Rhinehart had been living on the land, with no notice of adverse claims, for some time. His attorneys contended the revenue laws of the state were unconstitutional; that the auditor's deed did not comply with the necessary procedure and form for a valid deed; and that a statute of limitations of seven years had been enacted by the legislature in 1835, which was a defense against any other claim of title. The Adams County Circuit Court, Judge Jesse B. Thomas presiding, rejected those claims, and rendered judgment for Schuyler *et al.* The court records list N. H. Purple, J. Butterfield, and A. Williams as representing Rhinehart. O. H. Browning, E. D. Baker, and Logan represented Schuyler *et al.*

The Supreme Court, in an opinion written by Justice Young, affirmed the judgment. The majority opinion, which was thirty-four pages, cited many precedents justifying the taxation, including the twenty-ninth chapter of the *Magna Carta* in its original Latin language (English translation was also furnished), and concluded that the taxing statutes were constitutional. Additionally, the registry laws prescribing how land titles had to be conveyed between private individuals did not apply to deeds emanating directly from a state. Also, the statute of limitations specified that any person who held possession of land for seven years, with no knowledge of any adverse title, had a valid defense against anyone else who claimed title. Rhinehart had lived on the land for over seven years, but some of these were before 1835, and the only time allowed to justify adverse possession was that time after the passage of the legislation.

Justice Caton dissented in a ten-page opinion, contending the method of assessment prescribed in the revenue acts which specified land would be divided into three valuation classes (the first class would be valued at four dollars and taxed at two cents per acre, the second class valued at three dollars an acre and taxed at one and one-half cents, and the third class valued at two dollars an acre and taxed at one cent) and did not meet the constitutional requirement that property taxed must be valued so each person would pay a tax in proportion to the value of his property. The method prescribed was too arbitrary and excluded town lots and improvements to the land. Justice Treat simply concurred in Justice Caton's dissenting opinion.

This case includes six briefs, three by attorneys on each side. Logan represented Schuyler *et al.* who claimed title though Munn, who had bought the land at a tax sale. Logan started his brief with the following observation: "The substance of the argument seems to be that if the court can in any way destroy tax titles, it should do so. Now, whatever may be the nature of the contest about tax titles in other states and counties, in this state it is a mere contest between speculators; speculators in tax titles on one side, and speculators in tax titles on the other."

Justice Young recognized the importance of the issue, commenting as follows: "This case throughout, has been treated as it deserves to be, on all sides, as one of very great importance; not on account of the value of the property involved in the result of the present controversy, but of settling principles of the first magnitude, which, in their effects as precedents, are to control and determine the relative rights of numerous individuals, to a very large class of some of the most valuable property in the country."

This power was also recited in *Compher et al. v. People*,[29] December term 1850, an action brought on a bond executed by William Compher, as collector of Peoria County. The other defendants were his sureties. The sureties argued they should be discharged from their liabilities because the legislature changed the revenue laws after they agreed to be sureties for a collector. The Tazewell County Circuit Court, with Judge Davis presiding, held for The People and did not discharge the sureties. Lincoln & Herndon, Stuart & Edwards, D. B. Campbell, and D. L. Gregg represented The People on the appeal, and submitted a brief which contained the argument used by the Supreme Court in its opinion. N. H. Purple and R. S. Blackwell represented Compher *et al.*

The Supreme Court, in an opinion written by Justice Trumbull, affirmed the judgment stating that the changes did not prejudice the sureties:

> The power to control the revenue is one of the highest attributes of sovereignty. Without this power, no government could exist, and it cannot be supposed that the general assembly intended to part with this important prerogative, or to contract that no change should be made in the manner of collecting the revenue, during the continuance in office of any of its collectors. Parties who go security upon bonds of this character, do so with the full knowledge and expectation that the revenue laws will be changed, and the duties of the collectors altered as the public interests may require, and they have no right to complain of any duties of this principal, especially when such alterations are in nowise prejudicial to their interest. Such are the changes of the law under consideration.

(This case is also cited in chapter twelve as an example of responsibilities of sureties.)

NOTES

1. 3 *Ill.*, 79; *LCL*, 8.
2. Pratt, Harry E., *Lincoln's Supreme Court Cases*. Quoted in the *Illinois Bar Journal*, 32, November 1943, 23–35.
3. Howard, Robert, *Illinois: A History of the Prairie State*. 1972, 211.
4. 6 *Ill.*, 581; *LCL*, 76.
5. 9 Wheat, 680.
6. 8 *Ill.*, 502; *LCL*, 119.
7. 19 *Ill.*, 229; *LCL*, 204.
8. *Ibid.*, 282; *LCL*, 206.
9. 24 *Ill.*, 64; *LCL*, 210.
10. 12 *Ill.*, 391; *LCL*, 147.
11. 17 *Ill.*, 150; *LCL*, 185.
12. 23 *Ill.*, 498; *LCL*, 228.
13. 14 *Ill.*, 196; *LCL*, 167.
14. 5 Howard, 504.
15. 11 *Ill.*, 337; *LCL*, 132.
16. 13 *Ill.*, 457; *LCL*, 157.
17. 5 *Ill.*, 182; *LCL*, 52.
18. 7 *Ill.*, 241; *LCL*, 88.
19. 17 *Ill.*, 142; *LCL*, 185.
20. 25 *Ill.*, 169; *LCL*, 232.
21. 15 *Ill.*, 87; *LCL*, 171.
22. 14 *Ill.*, 193; *LCL*, 167.
23. 21 *Ill.*, 204; *LCL*, 213.
24. 11 *Ill.*, 479; *LCL*, 134.
25. 15 *Ill.*, 203; *LCL*, 175.
26. 21 *Ill.*, 120; *LCL*, 212.
27. 15 *Ill.*, 110; *LCL*, 172.
28. 7 *Ill.*, 473; *LCL*, 98.
29. 12 *Ill.*, 289; *LCL*, 145.

Chapter Six

Animals

ANIMALS WERE THE MOST IMPORTANT personal property owned in antebellum Illinois. Since this had also been true in England for hundreds of years, the common law of England, adopted by Illinois in 1819, was more than ample to protect property rights in animals. Some acts against animals were criminal, and the criminal law, as enacted, took care of that aspect of retribution. But the owners of animals also wanted compensation for loss or injury to their animals, or to recover possession of an animal, and that is the role the common law played. All the cases Lincoln handled before the Illinois Supreme Court were civil cases, with most of them involving ownership or possession of animals—primarily horses.

The first case of this kind was *Cannon v. Kenney*,[1] July term 1841, which was a case of trespass brought in the Sangamon County Circuit Court by Manly F. Cannon against Matthew P. Kenney before Judge Treat. Lincoln represented Cannon, and S.T. Logan represented Kenney. Kenney won in the circuit court; but upon appeal at the July term 1841, the judgment was reversed.

Cannon owned a horse that he gratuitously loaned to John Harris to be "rode" by him from Lead Mines to Sangamon County. John Harris rode the horse to Sangamon County, and put the horse in the hands of his brother James, to feed and keep for a fee. James transferred the horse's care to another brother, Robert, who "after feeding and keeping him until the grass came, turned him on the prairie with his own horses, occasionally salting him." That's when Kenney took the horse, which was worth sixty-five dollars at the time. Kenney argued there was no evidence that he took the horse from the possession of Cannon, which position the court sustained and rendered judgment for Kenney, dismissing the case.

Lincoln submitted in his appellate brief a virtual primer on ownership of personal property—including what constitutes possession, constructive possession, bailments of several kinds, liens against personal property, and when trespass or trover is the proper remedy when personal property has been taken. Justice Breese delivered this opinion, using Lincoln's brief to support the court's reasoning, and reversed the lower court holding that the absolute owner (Cannon) still had absolute ownership despite the transfers. Thus, Kenney took the horse from Cannon's possession and had committed trespass. The judgment was reversed and remanded for a new trial.

The next case, *Watkins v. White*,[2] December term 1842, was an action of *replevin*. It was brought by Lincoln's client, Thomas Watkins, against John White, for a certain mare, in the Sangamon County Circuit Court before Judge Treat and a jury. E. D. Baker and A. T. Bledsoe represented White. Verdict and judgment were rendered for defendant White. The appeal was based on improper instructions by Judge Treat to the jury.

Watkins had bought the mare when it was a colt, and sold it to a man with the name of Ferguson. Ferguson kept it for six or eight months, and sold it back to Watkins for seventy-five dollars in cash notes and thirty barrels of corn. Watkins kept the mare in a lot surrounded by a good fence at night, but the mare was missing one morning, "the fence being laid down as by human hands." Shortly thereafter, some time in 1838, Watkins' son, who was under age and had left home, sold the mare to James Maxey in Springfield for ten dollars in money and forty dollars in county orders. Maxey sold her to John Constant, who sold her to White. Subsequently, Watkins looked for the horse in livery stables in Springfield where the mare was normally housed, but not at the particular times Watkins looked for her. There was also testimony that Watkins knew someone had ridden the mare to some races he had attended in 1840. The jury was instructed that if Watkins knew the mare was in Springfield in possession of other people, who were exercising acts of ownership over her for more than a reasonable time to claim her, the jury might infer he ratified the sale by his son, and find for the defendant although the statue of limitations had not expired.

The Supreme Court, Justice James Semple writing the opinion, reversed the Circuit Court's ruling and ordered a new trial on the grounds that the instructions given by Judge Treat to the jury were too general. Lincoln argued that a party is not bound to sue immediately for any injury he may sustain. He may consult his own convenience as to when he will assert his rights, provided he is not barred by the statute of limitations, or such length of time as will amount to presumption of payment or satisfaction. The court held that the jury should have been allowed to make their verdict as to the real ownership of the mare, from the evidence before them; without being instructed that there was any presumption of the ratification of the sale, as the jury was charged in this case.

In *England v. Clark*,[3] December term 1843, Lincoln and J. D. Urquhart represented George England, who had purchased a horse from a constable who sold it by the execution of a judgment obtained by Henry Clark against a third party. E. D. Baker, A. T. Bledsoe and B. S. Edwards represented Clark. The constable believed the horse belonged to that third party. Clark received the money from the sale. However, the real owner of the horse (who is not identified in the opinion) brought an action against England for the horse, and he had to give it up. England sued Clark to recover the purchase price, in the Menard County Circuit Court before Judge Treat. The court held for Clark.

Lincoln based his request for reversal of the lower court decision on a precedent from the English common law of *ex aequo et bono* (according to what is just and good) first pronounced by Lord Mansfield in *Moses v. M'Ferlan.*[4] This case held that if a plaintiff is better entitled to have a thing than the defendant is to withhold it from him, he has a remedy to recover it. Justice Scates, writing for the Court, stated that the rule of *caveat emptor* (let the buyer beware) applied to all judicial sales, as long as the representative of the court making the sale had proper authority. The buyer would acquire only whatever title the judgment debtor had, without any additional warranties. The lower court judgment was affirmed.

Chief Justice Wilson wrote a concurring opinion, apparently because he wanted to state clearly what he thought of the *Moses v. M'Ferlan* case, and the *ex aequo et bono* rule. He stated "this is a most comprehensive rule, but I believe it has never been recognized in any subsequent case, to the extent its terms would seem to imply, and does not, conceivably, apply to this case."

The impression is that Lincoln made an ingenious argument to seek a victory for his client. Clark had a valid judgment against the third party, and was entitled to have it executed against any property owned by the third party. The constable thought the third party owned the horse, probably because the horse was in his possession, and levied the execution. England really learned what *caveat emptor* meant, and perhaps he had a better entitlement to the purchase price than Clark, but the court didn't agree.

Brundage v. Camp,[5] January term 1859, was another case involving animal ownership. James A. Brundage agreed to sell two mules to a man named Crouch for $300. Crouch wanted to take the mules with him, and offered Brundage a note to be delivered a few days later. Crouch took the mules, sold them to Camp, and never delivered a note or any money to Brundage. Brundage brought an action in the Sangamon County Circuit Court to recover possession of the mules. Judgment was entered for Camp, who was represented by Logan & Hay; Lincoln & Herndon represented Brundage.

The Supreme Court, in an opinion written by Justice Breese, affirmed the judgment. Breese reviewed many pertinent cases submitted by counsel for each side, and concluded the most recent cases supported the rights of a good faith purchaser (such as Camp). The sale was conditional upon Crouch paying for the mules, while the delivery of the mules was not. The good-faith purchaser should be protected. Breese summed it up as follows: "It seems to us that any other rule would be attended with great inconvenience and embarrassment, in such a community as ours, where it is impossible to inquire into the various neighborhood transactions of our people, of which the sale of personal property forms so important a part. Information cannot be had of the private arrangements between parties, not placed on record, and is only to be established through imperfect memories. A sale and delivery of a chattel, so far as a *bona fide* purchaser from the first vendor is concerned, without any notice of any reserved claims or rights on the property, ought to be sufficient for his protection."

In the following case, Lincoln's client, who had lawful custody of another's horse, rode it fifteen miles when it died. The horse's owner sued to recover the value of the horse. In *Johnson v. Weedman,*[6] December term 1843, Lincoln was successful in defending his client John Weedman in this action in DeWitt County Circuit Court, before Judge Treat. Wells Coulton represented Johnson.

Justice Scates wrote the opinion, and if all the opinions were written as succinctly as this one, the time required to write these observations about Lincoln's cases would have been reduced by at least one-third. He started the opinion as follows: "Trover, for a horse: issue not guilty: trial and verdict not guilty. The plaintiff moved for a new trial, which the court denied, and rendered a judgment for costs. The agreed case shows the following facts: that the plaintiff bailed a horse to the defendant to be *agisted* (to pasture livestock for a fee) and fed, for a valuable consideration; that while the horse was so in defendant's possession, he rode the horse fifteen miles; that the horse died within a few hours afterwards, but not in consequence of the riding. And the cause is submitted for the opinion of the court upon two questions: First; is the plaintiff entitled to recover upon the facts stated? and Secondly; ought a new trial to have been granted?"

Justice Scates answered "no" to both questions. In the first place, Andrew Johnson, the owner, tried to recover the value of the horse since it could not be returned. Lincoln argued that the riding of the horse was not an unlawful conversion. Failing in that, he cited *Murray v. Barling,*[7] arguing that "if the riding was a conversion, the injury done by the riding, and not the value of the horse, is the measure of damages." The cited case said, "as if a man takes my horse to ride, and leaves it at an inn, that is a conversion; for though I may have him by sending for him, and paying for his keeping, yet it brings a charge upon me. It is this charge that is to regulate the damages." Johnston was only entitled to nominal damages, which he couldn't recover in this form of action. Since a new trial could not be awarded to seek only nominal damages, the motion for same was properly dismissed. Lincoln's opponent brought the wrong form of action, and recovered nothing.

Ownership of hogs sometimes resulted in lawsuits as well. In *Byrne v. Stout,*[8] December term 1853, Lincoln represented Stout who sued Byrne in the Bond County Circuit Court, Judge Underwood presiding, in an action of trover and conversion, and recovered a judgment for $3. J. and D. Gillespie represented Byrne.

The evidence was somewhat conflicting, but it clearly involved a hog which Andrew J. Stout said he owned. The animal apparently wandered from home frequently, and during one of these wanderings, mixed with hogs belonging to Patrick O. Byrne. Stout came over to Byrne's property to get the hog, but the hog was not there at the time. Byrne told Stout he could have his hog; and Stout said when the hog returned, Byrne should bring him to Stout's place. Stout said, in effect: "that he had a hold upon plaintiff (Byrne); that he intended to chastise him; and that he would send plaintiff to the penitentiary, and would make him pay for the hog."

The Supreme Court, in a short opinion written by Justice Caton and containing mostly a recitation of abbreviated facts, reversed the judgment. Stout failed to show either an unlawful taking, or an actual conversion. "Castrating a scrub male hog running around one's stock is not such a proof of change of property as to be evidence of a conversion or appropriation to plaintiff's use.... Every element of a conversion is wanting." Then, for good measure: "Besides, there are very strong reasons, from the whole evidence, to doubt the defendant's (Stout) title to the hog." The judgment was reversed, and cause remanded for a new trial.

Horse trading sometimes left one of the parties disappointed. In the case of *McKinley v. Watkins*,[9] December term 1951, Joseph Watkins and William R. McKinley traded horses in 1845; afterwards they had some dispute about the trade, and Watkins threatened to sue. Since the horse Watkins had received in the trade died, he demanded that McKinley replace the horse or give to Watkins the monetary value of the horse. McKinley promised that, if Watkins would not sue, he would give him $50 or a horse worth that sum. Herndon represented Watkins, who brought this action against McKinley anyway. T. L. Harris represented Watkins. A judgment in the sum of $50 was awarded to Watkins by the Logan County Circuit Court, Judge Davis presiding.

The Supreme Court, in an opinion written by Justice Trumbull, reversed the judgment and remanded the cause. There was no evidence that Watkins had assented to McKinley's statement. The promise of McKinley to pay $50 if Watkins would not sue was incomplete until accepted by Watkins. He then quoted Story on *Contracts:* "A mere offer, not assented to, constitutes no contract; for there must be not only a proposal, but an acceptance thereof." Justice Treat dissented.

The major issue in *Crabtree v. Kile & Nichols*,[10] January term 1859, which involved a sale of cattle which were shipped on a railroad, was a warranty given in a sale. Lincoln & Herndon represented Kile Nichols, who sold John Crabtree eighty-one head of fat cattle; in return, Crabtree gave them a note for $2,550. Kile Nichols warranted the cattle to be free from a disease, called "milk sick or trembles," and Crabtree shipped them to New York City. During the journey about forty of the cattle died, and many of the rest were sick. Witnesses were allowed to impeach the credibility of one of Crabtree's witnesses at the trial. Kile and Nichols brought an action in *assumpsit* on the note, and the Edgar County Circuit Court, Judge Emerson presiding, awarded them a judgment for the total amount. A. Green, and Read and Blackburn represented Crabtree.

The Supreme Court, in an opinion written by Justice Walker, reversed the judgment and remanded the cause. When a vendor having title sells with warranty as to quality, when a consideration is given and possession is taken under the sale, the vendee may rely upon the contract of warranty to recover for any loss resulting from effects covered by it. An independent suit may be brought, or it may be set off, in an action on the contract for the sale of them. Damages represent the difference between the contract price agreed upon for healthy animals and their value as diseased animals at the time of delivery, together with any other immediate injury resulting from the breach of warranty. As for the court allowing witnesses to impeach the credibility of one of Crabtree's witnesses, a well-established rule of law is that the credit of a witness for veracity may be impeached by general evidence. But the general reputation of the witness is the subject of inquiry, not particular facts as were stated in this trial. The impeaching witness must be able to state what is generally said of the person to be impeached among his associates. That was not done here, so the impeaching witnesses should not have been heard.

Another case involves cattle trespassing and eating corn in a neighbor's field. The case really involved whether or not a justice of peace court had jurisdiction over the claim, but it is included to demonstrate the scope of animal-related legal disputes. In *Reed v. Johnson*,[11] December term 1852, Herndon and T. L. Harris represented Thomas Reed who brought an action against Archibald Johnson for trespass for injury done by Johnson's cattle to Reed's growing corn, before a justice of the peace. W. Brown represented Johnson.The circuit court in Menard County, Judge Woodson presiding, dismissed the action, stating that corn was real estate, and the justice of the peace only had jurisdiction over personal property.

The Supreme Court, in an opinion written by Justice Trumbull, reversed the judgment, and remanded the cause. The court traced some of the history of the evolution of the definitions of what constituted personal property and concluded: "There is no fixed rule by which to determine in every case, when they [growing crops] are to be deemed personal, and when real estate; and the present case may, as we conceive, be decided either way without any violation of principle, and upon respectable authorities."

The court continued the pragmatic view of this case as follows: "It will certainly be more convenient to allow justices of the peace to entertain jurisdiction of such cases. It often happens that the owner of a field of corn has no other interest in the land where it grows than to raise the crop from it; and if compelled to resort to an action of trespass *quare clausum fregit* (whereas he broke the close [boundary line]) in the circuit court, for every injury to the corn while maturing, the expense and delay of the proceeding will often deter him from an attempt to assert his rights. In this very case, for aught that appears, the owner of the corn may have been a mere tenant, and had no interest in the land except to raise the crop of corn. The bill of exceptions shows that the corn was protected by a good and sufficient fence; that the cattle of the defendant came over the fence and committed the injury to the corn, for which alone damages were claimed; and we see nothing either in the law, or the subject-matter of the suit, which should prevent a justice of the peace from entertaining jurisdiction of the case."

(There are two cases[12] involving animals in chapter seven because we believed the most important issues of these cases were the liability of the railroads, not the character of the goods transported. A third case,[13] not included here, is about fencing responsibilities and is such an important common law case we have included it in chapter twelve.)

NOTES

1. 4 *Ill.*, 8; *LCL*, 12.
2. 4 *Ill.*, 548; *LCL*, 44.
3. 5 *Ill.*, 487; *LCL*, 60.
4, 2 Burr. 12.
5. 21 *Ill.*, 339; *LCL*, 216.
6. 5 *Ill.*, 495; *LCL*, 61.
7. 10 Johns 176.
8. 15 *Ill.*, 181; *LCL*, 175.
9. 13 *Ill.*, 140; *LCL*, 152.
10. 21 *Ill.*, 180; *LCL*, 213.
11. 14 *Ill.*, 257; *LCL*, 169.
12. *Illinois Central RR Co. v. Morrison & Crabtree*, 19 *Ill.*, 136; *LCL*, 200. *Illinois Central RR Co. v. Hayes et al.*, 19 *Ill.*, 166; *LCL*, 201.
13. *Seeley v. Peters* 10 *Ill.*, 130, *LCL*, 127.

Chapter Seven

Railroads

LINCOLN PARTICIPATED IN NINETEEN CASES regarding railroad matters which were argued before the Illinois Supreme Court. The first railroads in other parts of the country were introduced during the early years of Lincoln's law practice. His admission to the bar in 1836 coincided with his election to a second term in the Illinois legislature. He was a major supporter of internal improvement legislation known by its detractors as the "internal improvement follies of 1837." This legislation provided the impetus for the funding of railroad construction. Ambitious plans for railroads, turnpikes, and canals were approved, together with allocation of $12,000,000 of state funds to guarantee the construction—a sum which proved to be grossly inadequate—and various abortive railroad projects were commenced.

The legislation provided for a railroad which would run from Galena in the northwest corner of Illinois, continue south, intersecting the terminus of the Illinois and Michigan Canal at the Illinois River, then continue through Springfield and Vandalia to Cairo, in the southwest corner of the state where the Ohio and Mississippi rivers meet. This was the beginning of the Illinois Central Railroad. The legislation also provided for three railroads to emanate from Alton—the largest city in Illinois at that time. Alton, with its prime location at the proximate confluence of the Missouri, Illinois, and Mississippi Rivers, was a serious contender with St. Louis; it was not certain which city would be the dominant trading city at the important juncture of those major rivers. One of these planned railroads became the Alton and Chicago Railroad. A third railroad system was proposed—one which would run between Quincy, on the Mississippi River, and Danville, close to the Indiana line. This became the Northern Cross Railroad.

These projects, while important and necessary in the development of Illinois, were too ambitious in light of the realities of that time. Lincoln, a staunch supporter of the projects, recognized the necessity for vast improvement in the public transportation of the state. It has been suggested that his support of these programs was a trade-off for support he received from legislators in moving the state capital from Vandalia to Springfield.

Political opposition developed as the projects were commenced, and the state developed serious fiscal problems. In February 1840, the legislature stopped all railroad work in the state, with only twenty-six miles of railroad constructed.

The first railroad to be built was the Northern Cross; its first twenty-four mile section which extended from Meredosia, east of Quincy on the Illinois River, to Jacksonville was completed in 1838. The line was continued to Springfield by May 13, 1842. The Northern Cross was operated by the state until 1847 when the governor, being unable to complete all the works authorized by the original act, conveyed the railroad property, by deed, to a combination of local individuals who reorganized it under the name Sangamon and Morgan Railroad Company. This company had been incorporated by the state legislature on March 1, 1845; it retained its name until 1853, when the legislature authorized it to change its name to the Great Western Railroad Company. Later, by various sales or consolidations, the road became part of the Wabash system, which literally follows the line surveyed and located by those old railroad pioneers of Illinois on that part of its route.

The ambitious major north-south railroad which became the Illinois Central was very significant in Lincoln's career. The idea of a major north-south railroad had been discussed for some time. In 1835 Sidney Breese, who was known as the "Father of the Illinois Central," disseminated his views favoring the subject. Finally, on January 18, 1836, a year before the notorious Illinois "internal-improvement legislature" passed its budget, the Central Railroad Company was incorporated to construct a railroad from "the mouth of the Ohio to a point on the Illinois River at or near the terminus of the Illinois-Michigan Canal." Little progress was made on this project until Breese took his seat in the United States Senate in 1843. Breese joined forces with fellow Illinoisan Stephen A. Douglas, who came to the United States Senate in 1847, and both senators worked to convince their colleagues of the importance to the entire country of a major north-south railroad in Illinois.

In September 1850, a bill on behalf of a land grant for this purpose was ratified by both houses of Congress and signed by President Millard Fillmore. Under its terms, the federal government granted to the state of Illinois alternate sections of public land for six miles on each side of a proposed railroad from Cairo to Galena, and from Chicago to a junction with the main line. The Illinois legislature met on January 1, 1851, and decided the best way to utilize the federal land grant was to create an entirely new private corporation and to transfer to it the land grant under certain restrictions and with certain payments to be made to the state. Under this plan, the company formed would assume entire responsibility for the completion of the road. A proposition to form the new private corporation was presented by a Massachusetts promoter, Robert Rantoul, acting in the interests of a group of eastern capitalists. Following considerable discussion and opposition, it was accepted by the legislature, and the bill was signed by Governor Augustus French.

The Alton and Sangamon Railroad Company was incorporated in 1847 to run between Alton and Springfield. The Tonica and Petersburg Railroad was also formed; after successive incorporations and consolidations, both lines became part of the St. Louis, Alton and Chicago Railroad Company. The Terre Haute and Alton Railroad Company was incorporated in 1851, and ran between these two cities. The Chicago, Burlington and Quincy Railroad was incorporated in 1855, and ran between East Burlington and West Chicago.

Lincoln represented the Illinois Central, the Alton and Chicago, and the Tonica and Petersburg railroads. He represented individuals in suits against the Alton and Chicago, the Northern Cross, the Chicago, Burlington and Quincy, the Illinois River railroad companies, as well as the Terre Haute and Alton Railroad Company.

Stock Subscriptions.

When private railroad corporations were formed, the first order of business was to raise capital through the sale of stock to the public. The standard method of purchase was for the purchaser (or subscriber) to obligate himself with a written contract to pay for the stock in a series of installments. Some of the subscribers changed their minds after initially obligating themselves, especially when they discovered the railroad had changed its plans and the anticipated ancillary profits based on the original plans dissolved. The railroads sought to enforce the contractual obligations of the subscribers, but there was no common law in Illinois to rely upon for this enforcement. Lincoln represented the railroads in establishing the law in the first of eight related cases. The court applied the precedent set in this case to three of the next seven cases. The first four of these cases were won by Lincoln, representing the railroads. The next two were lost when Lincoln represented a disgruntled subscriber. In the last of these cases, Lincoln represented a railroad and lost.

The leading case which established the precedent was *Barret v. The Alton & Sangamon Railroad Company*,[1] December term 1851. The original Supreme Court case called Barret "Banet," and in some later references to this case Banet is stated as the appellant. The details of the case are as follows. The Alton & Sangamon Railroad had been created under authority of an act of the legislature to complete a railroad from Alton to Springfield, and the articles of incorporation provided for stock to be issued for $100 per share, with subscribers to pay five percent down, and the balance at stated intervals to be specified by the board of directors. James A. Barret subscribed for thirty shares. He also had substantial real estate interests in New Berlin, through which the planned railroad would traverse. Before the completion of Barret's payments, the legislature authorized the company to change the location of the road, but without changing the termini. The railroad found it would be more efficient to shorten the line, eliminating the New Berlin stop. Barret saw economic detriment to himself by this move, and refused to pay any more installments on his stock. The railroad brought this action in *assumpsit* in the Sangamon County Circuit Court, and Judge Davis awarded it $1351. Lincoln represented the railroad, and Logan and E. B. Herndon represented Barret.

The Supreme Court, in an opinion written by Justice Treat, affirmed the judgment. Firstly, the alteration of the company charter did not excuse Barret from paying his subscription. The special reasons which may have influenced Barret to become a subscriber could not be taken into consideration. There was no fraud, and the subscription was not conditional. Although it was possible for an alteration in the charter to work a dissolution of the contract of subscription, this alteration was not material enough to do so. The general features of the project remained unchanged. Secondly, the power to make calls for additional payments was vested in the railroad's board of directors, who properly should make the calls.

The next case was *Klein v. The Alton and Sangamon Railroad Company*,[2] December term 1851, in which Lincoln again represented the railroad, and S. T. Logan and E. B. Herndon represented Klein. The action was brought in the Sangamon County Circuit Court, with Judge Davis presiding. The opinion on the case begins as follows: "This record presents the same state of facts as the Banet case, except in the following particulars. It did not appear that the defendant had any interest in property, the value of which would be affected by the location of the road through New Berlin. He subscribed for five shares of the capital stock, received a certificate therefore, and gave his promissory note to the agent of the commissioners, for the amount of the five per cent required to be paid by the charter. He paid the note before the books of subscription were closed." The opinion describes the action brought to collect the balance due and presents two questions which did not arise in the Barret case. First, Joseph Klein contended that giving a promissory note, rather than cash, when he subscribed did not bind him. Justice Treat said that the payment of money before the books of subscription were closed concluded him from raising any such objection. Second, Klein was willing to forfeit the five per cent paid to excuse himself from further payment. Justice Treat said the right of forfeiture belonged exclusively to the corporation stating: "This principle is abundantly sustained by authority." Treat cited seven cases from both the U. S. Supreme Court and other state supreme courts.

Lincoln had obviously researched this point thoroughly and had presented the seven cases as authorities to prove his case.

The next case, *Ryder v. Alton and Sangamon RR Co.*,[3] December term 1851, brought in the Madison County Circuit Court, did not rely on the precedent of the Barret case since no change from the original plan was involved. Simeon Ryder was president of the board of commissioners appointed to sell the railroad's stock. For some reason, he became disenchanted with the project after subscribing for fifty shares for himself. His stated reason for changing his mind was that the city of Alton had subscribed for one thousand shares for itself, and "certain persons in the City of New York" had subscribed for two thousand shares "upon the express agreement that the New York subscribers should have the proxy of the city of Alton, in all votes of the company, for the period of eight years; and that the stock of the New York subscribers should be preferred at six per cent [sic] for a like period." Ryder knew this would give the New York people control of the railroad for eight years, which possibly thwarted some hope on his part that he would have a major role with the company. The court said this presented no defense to the action. "The agreement between the city and the New York subscribers, that they should receive six per cent [sic] interest on their investments, for a period of eight years, is not binding on the corporation or other stockholders. At the most, it amounts to but a guaranty on the part of the city that the dividends on the common stock, for that length of time, shall be equal to an interest of six per cent [sic] per annum. And this is a matter exclusively between the city and those subscribers. It does not operate to the prejudice of the remaining stockholders." His other defenses were also dismissed by the Illinois Supreme Court. Levi Davis represented Ryder, and W. Martin and H. W. Billings represented the railroad.

Lincoln represented the railroad in the *Tonica and Petersburg Railroad Company v. McNeely*,[4] January term 1859, with the favorable decision based on contract law. Sathoff subscribed for two shares, but died before full payment was made. The railroad sued the administrator of the estate (William McNeely), and the Menard County Circuit Court held against the railroad. This was reversed on appeal. Justice Caton said it was a valid contract based upon a valid purpose and was founded on good consideration which created a legal obligation. He said, "we know of no law against this proposition, but are familiar with a great deal for its support." The attorneys of record were D. A. and T. W. Smith for the railroad, and McNeeley and Walker for McNeeley.

The case of the *Tonica and Petersburg Railroad Company v. Stein*,[5] January 1859, in which Lincoln and Herndon represented the railroad and won, also relied on contract law—specifically, the principle that parol (oral) evidence could not be used to alter the terms of a contract. Jacob Stein had authorized the secretary of the subscription meetings to subscribe for stock for him, and he signed his name on a blank sheet of paper. The Menard County Circuit Court, with Judge Harriott presiding, held that he could prove by oral evidence he had attached certain conditions to the subscription, which he had done, and he won the case. There was evidence for Stein by one J. M. Miles, who testified that the railroad representatives said, "the road [railroad] would locate the depot in the bottom, in Maj. Harris' cornfield . . . and the depot should be in the bottom at all events.... The depot is not in the town [Petersburg] as represented. It is about three hundred yards further off." Apparently this was too much of a deviation to please Stein, so he changed his mind. This case did not involve a change of plans after incorporation like the Barret case, but simply contract law. Stein proved his point by oral evidence, which the trial court, and the Supreme Court in affirming the trial court, both viewed as proper in this situation. Had the oral evidence been offered to explain a written instrument, it would have not been properly received. Stuart & Edwards, and Thomas P. Cowan represented Stein.

The first of two cases in which Lincoln represented an individual being sued by a railroad, and who sought to enforce an agreement to buy stock in the corporation, is *Sprague v. The Illinois River Railroad Company et al.*,[6] December term 1857, six years after the Barret case. Lincoln & Herndon, and H. E. Dummer represented Charles Sprague. Sprague was a resident of Cass County, which had voted to buy $50,000 worth of stock in the railroad. The railroad was organized to build a line from Jacksonville in Morgan County, Illinois, to La Salle in La Salle County, Illinois, passing through Cass County, which is contiguous to Morgan County on the north. Sprague sought an injunction to void the impending purchase of the stock by the county because the railroad had amended its original plan to build a line from Jacksonville, going directly to LaSalle. The new plan called the line to run through Cass County, cross the Illinois River, and then join with the Peoria and Hannibal Railroad, which ran from the river to La Salle. Lincoln recognized the court would rely on the Barret case, which in fact it did; but, in order to properly represent his client, he had to believe this was a material enough change to allow a stock subscriber to back out of the deal. The Cass County Circuit Court, with Judge Harriott presiding, held for the railroad, and this was affirmed by the Illinois Supreme Court. S. T. Logan and D. A. Smith represented the railroad.

Justice Caton, writing the opinion for the Supreme Court, said:

> We have nowhere met with a more satisfactory exposition of the general principle of the law, governing the respective rights of corporations and individual stockholders therein, as connected with subject, than in the case of *Barret v. The Alton and Sangamon Railroad Company,* 13 *Ill.,* 504. In determining the question as to how far the original purposes of a corporation may be departed from, after subscriptions have been made to its stock, without violating the rights of the stockholders individually, we must first consider with what intention, and in view of what advantages, the law must presume such subscriptions were made. As it is clearly manifest from the decision of the case above referred to, the conclusive presumption is that it was with a view to the profits to be derived from the stocks thus subscribed, and as an investment, and not in reference to any

incidental advantages which may accrue to the stockholder by reason of the construction of the improvement, in consequence of any anticipated enhancement of any other property which the stockholder may own, or otherwise."

There is no indication what personal interests, if any, Sprague had in wanting the railroad to build a line directly to La Salle County. Probably he changed his mind on the value of the county's investment, and sought an "out." In any event, he lost, and Lincoln, who had established the rule in his successful action against Barret, was wrong in believing the railroad had made such a significant change that the county could be excused. Lincoln learned the meaning of Shakespeare's phrase, being "hoisted by one's own petard."

Again in 1859, Lincoln & Herndon represented an individual who wanted to renege on his promise to subscribe to railroad corporation stock. J. Gillespie, S. W. Moulton, and Levi Davis represented the railroad. In *Terre Haute and Alton RR Co. v. Earp*,[7] January term 1859. Lincoln again tried to justify an exception to the Barret rule he had persuaded the court to adopt in that ruling case. Again he failed. He was successful in the trial in the Shelby County Circuit Court, but the decision was overruled in the Illinois Supreme Court.

John Starr summarizes the facts of this case, as follows:

The Terre Haute and Alton Railroad, to run between Terre Haute, Indiana, and Alton, Illinois, was incorporated in both states in 1851, and opened for business March 1, 1856. Later that year a consolidation was affected with the Belleville and Illinoistown Railroad Company, running from Belleville to what was then called Illinoistown, but is now known as East St. Louis, with an extension from the latter point to East Alton, the new organization being known as the Terre Haute, Alton and St. Louis Railroad Company . . . Daniel Earp's attorney sought to avoid payment on the ground the 'new and deflected road' had thereby made the real terminus . . . to be at said Illinoistown, and not at Alton as aforesaid, and that the same was done without the consent of the defendant. Despite this argument, however, the case went against Lincoln, the Supreme Court reversing the judgment of the lower tribunal.[8]

Justice Caton, writing the majority opinion, said:

If what we have said in the cases of (Barret, Sprague and two other cases in which Lincoln was not involved that relied upon it) has not shown satisfactory reasons for the rule of law which we hold on this subject, we despair of doing so now.

Justice Walker was the only justice who accepted Lincoln's arguments that this should be an exception to the Barret rule, and wrote a strong dissenting opinion. This had to be of little solace to Lincoln and his client, with Lincoln suffering the additional indignity of once again being "hoisted by his own petard."

The last case in the series of stock subscription cases is *Tomlin v. Tonica and Petersburg RR Co.,*[9] January term 1860, in which the railroad brought action in *assumpsit* against Thompson Tomlin for failing to complete his subscription to buy ten shares of stock at $100 per share. The pleadings recited the various formalities of the procedure, several of which were held inadequate on the appeal. Tomlin thought the railroad was going to be built on property adjoining his, but it was built a mile-and-a-half further away, which explains his reluctance to pay for his subscription. The Mason County Circuit Court held for the railroad. Herndon and T. P. Cowan represented the railroad. Lyman Lacey and Goudy & Judd represented Tomlin.

The Supreme Court, in an opinion written by Justice Caton, reversed the judgment and remanded the cause. As the case was presented, the railroad did not adequately prove the procedure in seeking the subscription as proper. Perhaps it was, or perhaps it wasn't. In either event when, and if, the case were retried, the attorneys for the railroad had to do a better job of presentation to prevail. There is no record of a retrial.

This case should have been won—the law of the applicability of the Barret case was clear. In chapter fourteen, I postulate that Herndon handled this case without Lincoln's support, and it appears it may have been mishandled. The pleadings should have followed those used in the Barret case.

Carriage of Animals

Under the common law of England which was adopted by Illinois, a common carrier, like a railroad, was in effect an insurer of property transported by it. It was not only liable for its own negligence, but also for unavoidable accidents and any casualty, with a few exceptions to this absolute liability for catastrophic-type events. In a leading Illinois case on the liability of railroads as common carriers, two shippers brought an action against the Illinois Central under the common-law rule for damages suffered by cattle entrusted to the railroad for transit. The shippers had been charged a reduced rate because they had agreed that the railroad would not have strict common-carrier liability. Lincoln represented the railroad, won the case for them, and the court established new precedent for the future.

The general common law rule and history of the reason for the rule is stated in *American Jurisprudence* as follows:

> In common law, a common carrier is an insurer against the loss, or

damage to, property received by it for transportation, except for loss or damage arising from an act of God, the public enemy, the inherent nature of the property shipped, the act or fault of the shipper, or an act or mandate of public authority. It is liable not only for its own negligence, but even for losses occasioned by the unavoidable accident or by any casualty whatever, except those above mentioned. The rule of the common law respecting a carrier's responsibility for goods entrusted to its charge for transportation is admitted everywhere in its full vigor, in the states governed by the jurisprudence of the common law.

The rule that a common carrier is answerable for all losses or damage to property transported which do not fall within the excepted cases had its origin in what were supposed to be the commercial necessities of England at a time when government afforded imperfect protection to goods in transit, and when robberies were of frequent occurrence. Before England became a commercial country, the laws of carriers were conformable to the general principles of bailment, that is to say, the carrier was liable only where he had not used ordinary care and vigilance, but when commerce became extended under the flourishing reign of Elizabeth, it was thought expedient to adopt a stricter rule, in order to guard against frauds and collusions, easily practiced, but hard to prove. It has been said that the reasons for adhering to the rule still exist in the main, although changing conditions may possibly have lessened the force of some, and at the same time furnished somewhat broader grounds for upholding the general doctrine. Collusion with thieves and robbers is less to be apprehended now than in times when the rule was first established. On the other hand, the immense increase of business, the inestimable value of the commodities now entrusted to the charge of common carriers, and the vast distances to which they are transported have multiplied the difficulties of the owner who seeks to recover for the loss of his goods, and have added greatly to the opportunities and temptations of the carrier who might be disposed to neglect or violate its trust. Furthermore it is apparent that while the danger of embezzlement and collusion with thieves, generally given as the cause, might be sufficient when the property is lost, such a reason has no application when it is delivered to its place of destination in a damaged condition. The carrier's exclusive possession of evidence, the difficulties under which the shipper might labor in discovering and proving the carrier's fault, his inability to contradict the carrier's witnesses, the necessity of avoiding the investigation of circumstances impossible to be unraveled, the importance of stimulating the care and fidelity of the carrier, and the convenience of a simple, intelligible, and uniform rule in so extensive a business—in other words, commercial necessity plus public policy and convenience—constitute much broader grounds and are the basis for the acceptance of the rule at the present time. While some courts have declared the rule to be harsh and unjust, there is, in its application, less hardship than might be supposed; for while the law holds the carrier to an extraordinary degree of diligence and treats it as an insurer of the property, it allows the carrier, like other insurers, to demand a premium proportionate to the hazards of its employment.

Notwithstanding the great rigor with which the courts have always enforced the common law obligations of common carriers, the law does not forbid certain contracts between carriers and shippers which aim to fix the terms on which goods shall be carried, and when there is such a special contract it takes the place of the contract which the law, in the absence of a special agreement implies; and insofar as it speaks, it is to be resorted to for the purpose of ascertaining the rights and liabilities of the parties. Therefore, when a specific contract is proved, the shipper cannot rely on the common law liability of the carrier; his only remedy in the event of loss is to sue on such contract for the breach thereof. Special agreements between shipper and carrier usually take the form of limitations on the latter's liability.[10]

The precedent-setting case was *Illinois Central RR Co. v. Morrison and Crabtree,*[11] December term 1857. The case was tried in the Coles County Circuit Court, with Judge Emerson presiding. In this case, David A. Morrison and John Crabtree contracted with the railroad to ship 400 head of cattle from Urbana, Illinois, to Chicago, at a rate less than the first-class rate because they signed a release to the railroad of its liability for any claims resulting from any damage or injury to the stock except if the damage should be the result of gross negligence of the railroad. During the shipment a few cattle died, and many suffered greater weight reduction than normal because of delays and hardships on the trip. At the trial, the plaintiffs—Morrison and Crabtree—proved the facts regarding the shipment of the cattle, the fatalities of some of the cattle, and that the loss of weight by the live ones was 150 to 170 pounds more than would have been normal if the cattle had been transported in reasonable time and in proper railroad equipment.

The attorneys for the railroad (Lincoln did not represent the railroad at the trial) argued the plaintiffs had been charged less than the normal fare because they had released the railroad from liability under these circumstances and consequently were not liable for damages. The trial judge refused to allow evidence of these releases to be admitted in evidence on the grounds that a railroad, being a common carrier, could not as such relieve its legal responsibilities by agreement of the shippers. Since the releases were inadmissable, the jury found a verdict for the plaintiffs and awarded them damages of $1200. Lincoln, O. B. Ficklin, and H. C. Whitney represented the railroad on the appeal, which was based on alleged error in the judge's ruling on the releases. C. H. Constable and A. Green represented Morrison and Crabtree.

Justice Breese wrote the opinion for the Supreme Court, reversing the lower court, stating: "As the Circuit Court seemed to have entertained views of law different from those here expressed, the judgment is reversed, and the cause remanded for further proceedings not inconsistent with this opinion."

Justice Breese and his cohorts did not have the benefit of *American Jurisprudence* 2nd or any other modern text; they had to rely, initially at least, on the presentation of Lincoln on behalf of his client to hold contrary to the trial court. Lincoln showed the reasoning for the reversal and, as we shall see in the opinion, there were already some precedents from both England and other states to support his side. The opinion starts as follows:

> The question presented in this case is one of importance to the business public, and to the railroad interests, and has received due attention from the court. . . . That railroad companies are common carriers cannot be disputed, and, being so, they are bound and controlled, as a general principle, by all the common law rules applicable to such a position—they becoming, in fact, insurers.
>
> Until the establishment and use of railroads for the conveyance of property, it was not generally considered that common carriers could, by special contract, limit their liability, or take themselves out of the severe rules which governed such business.
>
> At this time, railroads have acquired much of the carrying trade of the country, and reversing the former order of things, now carry the very animals which propelled the old machines used for that purpose. It was quite an era in trade and transportation, when speedy means were devised by railroads for carrying live stock from one extreme of the country to the other, and, on its origination new rules were found necessary, or modifications of old ones, as applicable to this new system, which, whilst protecting these magnificent and costly enterprises, should be so guarded that no injury to the public should flow from them.
>
> Transportation of live stock in railroad cars, in their rapid motion, is attended with great hazard, against which, if the companies owning them had no power of protection, irretrievable ruin to them might be the necessary consequence. Accordingly, we see that the courts in England, where the railroad system, though yet perhaps in its infancy even there, has been brought to great perfection, and in most of the older and well regulated, and highly commercial States of our Union, have declared that these companies may protect themselves from their general liability as common carriers, by special contracts.

Lincoln had been contacted to represent Morrison in this case, but because he had prior legal relationships with the Illinois Central, he had an obligation to check with it before taking an adversary position against an old and valuable client. John J. Duff, in *A. Lincoln, Prairie Lawyer* (1960), speaks of this as follows:

> It is of interest to note that Lincoln had first been approached by James Steele and Charles Summers, Morrison's local lawyers, in Paris, Illinois, to represent Morrison, on the appeal, against the Illinois Central. At the time, Lincoln's claim for his fee in the McLean County tax case was pending against the road. The fee was $5000. Lincoln successfully represented the railroad, the chief executive officer of which was one George B. McClellan—later to be an important general—who refused to pay it [Lincoln successfully sued the railroad and recovered the full amount.] On February 12, 1857, Lincoln wrote to Morrison's lawyers, stating he had been in the regular retainer of the co. for two or three years, but he believed they did not wish to retain him any longer. He further stated that he was going to Chicago on February twenty-first, and when there would ascertain if the company wished to continue using him, and if not, as Lincoln had reason to expect, then he would handle the case on behalf of Morrison. Instead of being discharged by the road, Lincoln was engaged by it to handle the Morrison case, as well as others which followed, some of them of far-reaching importance.[12]

Duff goes on to summarize this case very well:

> Lincoln's position, as reflected in his notes and in the opinion of Judge Breese, reversing the judgment below, deserves some analysis. Charting an unprecedented course, he conceded that the common law rule was rigidly opposed to exemption of common carriers from liability, but, pitching his argument on the high plane of a changing economy, reasoned that the new era in trade and transportation called for a modification of the old order of things. Transportation of livestock was attendant with great hazards, he pointed out, and if the railroads had no power of protection by special contract, disastrous consequences would likely ensue. Such was the largeness of this view, in the latter years of his practice, the period of his greatest intellectual growth, that in his appeals to the appellate bench Lincoln so often stressed the broad issue involved in the case, at times minimizing its importance in the case at hand. This was advocacy in the grand manner.[13]

Lincoln and Henry Clay Whitney represented the Illinois Central in defending it in an action brought by another shipper of livestock. The case is *Illinois Central RR Co. v. Hayes et al.*,[14] December term 1857, and was brought in the Champaign County Circuit Court. This case involved full common law-common carrier liability because Brock Hayes *et al.* paid the full fare. In this case Hayes shipped live fat hogs from Okaw, Illinois, to Chicago. The trip took three days when the normal time would have been one day. The weather was excessively cold, many hogs died, and the remaining ones lost about twenty-five pounds, when the normal expectation of weight loss would have been two and one-half pounds. The liability was clear, and the jury found for Hayes *et al.* and awarded $860.25 in damages. Lincoln, representing the railroad, contended the damages were excessive. C. H. Constable represented Hayes *et al.* The Supreme Court, in affirming the judgment, said the only question was in the amount of damages and whether the evidence justified the verdict. It did.

Taxation

Lincoln represented the Illinois Central in two major tax cases. Both of these cases had long-term benefits to the railroad, represented major victories, and confirmed Lincoln's status as one of the outstanding appellate attorneys of his time.

The first case is *Illinois Central RR Co. v. County of McLean et al.*,[15] December term 1855. This was an action in chancery brought in the McLean County Circuit Court by the Illinois Central Railroad to enjoin the collection of a tax assessed by the County of McLean upon the property of the railroad company in that county. The court held for the County of McLean. Lincoln, M. Brayman, and J. F. Joy represented the railroad, and Logan, along with Stuart & Edwards, represented McLean County.

The Supreme Court, in an opinion written by Justice Scates, reversed the decree, and made the injunction against the collection of the tax perpetual. The legislature had enacted a special state tax for railroads, exempting its property from taxation, upon the payment of a certain proportion of its earnings (to the state). McLean County contended this was unconstitutional, since the general rule of the constitution intended to apportion the burden upon the actual appraised value of all property in a manner which would, as far as possible, make its operation "uniform in respect to persons and property within the jurisdiction of the body imposing the same." Justice Scates said, "had the rule stopped here, there could be little room left for construction. But there are exceptions to it (in the constitution), which show that an inflexible, universal rule was not intended. And it becomes a question how far the legislature may depart from it—in what instances—and whether the present is warranted as one falling within the exceptions." He stated this was a proper exception, and it was for the legislature and not the court to make the exceptions. The only duty of the court was to make certain the legislature did not make an exception "in palpable violation of the constitutional rights of the tax-payer."

Justice Skinner wrote a separate, concurring opinion, agreeing with the reversal but questioning some of the reasoning. Lincoln had to sue the Illinois Central Railroad company to recover his $5000 legal fee.

Starr mentions in *Lincoln and the Railroads* that several counties, including McLean and Champaign, had sought Lincoln's services to represent McLean County in pressing the collection of its tax on railroad property in the courts. Lincoln, having represented the Illinois Central, consulted with the railroad about this solicitation of his services, and the railroad hired him to protect its interests in the matter to resist this taxation. The case was first argued in the circuit court in McLean County in August of 1853, with the Supreme Court finally settling the matter in 1855.

Starr reports several versions as to how the $5000 legal fee was arrived at, and how it was collected. He quotes Billy Herndon:

> [After the Supreme Court decision] Mr. Lincoln soon went to Chicago and presented our bill for legal services. We only asked for $2000 more (a retainer of $250 had already been paid). The official to whom he had been referred—supposed to have been the Superintendent George B. McClellan who afterwards became the eminent general—looking at the bill expressed great surprise.
>
> "Why, sir," he exclaimed, "this is as much as Daniel Webster himself would have charged. We cannot allow such a claim!"
>
> Stung by this rebuff, Lincoln withdrew the bill, and started for home. On the way home he stopped at Bloomington. There he met Grant Goodrich, Archibald Williams, Norman B. Judd, O. H. Browning and other attorneys, who, on learning of his modest charge for such valuable services rendered the railroad, induced him to increase the demand to $5000, and to bring suit for that sum.
>
> This was done at once. On the trial six lawyers certified that the bill was reasonable, and judgment for that amount went by default. The judgment was promptly paid. Lincoln gave me my half, and much as we deprecated the avarice of great corporations, we both thanked the Lord for letting the Illinois Central fall into our hands.[16]

Starr further presents the Illinois Central version of that same transaction as it appeared in a 1905 publication. The railroad claimed that when Lincoln presented his bill for $5000, "the then general counsel of the road advised Mr. Lincoln that while he recognized the value of his services, still, the payment of so large a fee to a western country lawyer without protest would embarrass the general counsel with the board of directors in New York, who would not understand, as would a lawyer, the importance of the case and the consequent value of Mr. Lincoln's services."[17]

Whatever the proper version—and there are other nuances in Starr's report—the incontrovertible fact is that the professional relationship of attorney and railroad was not severed. Abraham Lincoln continued to handle its litigation afterwards, the same as he had done before.

The second major tax case Lincoln won for the railroad was *The State of Illinois v. Illinois Central Railroad,*[18] November term 1861. In this case the State brought action against the railroad for unpaid taxes alleged to be due the state for the year 1857. The railroad charter provided it would pay five percent of is gross proceeds to the state; and after the expiration of six years from the grant of its charter, the railroad was required to furnish a list of its stock, property, and other assets so that additional taxes could be assessed. The railroad provided such a list for 1857, and the State assessed taxes of $108,000 (five percent of its gross revenues), and $132,000, based on its list of property. The major question in the case concerns the evaluation of the railroad's property. The railroad paid $37,600 (in addition to the $108,000) based upon its valuation of its property. This is an original suit in the Supreme Court, with agreed facts, to determine the proper evaluation of the property. This action was first argued by Lincoln during the January term, 1860. The Supreme Court finished its deliberations and rendered its opinion in the November term, 1861—after Lincoln had assumed the presidency. States Attorney S. B. White, Logan, and Hay represented the state, and J. M. Douglas and Lincoln represented the railroad.

The Supreme Court, in an opinion written by Justice Breese, held for the railroad. The basic difference between the arguments of each suit was that the state assessed the land at prospective value, and the railroad at its present value. Breese said: "The most experienced and intelligent railroad men in the West were fully examined on all the elements of value, as subsisting in a railroad concern, and in this road particularly. Present value should be used; as the railroad property increases in amount and in profitable use, it will be evaluated each year on the same basis." Justice Breese then observed:

> In this country at least, hope is so seductive, and the future so bright, and so full of promise, there is the greatest danger that the most prudent man may be mistaken, and the most considerate be misled, and it is much safer to rely upon practical demonstration, to determine the present value of such property, rather than speculatively, enter into the unknown future, whose dark veil is not given to us to lift, and look beyond. It is safer surely, to say, that, when the future shall be revealed, and practically exhibit an increased value of the property, then would be the proper time to assess it at such increased value. The road is doing its best, and it is proved, it has no net income—no profit on its cost, and is not a good investment at a value greater than that fixed by its owners, and proved on the trial.

This was the last case Lincoln argued before the Illinois Supreme Court, and the final decision was not made until after he was serving as president. The case was argued before the Supreme Court on January 12, 1860, and at the conclusion of the arguments, the court took the case under advisement—rendering its opinion at the November term, 1861. Starr quotes an official of the railroad as follows: "This was a case of considerable importance and it was largely due to the efforts of Mr. Lincoln that judgment was rendered in favor of the company."[19]

Beveridge offers additional details on these two cases and on Lincoln's relationships with the Illinois Central Railroad and with Captain George McClellan, when he was in its employ; and attributes the reluctance of the Illinois Central to pay Lincoln's fee to financial difficulties. The fee was paid in August 1857. The Great Panic of October 1857 prostrated business generally, and the Illinois Central was forced to suspend payment of major expenses for over a year.[20]

Mundane Miscellany

Lincoln had seven other cases before the Illinois Supreme Court. Two of them involved the Northern Cross Railroad, both of which being reported at the December term, 1842.

In *Taylor et al. v. Whitney*,[21] Logan & Lincoln and L. Trumbull represented Jonas Whitney, who had donated certain land in Springfield to be used by the Northern Cross Railroad for a station or turnout, which would have benefited his other land adjacent to that given to the railroad. However, the railroad chose other sites for these purposes which it deemed more efficient and less expensive. Whitney brought this action against Edmund D. Taylor and others who were the agents of the commissioner of state railroad construction funds and contractors working for the state on this project, to compel them to use his site and no other for the station and turnouts. Whitney secured his injunction in the Sangamon County Circuit Court, Judge Treat presiding, but it was reversed by the Illinois Supreme Court. There was nothing in the acts of the legislature authorizing the railroad construction to require the railroad to use donated lands, unless such use would be the most efficient and least expensive for the railroad project. J. Lamborn represented Taylor.

In the second case, *Paine & Alexander v. Frazier et al.*,[22] Lincoln represented the Fraziers, who had purchased certain tracts of land on which the Northern Cross Railroad was located, from Morgan L. Paine. Paine had obtained a $150 judgment against the state of Illinois for damages occasioned by the location of the railroad, which Paine agreed to pay the Fraziers. This action sought an injunction to restrain the payment to Paine and to require that M. K. Alexander, commissioner of the Board of Public Works, pay the money to the Fraziers. An injunction was granted. Alexander filed his answer, acknowledging recovery of the judgment by Paine, and denying all knowledge of the sale by Paine to the Fraziers. He also said that before he had any knowledge of the pendency of his suit, he paid Paine $50 in full satisfaction of the judgment, and received from him a relinquishment to the state of the right of way over the land. The Vermilion County Circuit Court ordered Alexander to pay $150 to the Fraziers. O. B. Fickland represented Paine, *et al.* This decree was reversed on appeal, and remanded to be tried again since Alexander's defense was not adequately considered in the trial. There is no record in the Illinois Supreme Court to tell us what later developed in this case.

The next three cases involved actions seeking damages from railroads condemning land or because of railroad construction. In the first two, which he won, Lincoln represented the Alton & Sangamon Railroad. The other one, against the Chicago, Burlington & Quincy Railroad, he lost.

The *Alton & Sangamon Railroad Company v. Carpenter,*[23] December term, 1852, was a proceeding in the Sangamon County Circuit Court, before Judge T. L. Dickey, to condemn the railroad company's right of way over William Carpenter's land. The only question on appeal was the proper measure of damages in the case. Carpenter was awarded $326.96. Logan represented Carpenter. Lincoln & Herndon represented the railroad, and requested the following instruction to the jury (which was refused):

> That, in estimating the damage done to the land by the construction of the railroad, they are to deduct the advantage which they believe the land will derive from its construction; and in estimating such advantages, they are not to be confined to the advantages peculiar to this tract of land, but they are to consider as such advantage, whatever increased value they may believe the land bears in common with other land beyond what they may believe it would bear if the road was not constructed, nor to be constructed at all; and that if in their opinion, such increased value is equal to, or greater than the damage done, they are to give no damage at all.

The Supreme Court, in an opinion written by Justice Trumbull, reversed the judgment and remanded the cause. It is obvious from reading the pertinent statutes that the legislature never contemplated the payment of damages to the owner of a tract of land for the privilege of constructing the railroad through it when the additional value to be given to the land by its construction was fully equal to the injury which it would occasion.

After these proceedings were instituted, the legislature passed a statute amending the law condemning right of way for purpose of internal improvement, as follows: "it is expressly declared that no benefits or advantages shall be estimated which may accrue to land affected in common with adjoining lands on which the public work does not pass." Whether this was allowed as a limitation on the requested instruction to the jury at the rehearing is not known, and there is nothing in the Supreme Court records subsequent to this case to give the answer.

The *Alton and Sangamon RR Co. v. Baugh*,[24] December term 1852, was a case where the railroad was assessed damages of $480 for the company's right of way over George Baugh's land. The case was heard in the Sangamon County Circuit Court before Judge T. L. Dickey. Lincoln & Herndon represented the railroad, and Logan represented Baugh. The appeal is based on the railroad's contention that the following instructions given the jury were improperly given and, consequently, a new trial should be awarded. The challenged instruction was "that after the assessment and payment of damages in the case, the railroad company will not be bound to make fences for Baugh, on either side of the road to make cattle guards for him across the road; nor will Baugh have the right without consent of the company, to make cattle guards across or under said road."

The Illinois Supreme Court, in an opinion written by Justice Trumbull, affirmed the judgment. The first part of the instruction does not seem to prejudice the railroad in any fashion. I assume the railroad did not want the obligation to build fences or cattle guards. Perhaps that part of the instruction was included in the appeal because it was not deemed severable from the instruction dealing with potential problems to the railroad (which gave the right to the land owner to build fences and cattle guards which might obstruct the right of way). Perhaps the purpose of the objection and appeal was to get another chance to try the action, with the expectations of lowering the amount of damages the second time around. Since the appeal was not allowed, the $450 stands, and Baugh could not build fences or cattle guards on the right of way without the consent of the railroad.

In the next case, Lincoln and G. Goodrich lost when they represented a landowner against the railroad—*Chicago, Burlington & Quincy RR Co. v. Wilson*,[25] December term 1855. In this case, an application for a *mandamus* was filed with Judge I. G. Wilson asking for the appointment of commissioners to fix compensation to be made for appropriating certain lands for use of the railroad, as provided in the legislative act establishing the railroad. Judge Wilson denied the petition, so the application for *mandamus* was brought to the Supreme Court. Lincoln and Goodrich represented Isaac Wilson, who owned some of the land to be acquired, and objected. J. F. Joy represented the railroad.

The court, in an opinion written by Justice Caton, granted the *mandamus*. Its charter authorized the Chicago, Burlington, and Quincy Railroad to construct a railroad on the prescribed route "with such appendages as may be deemed necessary for the convenient use of the same," and to acquire the right of way or title to land necessary thereby. The railroad sought this land to build workshops, and such are necessary appendages. Also this power is not exhausted by an apparent completion of the road, if an increase of business shall demand other appendages, or more room for tracks.

It was also contended that Judge Wilson acted in his judicial capacity, and that the Supreme Court did not have the power to force him to reverse his decision. Caton said, "We cannot by *mandamus* control the judicial action of any inferior tribunal. We can, in such a case, only set it in motion, and require it to act one way or the other, but without determining how it shall act." However, here the judge was acting as a ministerial officer rather than judicial. He is compelled to act, if such a case is made as the statute directs. Such was the case here.

Justice Onias C. Skinner wrote a concurring opinion. He wanted it made clear that property sought to be condemned is a decision to be made by the courts, as it is not the sole province of the corporation to determine what property its exigencies require.

The last case in this section is *Illinois Central RR Co. v. Allen*,[26] January term 1866. As we all know, Lincoln left Springfield in 1861, never to return. I include it because he was involved in the case in the original trial in 1859 in the Macon County Circuit Court before Judge Charles Emerson. Wilson Allen brought this action in 1859 against the railroad for damages caused by a pond forming on one section of his land due to a ditch being clogged by the railroad, and to another section of land due to washing of mud and improper construction of the railroad. The railroad defended itself by proving Allen had brought an action of trespass against it in 1854 due to mud washing down onto the same section of land for which he made this new claim, and was awarded $762.50. Judgment was awarded him in this case of $25. Moore & Greene represented the railroad, and L. Weldon represented Allen on the appeal.

The Supreme Court reversed the judgment in an opinion written by Justice Lawrence. The recovery of the prior damages precluded any further action against the railroad for injury to the same tract of land covered by the prior suit; the change in the ditch was at the request of Allen, and thus he is precluded from bringing a suit for damages caused by such change.

Joseph Dalby

The following account was first published in Volume XII, Number 3 of *The Lincoln Newsletter*. The summary of the *St. Louis, Alton & Chicago Railroad Company v. Dalby*,[27] December term 1857, follows:

> One of Abraham Lincoln's most intriguing and lucrative clients was Joseph A. Dalby of Elkhart, Illinois. Elkhart is about twenty miles from Lincoln, the home of Lincoln College since 1865. In fact, Dalby and his wife were riding on a train from Elkhart to Lincoln when a most unusual event transpired. During that short journey, Dalby was severely injured in

a fracas with three railroad employees. The story might be described as a situation of a comparatively modern *David v. three Goliaths,* simultaneously.

The railroad employees were attempting to enforce the rules of the railroad as they understood them. Dalby had a different opinion of these rules, sought mightily to convince his opponents of the justice of his side, but failed and had the severe bruises and contusions to prove it.

Lincoln & Herndon represented Dalby in an action of assault against the St. Louis, Alton & Chicago Railroad Company. It resulted in Dalby being awarded a judgment in the Logan County Circuit Court for $1000—which was a lot of money in 1857. This was one of the largest judgments Lincoln ever won for a client. (Stuart & Edwards represented the railroad.)

Dalby and his wife boarded the train at Elkhart. The railroad required a fare of four cents per mile, unless the ticket was purchased in the station, where only three cents a mile was charged. Dalby tried to purchase the tickets in the station, but was told that none were available. When the conductor on the train asked the Dalbys for their tickets, Dalby told him his sad story—to no avail, since the conductor still insisted on collecting the full fare of four cents per mile. Dalby said he would pay no more than three cents and a fight ensued. Dalby lost the argument and the fight, and paid the four cents a mile. But he still believed he was right, and sought monetary redress for his injuries through legal action.

Lincoln lined up four witnesses. William Miller testified to the sequence of events leading up to and including the fight. When the railroad employees were very emphatically told by Dalby that he would pay the fare only at the three-cent rate, the three men grabbed him to throw him off the train. Their intention was to eject him at the next stop, which was Broadwell.

According to Miller, "Conductor and both brakemen had told of Dalby at the same time; one of the men had his head drawn over the arm of the seat, while the others were holding him, and pounded him in the face ten or a dozen licks ... in the scuffle, Dalby tore one of the men's coats and the man said, 'Damn you, you tore my coat. I will tear your hide.' Dalby's face [was] pretty badly bruised up, his face black under the eyes; bruised up considerably; some bloody; bled considerable."

Charles Gear said, "I was four or five seats back, and got up and went nearer, to the second seat back; when I got there the brakeman had Dalby by the hair with his left hand and was striking him in the face ... eight or ten times."

Another witness, Dr. Thomas H. Fowler, like Charles Geer, wanted a better view of the fight. He testified that the "fracas induced me to move forward. . . . [The] conductor and one brakeman both had hold of Dalby by the hair of his head, and the other brakeman was striking Dalby in the head as hard as he could." William Snodgrass, the fourth witness to testify in court, already had a good seat. He told the court that he "[w]as on the cars when the affair took place; was forward of Dalby, on [the] next seat; saw all the fracas." Apparently, these witnesses with ring-side seats took the opinion that this was a sporting event staged for their amusement and thought it would be inappropriate to assist Dalby.

The lawyers for the railroad based the defense on three points—all of which Lincoln refuted. First, they held that the railroad employees had the authority and responsibility to enforce its rules, using reasonable force if necessary. Lincoln disagreed, and the court agreed with him that the force exerted against Dalby was "unjustified, unreasonable and actionable."

The railroad then pleaded the special defenses based on its status as a corporation. Justice John D. Caton, writing the opinion for the court, addressed this issue, recognizing that private corporations had been known for some time but were few in number and were "little studied by the courts." One of the railroad's contentions held that since a corporation was an inanimate body, it could not be assaulted, and therefore could not commit an assault.

Caton said that there was some precedent in the English common law holding that assault against a person could not lie against a corporation, that "a corporation cannot beat or be beaten." However, "[t]he idea that a corporation can not be liable for beating because it has no body to be beaten, must be founded on the assumption that no party can inflict an injury which it is not capable of receiving. We confess to a want of respect when such whimsical notions are advanced by grave and learned judges. As well might it be said that a man cannot commit a rape because he cannot be the subject of one."

Justice Caton went on to say: "It is not to be presumed that the legislature would ever grant or suffer such [corporate] rights to exist, if the restraining influences of a just responsibility for the abuse of those powers were not to attach to their exercise . . . it follows, as necessary legal consequence, that if, by the exercise of the powers either express or implied, which they possess, they commit a particular wrong, they must be held responsible for such wrong, and the courts must necessarily adopt the known and appropriate remedy for the redress of such wrong."

The railroad then offered its third point: the corporation had no authority to order an unlawful act to be done, thus any unlawful act done by any one of its employees was his responsibility and not the corporation's. Caton dismissed this one quickly, based on his statements regarding the previous point. Lincoln recognized this argument would be made, so he didn't include the employees of the railroad in the suit. He reasoned that these employees didn't have the deep pockets the railroad had to pay damages. Furthermore, he did not want to make it easy for the jury to assuage its sympathy if it was prone to believe either one of the railroad's corporate yarns, by giving it alternative defendants to pay the damages.

Jim Hickey, eminent Lincoln scholar, chairman of the Heritage Committee at Lincoln College, and probably the best current authority on Joseph Dalby's life, has provided us with a copy of the 1873 *Logan County Atlas* which devoted several pages to Dalby. The article is written in a genteel, mannerly way and fails to mention one of the major events of Dalby's life—when he tried to protect himself against the ungentlemanly ruffians on a train. (Undoubtedly, the publication was not targeted for sale in the "supermarkets" of that time!)

Dalby was born in 1820, moved to Elkhart in 1852, died in 1873, and is buried in Elkhart in a beautiful cemetery on a wooded hill. Cogent comments which might help us understand why he persisted in his concept of right, against serious opposition, can be gleaned from these excerpts from the *Atlas:* "[In Elkhart] he gained a favorable reputation...honest in his life and honorable in his practice.... Free thought and free expression he looked upon as sacred rights of human kind.... Joseph A. Dalby would not curb or be curbed—would not subscribe to a theory or accept a doctrine, simply because it found support in favored places. Within the shadow of truth he stood, and diverged only where it pointed."

Joseph and Sarah Dalby had eight children. Number seven, George W., was born on August 3, 1857; number eight, A. Lincoln was born June 15, 1858. Dalby's case against the St. Louis, Alton & Chicago Railroad Company was finally concluded when the Illinois Supreme Court affirmed the trial court's $1000 judgment at the December 1857 term. Perhaps if the case had been finalized before August 1857, child number seven would have been named after the future sixteenth president rather than the first. Obviously, though, Joe and Sarah were pleased with Lincoln's work.

Abraham Lincoln was involved in 333 cases before the Illinois Supreme Court, many of which setting for the first time the common law of Illinois. The Dalby case set a precedent for liability of corporations for assaults against persons, which is still the law in Illinois and other civilized areas. We don't know what Lincoln's fee was in this case. We assume it was more than a promise to name their next son for him.

Contingency fees with large percentages of a judgment ear-marked for the successful lawyer were not prevalent in those days. We know Lincoln was wise enough to set the hourly rate for his services in advance, and if it was four dollars an hour, he made sure Dalby did not think it was three dollars.

Lincoln really did distinguish himself in this case. And his importance to the St. Louis, Alton and Chicago Railroad was indicated in the early stock subscription cases he won for them, and in later related cases. Despite his winning the Dalby case against it, the railroad still considered Lincoln as its counsel. Starr references this relationship as follows:

> A letter addressed to Joel A. Matteson, in control of the St. Louis, Alton and Chicago Railroad, as it was then called, written by Lincoln in the fall of 1858, shortly after the close of the Lincoln-Douglas Debates, testifies to the fact that the Springfield attorney was undoubtedly engaged at that period to handle certain litigation for the road....

This Joel A. Matteson was Governor of Illinois from 1853 to 1857, and it was largely through Lincoln's influence that he had been defeated for United States Senate by the Legislature in 1855. Although undoubtedly aware of Lincoln's action, and of the fact he had appeared against the railroad in the Dalby case six months before, Matteson's engagement of Lincoln in the summer of 1858 speaks volumes for the high legal reputation which Abraham Lincoln had attained at the time.[28]

NOTES

1. 13 *Ill.*, 504; *LCL*, 158.
2. 13 *Ill.*, 514; *LCL*, 159.
3. 13 *Ill.*, 516; *LCL*, 160.
4. 21 *Ill.*, 71; *LCL*, 211.
5. 21 *Ill.*, 96; *LCL*, 211.
6. 19 *Ill.*, 173; *LCL*, 202.
7. 21 *Ill.*, 290; *LCL*, 215.
8. Starr, John W., Jr., *Lincoln and the Railroads*. New York: Dodd, Mead & Company, 1927, 124–25.
9. 23 *Ill.*, 374; *LCL*, 221.
10. *American Jurisprudence* 2nd. Rochester, New York: Lawyer's Cooperative Publishing Company, 1950, §§ 508–10, 39–42.
11. 19 *Ill.*, 135; *LCL*, 200.
12. Duff, John J., *A. Lincoln, Prairie Lawyer*. New York and Toronto: Rinehart & Co., 1960, 266.
13. *Ibid.*, 267.
14. 19 *Ill.*, 166; *LCL*, 201.
15. 17 *Ill.*, 290; *LCL*, 193.
16. Starr, 75.
17. *Ibid.*, 76, 77.
18. 27 *Ill.*, 64; *LCL*, 234.
19. Starr, 69.
20. Beveridge, Albert J., *Abraham Lincoln, 1807–1858*. Boston and New York: Houghton Mifflin Company, 1928, Vol. 1, 584–97.
21. 5 *Ill.*, 61; *LCL*, 47.
22. 5 *Ill.*, 55; *LCL*, 46.
23. 14 *Ill.*, 189; *LCL*, 166.
24. 14 *Ill.*, 210; *LCL*, 168.
25. 17 *Ill.*, 122; *LCL*, 184.
26. 39 *Ill.*, 205; *LCL*, 243.
27. 19 *Ill.*, 352; *LCL*, 208.
28. Starr, 83–84.

Chapter Eight

Agency

"AGENCY" EXISTS WHEN ONE PERSON acts for another (the principal) under the latter's authority. The agent's obligation is to protect the interests of his principal, and not use the position for his own unlawful gain. Lincoln was involved in three Supreme Court cases which covered various aspects of the agent/principal relationship.

The simplest and shortest one was *Rusk v. Newell*,[1] January term 1861. Here the agent used his principal's money to pay a personal debt. This is clearly wrong. William Newell's agent, Anderson Pruitt, collected $1000 from W. J. Rusk for some hogs Newell sold him. Pruitt was indebted to Rusk for $1000, so he gave Newell's money to Rusk to discharge that debt. Newell brought an action of *assumpsit* in the Richland County Circuit Court, with Judge A. Kitchell presiding, against Rusk to recover the $1000. Judgment was entered for Newell. The official opinion lists Stuart & Edwards, and Brown representing Rusk, and Milton Hay representing Newell.

The Supreme Court, in an opinion written by Justice Breese, affirmed the judgment. Rusk knew Pruitt was Newell's agent. Justice Breese, very generously, said, "We make no comment on the morality of the transaction."

Chase v. DeBolt,[2] December term 1845, involves an action against an agent by someone who claimed he properly thought the agent was really the principal. George DeBolt sued Henry J. Chase in a justice of the peace court in Peoria to recover payment for work done by DeBolt on Jubilee College. DeBolt was awarded $75.93 3/4. Chase appealed to the Peoria County Circuit Court and appeared before Judge Caton and a jury; the verdict and judgment were rendered for DeBolt for the same amount. Chase testified in the justice of the peace court that he had hired DeBolt on behalf of Bishop Chase for Jubilee College, but although he had not told DeBolt he was an agent rather than a principal, DeBolt knew it from other sources. Thus, as an agent, he was not liable to pay DeBolt, and DeBolt's remedy to collect money due him was to sue Jubilee College. There is no evidence in the case of any relationship between the Chases. Chase appealed to the Illinois Supreme Court, and in this matter DeBolt was represented by Lincoln and H.O. Merriman. Chase was represented by E. W. Powell and W. P. Bryan.

Justice Scates, writing for the court, reversed the judgment, and remanded the case for a new trial. Lincoln objected to the inclusion of testimony in the circuit court by the justice of the peace, stating that Chase testified he hired DeBolt, and DeBolt knew he was an agent from other sources. He said this was hearsay, and not admissible. Scates held that Chase's testimony was an admission, and thus proper as evidence. The two lower courts had said Chase was liable to pay because DeBolt believed him to be a principal, and not an agent. An agent is liable as a principal if he does not disclose this; but if the other party knows the agency status from other sources, he is not. New trials can be awarded if there is a strong preponderance of testimony that the judgment was improper, especially where apparent injustice has been done. Chase was not a principal and should not have been found liable as one. He was an agent, and DeBolt knew it.

I don't know when Lincoln joined this case, and presume it was only for the appeal. By this time in his career, his services were frequently sought for appeals to the Supreme Court, when he had not been involved in the trials. He argued every positive point he could, and cited pertinent cases and treatises on English common law to support his points. Once it was clear to the court that Chase was only an agent, it was impossible to affirm lower court opinion that he had been a principal.

In *Martin and Warfield v. Dryden et al.*,[3] December term 1844, an agent placed real property he held in trust for his principals on the records in his own name. A lien was placed against the property for a claim against the agent, and the principals lost their ownership rights. In 1836, Joshua Dryden *et al.* (a total of twenty-eight citizens of Baltimore, Maryland) entered into articles of co-partnership, in the name of "Baltimore and Western Land Association" for the purpose of buying and selling, and speculating in lands in the state of Illinois and elsewhere, with a capital of $20,000. They employed Charles A. Warfield as their agent. Warfield purchased the lands in controversy in 1836 and 1837, in his own name. He conveyed these lands to three members of the company—Dryden, Gasnell, and Wood—on March 11, 1840. The deed was recorded in Madison County, Illinois, on December 20, 1840.

John T. Martin sued out an attachment against Warfield on July 14, 1840, and on the same day it was levied upon the lands in controversy. Warfield denied the debt, but in September, 1841, judgment was rendered for $1666.35. In October, an execution was issued on the judgment, under which the lands were sold to Martin. Dryden *et al.* brought this action in equity to enjoin Martin from proceeding, and to remove his lien on the land. The Madison County Circuit Court, Judge James Semple presiding, granted the relief.

Martin appealed, and Lincoln and J. M. Krum represented Dryden. The opinion of the court cites extensive arguments on each side, including a seven-page printed brief on behalf of Dryden which is identified as follows:

> A. LINCOLN and J. M. KRUM, for the appellees.
> The following is a portion of a printed argument, presented by JOHN M. KRUM, Esq. who contended . . .

The lower court was reversed in the opinion written by Justice Scates, meaning Dryden *et al.* lost, and perhaps the results would have been different if Lincoln had argued the case. Martin and Warfield were represented by O. H. Browning, N. Bushnell, N. D. Strong, and J. Hall.

The heart of the case was the timing of the filing of the deed from Warfield (December 1840) and when Martin filed the levy under his action on debt against Warfield (July 1840). The statutes governing filing of liens on land had been in force for ten years at the time of this trial, but the definitions of a "creditor" under the law, having right to file a lien, and when the lien had to filed, had not been defined. Justice Scates examined cases from various states, discarding those of Kentucky and New York as being opposite extremes and not acceptable. He chose Massachusetts as the model for Illinois, stating the time of levy in an action on debt is the proper date. It would become binding when, and if, judgment is rendered, but at the date of the levy. Under this newly minted definition "of a creditor," the lien of Martin was established before he had constructive notice of the interests of Dryden *et al.* Martin had no actual notice of this interest, and since the deed wasn't filed until December of that year, his claim was prior and prevailed.

NOTES

1. 25 *Ill.*, 211; *LCL*, 233.
2. 7 *Ill.*, 371; *LCL*, 93.
3. 6 *Ill.*, 187; *LCL*, 66.

Chapter Nine

Family Relations Law

IN ANTEBELLUM ILLINOIS, the common law regarding family relations was a continuation of the English common law. The laws covering marital rights and obligations and rights of minor children were especially important because of their effect on the ownership of real estate.

The common law granted primacy in the ownership of property to the husband in the family. The wife had a dower right in any real estate property of the husband, which was generally defined as a life interest in one-third of the lands her husband owned during their marriage. Since most of the measurable wealth of any man generally consisted of his land and improvements he had made to it, this dower right was treated with great importance by the courts. Lincoln was reminded of how important this right was when he represented John Villars in *Leonard v. Villars*,[1] January term 1860, who brought an action to foreclose a mortgage against Peter R. Leonard, and did not include Leonard's wife as a necessary party. The decree of foreclosure was granted by the Vermilion County Circuit Court, Judge Davis presiding, with interest also granted. The interest amount included $16.80 of interest computed on interest. Logan, Hay, and G. T. Pierson represented Leonard.

The Supreme Court, in an opinion written by Justice Walker, reversed the decree and remanded the cause. Mrs. Leonard should have been included as a party. She had a right of dower along with her husband's right of redemption. A decree which would attempt to deprive her of these rights, unless she was a party to the record, and properly before the court, could not bind her any more than would a decree against any other person over whom the court had no jurisdiction. Also, to compute interest on interest has been found by all courts to be compounded interest, and in violation of law.

Lincoln, however, did a masterful job in representing Clarissa Wren, whose husband had been granted a divorce from her based on her proven misconduct. Her husband also tried to do her out of her dower right, but after two lawsuits Lincoln succeeded in protecting her interests. Aquilla Wren filed a bill of divorce from his wife, Clarissa; a divorce was decreed, and the question of alimony was continued to the next term of the court. However, before that next term, Aquilla made a will leaving his property to people other than his former wife, and then he died. Clarissa brought this action, *Wren v. Moss et al.,*[2] December term 1844, in the Peoria County Circuit Court, Judge Caton presiding, with Lincoln and E. N. Powell as her attorneys in a motion to the Supreme Court. A motion was made for a writ of *scire facias* (to show cause why a judgment should not be amended) and for a writ of error (to revise the decree of divorce). H. O. Merriman and J. B. Thomas represented Moss *et al.*

Lincoln contended that a question of property (the right of dower or alimony) was involved, as the decree a *vinculo* (a term descriptive of a kind of divorce which effects a complete dissolution of the marriage contract) barred her dower right. He contended that by abating the suit as to the pending motion, she was cut off from alimony, and therefore the action should survive on account of the nature of the interests involved.

The motion was allowed, with an order of publication of the motion to the non-resident defendants. Publication of this decision would constitute notice to non-residents of the state. Thus, in a subsequent action, a court would have jurisdiction over them as if they had made a personal appearance.

An executor had been appointed to carry out the provisions of Aquilla's will. The executor sold the land to William S. Moss and Smith Frye, although Clarissa had not released her right of dower. Clarissa, again represented by Lincoln and E. N. Powell, sought a writ of error to revise the decree of divorce in the Peoria County Circuit Court. This was granted, making all the persons involved in the sale of the land defendants. At the next term of the Supreme Court, this case—*Wren v. Moss et al.,*[3] December term 1845—was brought as an application for a rule upon the defendants to join in error, and the application was resisted on the ground that a writ of error did not lie in this case. J. B. Thomas and H. O. Merriman again represented Moss.

The Supreme Court, with Justice Scates writing the opinion, granted the motion. He stated the general rule was that a writ of error did not lie against any but him who was party to the first judgment, or to his heirs, executors or administrators. However, there are exceptions. Some of the parties who are defendants here did not meet the general definition, but they all had interests which could be influenced if the original decree of divorce were altered. Scates states that Clarissa believed she had been injured by an erroneous decree. Her only two remedies were appeal or writ of error. She could not appeal because the judgment against her was not $20 or more. There was no money involved in it, so her only remedy was a writ of error. Thus, a writ of error was granted, which in reality entitles her to a new trial, and all the interests of the various defendants must be included to protect their rights. Justice Young dissented; Justice Purple did not sit in this case because he had been one of the attorneys for Moss *et al.* in the first proceeding.

There is no record in the Supreme Court decisions of any subsequent activities between these parties. There apparently was enough property involved to justify these two proceedings. Lincoln's client prevailed after suffering an initial setback of having been the defendant in a successful divorce action based on her misconduct.

In another divorce case, *Shillinger v. Shillinger*,[4] December term 1852, there is no mention in the opinion about real property or dower rights, but we can presume that was one of the reasons for this husband seeking single status. George Jacob Shillinger came to Illinois from Philadelphia in 1848, leaving his wife, Elizabeth, who promised to move to Illinois when he asked her to join him. She failed to abide by this promise, and George brought this action for a divorce, under a statute providing that if a wife refuses to live with her husband for at least two years, a divorce will be granted.

The parties had stayed in touch in the interim, and George had sent her money. George's brother left Philadelphia in 1851 to come to Illinois, and at George's request, asked Elizabeth to accompany him. She refused. Since the suit was filed by publication, and Elizabeth was never served, the court appointed a master, as specified in the statute, to hear evidence. He reported he believed a divorce should be granted, and the Morgan County Circuit Court, Judge Woodson presiding, decreed a divorce at the March term, 1852. Herndon and D. Campbell represented George. S. W. Robbins represented Elizabeth.

The Supreme Court, in an opinion written by Justice Trumbull, reversed the decree. A court has no authority to decree a divorce when the other party does not appear, without proof to sustain its allegations. The general statement of the master is not enough. There was not enough evidence in the decree to grant the divorce. The master's report, so far as showing a refusal by Elizabeth to join George for a space of two years, fails to show any such refusal until 1851, only a few months before this bill was filed.

Another divorce definitely involved real estate—both land purchased by money the wife brought to the marriage, value added to that land by the husband's work during the marriage, and land she purchased with the proceeds of the sale of property he left her after he abandoned her. In *Stewartson v. Stewartson*,[5] December term 1853, all these varied purchases of land were addressed by the court. The action was brought in the Shelby County Circuit Court before Judge Emerson. Mary Jane Stewartson married William Stewartson in 1848, and had, at her marriage, "$320 and upwards, which afterwards came to the use of the appellee [William], and was appropriated by him." Shortly after the marriage, $40 of Mary Jane's money was used to buy land, which was purchased in her name. In 1850, William abandoned Mary Jane, and left her in possession of the dwelling-house, and a few articles of personal property, some of which she sold. She then bought, in her own name, another forty-acre tract of land, unimproved, but contiguous to appellee's [William's] farm. In 1852 Mary Jane filed for divorce, and obtained a decree of divorce and $50 a year alimony. This action was brought by William to change the terms of the financial settlement. The court heard the facts, and decreed that Mary Jane convey to William title in the last tract of land she bought, and the alimony was reduced to $30 per annum. Lincoln and S. W. Moulton represented Mary Jane on the appeal. A. Thornton represented William.

The Supreme Court, in an opinion written by Justice Caton, affirmed the decree. Caton said

> Before we should feel justified in disturbing a decree of this kind, we ought to be able to say that manifest injustice has been done.... We are not disposed to disturb the decision of the circuit court. There can be no question as to the propriety of that portion of the decree which directs the complainant to convey to the defendant the forty acres which she entered with the proceeds of the property which she had sold, belonging to him. It was bought with his money, and there can be no doubt he had the right to claim it as his own. While there is undoubted propriety in allowing her to retain the forty acres which he had entered in her name, with money she had brought to him at the marriage, it is worthy upon consideration upon the question of alimony, that that forty acre tract had all been improved by him and constituted a part of his farm and by those improvements its value must have been much enhanced, and rendered immediately available and productive for her support.

The case of *Young et al. v. Ward*,[6] January term 1859, enlightens us on how property of a husband and wife was treated by the common law. A note signed by J. L. Reim and William H. Young and others was made payable to Alfred Ward or Charity D. Ward, his wife, for $250, and was in default. An action of *assumpsit* was brought in the name of Charity D. Ward in the Logan County Circuit Court. Young *et al.* pleaded action brought only by Charity Ward was improper, and that Reim (not Young *et al.*) had defrauded them. Judgment was entered for Charity. Lincoln & Herndon and C. Parks represented Charity Ward, at least on the appeal. W. H. Young represented William.

The Supreme Court, in an opinion written by Justice Walker, affirmed the judgment. Walker said there was no doubt the suit should have been brought in the name of the husband alone, or in their joint names. However, "The husband and wife being in law regarded as one person, the legal effect of the note was that the husband was the payee, and the note was not payable in the alternative, to one of two persons, and the objection that there was uncertainty as to who was the payee, and therefore void, does not apply."

Secondly, Young and the other makers of the note claimed Reim had lied to them to induce them to join in the note. But since the Wards were innocent of any participation in any possible fraud, they were not affected by the fraud. "It is the duty of the maker to see that his negotiable paper does not improperly get into circulation, and failing to do so, he must suffer the consequences of his negligence."

Children's property rights were protected by guardians appointed by the court in legal matters when they were still of minor age status. In *Davis, adm. of Hains v. Harkness,*[7] December term 1844, the property of minor children in control of their mother when she remarried was protected when her new husband died. This was an action in equity in McLean County Circuit Court before Judge Treat, brought by the heirs of Samuel Harkness, to recover payment from the estate of Thomas Haines. Logan & Lincoln represented the heirs. The judge awarded $1292.50 to the heirs. W. Colton and E. D. Baker represented Davis.

Samuel Harkness died in 1822 in Ohio, leaving a widow, Esther, and two children, Elisha and Hannah. The widow was appointed administrator, with $1000 in her control—which had been left specifically for the children. She married Thomas H. Haines, and the entire family moved to Illinois. Haines supported the family, and voluntarily brought up the children, "they doing service in his family as is common in such cases." Haines died, and there were not enough assets to pay all the claims. The children brought this action to be paid the estate ($1000) left them by their father, and to have priority in this claim against other creditors. They succeeded, and the decision was affirmed by the Supreme Court.

Justice Caton stated in his opinion that the general rule was that the expenses of a ward should be paid from the income from the estate, and not from the principal. While the children were technically not wards, with Haines as their formally-appointed guardian, his obligation was to protect the principal for the children—even more than if he had been officially appointed, because then the court would have supervised his stewardship.

The statute of wills was enacted by the Illinois legislature to formalize the disposition of estates. The 110th section provides for the priority of claims: (1) funeral expense; (2) expenses of administrators; (3) assets received in a representative capacity as guardian, etc.; (4) all other debts.

The court of equity had the power to treat the status of Haines in relation to the inheritances of the children, as being one of formal guardianship. Thus the assets were properly in the third class. Payment to the heirs was a proper priority over other creditors.

The opinion stated that "courts of equity are not bound down by the literal expressions of the statute, but where a case is found to be within the equity of the provision, it is held to be within the provision itself." This case, and others involving Lincoln's practice of law, could indicate that Lincoln had a sense of fairness which was expressed in the principles of equity courts. At least he convinced Judge Treat of this on numerous occasions.

Wright v. Bennett et al.,[8] December term 1845, dealt with the rights of, and responsibilities to, illegitimate children. Richard E. Bennett was convicted of being the father of an illegitimate child by one Jane Davidson, and was ordered by the court to pay the sum of forty dollars annually for seven years to support the child. Pursuant to an act of the legislature entitled an "Act to provide for the maintenance of illegitimate children," he entered into a bond with John Bennett as surety. Richard Bennett demanded the possession and control of the child, under the statute insisting if she did not give over custody, his obligation under the bond was discharged. Davidson insisted that a second bond was required under the statute before she must give up custody. Judge Treat in the Menard County Circuit Court held for Bennett, and that no second bond was required. Asa D. Wright, the Probate Justice of Menard county for the use of the child, appealed. Lincoln represented the Bennetts, and T. L. Harris represented Wright.

The court, with Justice Purple writing the opinion, agreed and affirmed the judgment, albeit reluctantly. Justice Purple, in commenting on the lack of necessity of a second bond, said: "I regret that, upon a careful and attentive consideration of the law, I can find nothing in its various provisions to warrant this construction, and am reluctantly compelled to admit that, if the reputed father of an illegitimate child, under the law as it existed at the time of the commencement of this suit, will have the inhumanity, in its helpless and dependent infancy, to demand its surrender by the mother, the law, upon her refusal, imposes upon him no further obligation to aid in its maintenance and support, at least so long as she persists in her refusal." By the common law, the reputed father was not entitled to custody of his illegitimate children. But this statute changed that; however, if he does take custody his obligation to the child does not end after the seven years stipulated in the statute. Judge Purple concluded: "and that the legislature did not intend that, when he had once so chosen to demand it of the mother, that his duties toward it should cease at the expiration of seven years, the time limited in the bond for its support, and then be at liberty to thrust it forth upon the world's charity, friendless and unprotected." (Also see *Cowls v. Cowls* in chapter twelve.)

NOTES

1. 23 *Ill.*, 322; *LCL*, 219.
2. 6 *Ill.*, 560; *LCL*, 74.
3. 7 *Ill.*, 72; *LCL*, 83.
4. 14 *Ill.*, 146; *LCL*, 164.
5. 15 *Ill.*, 146; *LCL*, 174.
6. 21 *Ill.*, 223; *LCL*, 214.
7. 6 *Ill.*, 173; *LCL*, 65.
8. 7 *Ill.*, 587; *LCL*, 100.

Chapter Ten

Torts

THIS CATEGORY EMBRACES all manner of private wrongs or injuries (other than breach of contract) for which the court will provide a remedy in the form of an action for damages. There are three elements of every tort action:
1. existence of a legal duty from defendant to plaintiff;
2. breach of that duty;
3. damage as approximate result.

The Lincoln tort cases before the Illinois Supreme Court involved injury to property (fraud or injuries to animals) and injury to persons (assault, slander, seduction, criminal conversation, and malpractice). Lincoln represented the party claiming to be wronged (the plaintiff) in most of these cases, perhaps reflecting his strong belief in the rights of individuals.

Cases of Fraud

The following elements must be present for an action to be defined as fraud:
1. false representation of a present or past fact made by defendant, with intention to deceive;
2. action in reliance thereupon by plaintiff;
3. damages resulting to plaintiff from such misrepresentations.

The first case in this category involving Lincoln was *Weatherford v. Fishback*,[1] December term 1841. Henry Fishback, represented by D. A. Smith, instituted this action against Jefferson Weatherford, who was represented by Logan and J. J. Hardin, for alleged fraudulent actions. Fishback desired to buy a tract of land owned by Harbard Weatherford, but he did not know the lines or boundaries of the land. Jefferson Weatherford (Harbard's brother) said he knew these, and would show them to Fishback. The two then inspected the land, and Jefferson showed him the lines and boundaries. Fishback bought the land from Harbard Weatherford for $400, with Jefferson Weatherford receiving nothing from the transaction. Fishback brought this action in the Macoupin County Circuit Court before Judge William Thomas, claiming that Jefferson Weatherford knowingly deceived him. The land he purchased was worth $10 an acre, whereas the land Jefferson showed him—the land he thought he was buying—was worth much more. Jefferson, in his own defense, said that Fishback was suing the wrong person. Harbard received the purchase price, and Jefferson received no benefit. Judgment was rendered for Fishback for $183.40.

The Supreme Court, in an opinion written by Justice Breese, affirmed the judgment. Jefferson, in his defense, said that even if all the facts in the complaint were true, Fishback was not entitled to a judgment as a matter of law. There were some old common law cases cited, stating the servant is not personally liable for any fraud he commits for the benefit of his master. In this instance, Jefferson was really acting as an unpaid servant of Harbard. However, this was no longer the law. Only two elements are necessary in an action of deceit—fraud and knowledge by the wrongdoer that what is being done is fraudulent. Both were present here against Jefferson. The fact that he had no personal interest in the fruits of the fraud was immaterial.

Another case involving suspected fraud in the sale of land is *McAtee v. Enyart*,[2] December term 1851, in which Lincoln, W. J. Ferguson, and Herndon represented William D. Enyart, with Logan and Stuart & Edwards representing Smith McAtee. In this case Enyart conveyed certain property to McAtee for a consideration of $350, while the land was actually worth $1000. Enyart had a serious drinking problem, and had been indicted for larceny for stealing a pair of shoes. McAtee befriended him, and Enyart contended that McAtee took fraudulent advantage of him. Judge David Davis, in the Sangamon County Circuit Court, heard the case and decreed the conveyance annulled, and required the land to be reconveyed to Enyart.

The Supreme Court, in an opinion written by Justice Treat, affirmed the decree. Treat said, "Inadequacy of consideration in the conveyance of land as between the vendor and the vendee would not justify the interposition of a court of equity to set aside a sale, unless the inequality was so gross and palpable as to shock the conscience and convince the judgment; but where fraudulent practices are used under such peculiar circumstances as to make the vendor a prey of the vendee, the aid of the court may be obtained." Such was the case here.

The case of *Casey v. Casey*,[3] December term 1852, is an action brought by the complainant against the defendant to set aside the sale of an inheritance on the grounds of fraud.

Sarah Piggot died in New York City, leaving an estate subsequently valued at $13,000. The first knowledge that Robert W. Casey, the complainant, had of this, or that he was an heir entitled to one-eighth of the estate, was brought to him by the defendant, Zadok Casey, who learned of the existence of the estate from a friend in New York. The defendant went to New York, and although he wasn't an heir himself, represented himself as acting for the heirs. He then visited Robert W. Casey in Tennessee, and depreciated the value of the estate, reciting potential problems and valuing the estate as worth about $3000. The complainant sold his one-eighth interest to the defendant for $75. The defendant then bought the other shares as well. No facts are given as to how much he paid for them or what was said to induce the sales. He was paid $13,000 from the estate. The complainant believed he had been ill-served, and the Jefferson County Circuit Court, Judge Marshall presiding, agreed, awarding a decree to the complainant for one-eighth of the total estate. W. B. Scates, Logan and Lincoln represented Zadok Casey, and R. S. Nelson represented Robert W. Casey.

The Illinois Supreme Court, with Justice Caton writing the opinion, affirmed the decree. Caton said:

> A party who voluntarily interferes with and manages an estate in behalf of heirs, as their representative, and as such acquires information to which a stranger would not have access, assumes the obligation to his principals which properly appertain to the character of the agent, and entreating with them for the estate, he is bound to disclose how he has acted, and every matter which it was important for them to know, unless such disclosures were distinctly dispensed with. . . . Where confidence is reasonably reposed, that confidence must not be abused. The party relied upon must see that he meets fully and fairly the responsibility of his position, and does not take any advantage, either to the injury of another or for his own gain.

Two of the cases involved alleged fraudulent purchases of land. Lincoln, Logan, and E. D. Baker represented William Fithian, who was believed by the plaintiffs in two related cases to have shamefully taken advantage of them. Lincoln usually represented the plaintiffs in tort cases, but here he successfully represented the defendant in both cases, and based on the evidence reported in the opinions, he did a superb job.

The first of the two is *McDonald v. Fithian et al.*,[4] December term 1844. Fithian had purchased a lot in Milwaukee, Wisconsin, from Solomon Juneau, who had also sold a lot to John H. Murphy. However, Juneau had been unable in either sale to deliver titles to the purchased lots to the buyer. Later, Fithian and three others (one being the agent for Alexander McDonald and another being Hezekiah Cunningham, who was the complainant in the next case involving Fithian) journeyed to Milwaukee to buy land. Fithian volunteered to talk to Juneau alone, since he knew him, and the others agreed. Juneau agreed to sell land to them, but only if the monetary transactions were handled through Fithian. This was agreed to, and the land was transferred. However, as time passed, McDonald felt he had paid too much, and became convinced that Fithian had defrauded him. He brought this action in equity to rescind the transaction and to get his money back. Judge William Wilson in the Vermilion County Circuit Court dismissed the complainant's bill. J. J. Brown and J. McRoberts represented McDonald in the appeal.

Justice Scates wrote the opinion of the court after listing eighteen pages of summations of testimony and depositions from the trial. He affirmed the decree of the circuit court and cited the rule of agency that an agent must disclose all relevant facts. However, since the arrangement among Fithian and the others was verbal, there could be no formal agency since this involves real estate, and any valid agency contract involving real estate must be in writing. However, "fraud is odious, and will not be tolerated under the guise of friendship or gratuitous service." If fraud is proven, the appropriate punishment should follow, whether as agent or friend, and with or without compensation for the trouble."

The testimony was bountiful and confusing. We assume Lincoln also represented Fithian in the lower court, and that his mastery of inquiry and confrontation of witnesses earned the victory. There were other indications of possible fraud by Fithian. For example, there was evidence of two sets of notes covering the same part of the purchase price. McDonald and the others were obligated to pay (to Fithian) the note of higher value; it is possible that Fithian paid a lesser amount to Juneau. Murphy, who had earlier dealings with Juneau, believed he had been ill-used, and that Fithian had withheld information from him. The court states some evidence on this as follows: "In 1838, Fithian was a candidate, and was charged with fraud in the matter by John H. Murphy, and in a handbill, when Fithian said he would not explain the two sets of notes if his election depended upon it."

Justice Scates reasoned from the question of the two notes that this was a private matter, with Juneau asking Fithian to conceal information from Murphy, and had no bearing on this case. Scates wrote, "It seems to me to be unfortunate for him (Fithian), that he assumed an obligation of secrecy, that prevented him from answering the legitimate inquiries of those concerned; and it should be an admonition, from its consequences, of that truth, that open confession is good for soul."

The case presents more evidence by way of summary of testimony and depositions than any case noted here to date. Most of it seems negative to Fithian, which prompts the observation Lincoln must have dominated the trial. Justices Treat, Shields, and Thomas dissented from the opinion, which is further indication there was a lot of evidence unfavorable to Fithian.

The next case, *Cunningham v. Fithian et al.*,[5] December term 1845, involves the same transaction which was the subject of *McDonald v. Fithian et al.* Hezekiah Cunningham sought injunctive relief from the land purchase deal involved in the earlier case. Again in the Vermilion County Circuit Court before Judge Wilson, Lincoln, S. T. Logan, and E. D. Baker represented Fithian *et al.* here as well, and J. J. Brown and J. B. Thomas represented Cunningham. The Supreme Court again upheld the lower court decision denying the requested relief.

Justice Lockwood, writing for the court, said "the questions have been very ably reargued at this term, and this court has been called on to review the former decision and pronounce in this case a different judgment. We have accordingly given important questions involved in the controversy between these parties a careful re-examination, but have been unable to discover any good reasons why the decision in the former case should be adhered to." This statement is awkward and misleading. The court held the same way in this case as it did in the *McDonald v. Fithian* case. To use a double negative, if that's what Lockwood intended, it might have been more clear had he said, "[We] have been unable to discover any good reasons why the decision in the former case should not be adhered to." Probably it was the reporter's error and not the justice's.

The court added an additional reason why the complainant in this case, Cunningham, should not be granted relief. He waited five years after suspecting he had been wronged, and he did not pay taxes for three of these years. Also the value of the land had declined, obviously influencing his decision to try to get out of the deal. "It is a well settled rule of equity that where a party seeks to rescind a contract for fraud, he must ask the aid of the court in a reasonable time, and be in a situation to restore to the opposite party whatever he may have received from him." Cunningham had waited too long, and could not restore the property as he received it because of the tax liens.

Treat dissented again; this time he was joined by Koerner, and deserted by Justices Shields and Thomas, who dissented in the McDonald case. Obviously a close case at each trial, and the effect of oral arguments (by Lincoln and possibly others on his side) again carried the day.

The next four cases are based on a common device—a "horological cradle" which had unique characteristics. Lincoln, sometimes with Stuart, Edwards, and Herndon, represented the losing side in all four. He represented the parties bringing the actions seeking relief because of alleged fraud.

The first case is *Edmunds v. Myers et al.*,[6] December term 1854, in which Lincoln represented John and George Myers. We have a description of this "horological cradle" in the pleadings Lincoln prepared for this suit against Alexander Edmunds, extracts of which follow: "The said Edmunds professed to have invented an horological cradle which was to be rocked by machinery, with a weight, running on one or more pulleys; the cradle constituting the pendulum, and which, being wound up, would rock itself until it run down, and so save the continual labor to mothers and nurses, of rocking the cradle." The pleadings further indicate Edmunds said he had a patent for such device, which "patents right would be universally valuable, and could be sold for a large sum of money." Then, "that they [the Complainants] have now discovered that Edmunds has really no letters patent for said horological cradle, or for its machinery, mode of operation, or its principal of action; but your orators have discovered, by procuring a copy of the letters patent to said Edmunds a design for a cradle, and the specifications of his claim for said letters patent only claims, as the production of said Edmunds, the design and configuration of the ornaments described and set forth, forming together an ornamental design for an horological cradle." Edmunds denied fraud had been intended or committed.

Myers *et al.* filled a bill in equity in the Logan County Circuit Court before Judge Davis, against Edmunds for a recision of a contract he made with Edmunds, whereby Edmunds assigned certain interests in a "horological cradle" for $2000, paid for by transferring title to a certain tract of land, plus $500. Myers *et al.* contended there was misrepresentation, as they thought he had a patent for the machinery that sustained motion of the cradle, when his patent merely covered the design. Judge David Davis decreed the contract should be rescinded, and the land reconveyed and the money returned. Williams and Lawrence represented Edmunds.

However, the Supreme Court, in an opinion written by Justice Scates, reversed the decree and dismissed the bill. Firstly, Myers and others had made some sales of the cradle, and did not offer to account for those. A basic principle in chancery is that he who seeks equity must do equity. Here the contract was executed by the performance of Myers and others, and to restore the status quo, a party seeking equity must account for the fruits of his execution. Secondly, fraud was not proved. Scates said, "But the defendants [Myers *et al.*] wholly failed in their evidence. No witness testifies to any representation whatever being made to them."

The second action—*Edmunds v. Hildreth et al.*,[7] December term 1854—covers substantially the same facts as the previous case against Edmunds except the latter case specifies sale of rights for several states for ten thousand dollars, and the prior case cites a sale of "certain interests" in the cradle for two thousand dollars; and the newer case claims that Edmunds sold these rights to McCarty Hildreth and William Turner. The latter case is an action brought by Hildreth and presumably the Myerses. Although the Myerses were not mentioned in the opinion as parties to the case, they are the only ones mentioned other than Hildreth who still had any interests, and who were represented by Lincoln. It is a request for recision of the sale of patent rights by Edmunds to Hildreth and Turner of the said patent for several states for ten thousand dollars, and that Turner had sold his interest to the Myerses for five thousand dollars. The Myerses were not parties to the agreement between Edmunds and Hildreth and Turner. Judge Davis in the Logan County Circuit Court rescinded the contract and ordered Edmunds to return the consideration. Williams and Lawrence again represented Edmunds.

The Supreme Court, in an opinion written by Justice Scates, reversed the lower court. Justice Scates said, "We are unable to find any ground to sustain this decree." Then, "I have already, in the other case, given my views of the supposed equities, upon the supposition that the fraud was established, and they apply equally to this case.... Suppose there was fraud, the party defrauded and those injured by the fraud, could alone take advantage of it to annul the contract." The Myerses had no contract with Edmunds, and therefore could not be parties in an action against him for fraud.

In *Myers et al. v. Turner,*[8] December term 1855, Lincoln was assisted by Stuart, Edwards, and Herndon, and continued to represent the Myerses. This case in the Logan County Circuit Court before Judge Davis, involved an action on the two promissory notes brought by Turner against John and George Myers. The Myerses had given the notes to Turner when they acquired certain rights in the "horological cradle" from him (which he had acquired from Edmunds). Since the notes were due and unpaid, Turner brought these actions against the assignees. They pleaded failure of consideration. A judgment was entered for Turner. J. P. Lacey represented Turner on the appeal.

The Supreme Court, in an opinion written by Justice Caton, affirmed the judgment. The language in the assignment of the rights was very clear. There was sufficient consideration, even if the invention may have had little value. *Caveat Emptor.* The Myerses also pleaded fraud. Caton said, "There is not near as much suspicion of fraud in this case as there was in *Edmunds v. Myers, 16 Ill. 207,* and yet in that case we reversed the decree and dismissed the bill because the charge of fraud was not sustained. That suit grew out of this same transaction."

The last case in the "horological cradle" saga is *Hildreth v. Turner,*[9] December term 1855—again in Logan County Circuit Court before Judge Davis. Turner had sold his interest at some point to Hildreth, who had given Turner promissory notes in exchange. Hildreth refused to pay, contending lack of consideration because of the underlying fraud. He also suspected a technical problem in the assignment of the patent. Hildreth was represented by Lincoln and his three associates in the previous case. Judgment was rendered for Turner. L. P. Lacey again represented Turner. The Supreme Court, in an opinion written by Justice Caton, affirmed the judgment. Caton said, "The first question in this case is precisely like that decided in *Myers v. Turner, ante,* and is determined in the same way for the reasons there assigned. This record presents the additional question: whether the assignment or transfer of a patent right is operative, until it is recorded as required by the patent laws of the United States.... This act has been repeatedly held by the federal courts to be merely directory as between the parties.... It is sufficient that the question has been settled by the federal courts, whose particular province it is to construe the acts of Congress. We follow these decisions, not only because they are authority, but also because we are satisfied they are sustained by sound legal reasoning."

By this time, the Myerses and Hildreth probably were tired of the whole "horological cradle" fiasco. Lincoln persuaded many people, including his clients and some trial judges, that fraud had been committed. Nevertheless, Justice Caton—who had the most important vote on the presence of fraud—remained unconvinced.

Another group of cases involving alleged fraud in the sale of a patented device like the "horological cradle" sold by Edmunds involves another entrepreneur, Reuben Miller. Miller patented a device which he called a "cast iron cemetery tomb." Lincoln & Herndon represented Miller in the first two cases, both of which were remanded for new trials in 1860, and later appealed and decided in 1864, when Herndon alone represented Miller.

The first two cases, *Miller v. Whittaker* and *Young v. Miller*,[10] January term 1860, involved the same basic facts and were combined on appeal; they were tried in the Logan County Circuit Court. The first case was brought by Nathaniel M. Whittaker against Reuben Miller to rescind a contract. Lincoln & Herndon, and Logan & Hay represented Miller, on the appeal at least, and Stuart & Edwards, and W. W. Young represented Whittaker and William H. Young. Miller, as agent for Henry R. Flinchbaugh, sold the exclusive patent rights to a cast iron cemetery monument for most of the counties in Illinois. Whittaker transferred title in certain land and gave notes to Miller. Whittaker contended fraud was present, and that "at the time of the purchase, [he] was so intoxicated and stupefied by the use of liquor as to not know what he was doing; that Miller not only knew this, but in a great measure caused and prolonged it to enable him to get an advantage." A decree was entered rescinding the contract, thus causing Miller to surrender the notes and reconvey the land.

The second case was also a motion in chancery, by William H. Young against Miller, to set aside the exclusive rights to the same patent for the state of Michigan again alleging fraud. Young transferred title to 160 acres of land as consideration. Miller admitted the sale and the representations, but claimed they were but the expression of opinions, and denied the charge. The court here held for Miller, and dismissed the bill. There is no evidence of intoxication in this case, which is possibly the reason the outcome was different from that in the Whittaker case.

The Supreme Court, in an opinion written by Justice Caton, wrote a short opinion, reversing both decrees. Flinchbaugh was a necessary party. The consideration received in the Whittaker case was received in trust for Flinchbaugh, as his rights could not be protected without his presence. Also, Whittaker did not offer to reconvey the title to the patents to Miller in the pleading, which was necessary. The Young case was also reversed, because

Flinchbaugh was not a party. Both cases were reversed, and the suits remanded with leave to the complainants (Whittaker and Young) to amend their bills and make Flinchbaugh a party.

The next record of these cases resurfacing in the Supreme Court was during the January term, 1864, when each case was retried in Logan County Circuit Court in accordance with the orders from the Supreme Court. Decrees were rendered at those trials, and each appealed separately. *Miller v. Young,*[11] was the first to be reported. In the earlier case, Young's bill was amended to include Flinchbaugh, and to offer to reconvey the patent rights. The court entered a decree against Flinchbaugh (who didn't enter an answer) and Miller for a recision and reconveyance of the land and notes. Miller made this appeal on the ground the decree was not supported by the evidence. Herndon represented Miller on this appeal and Morrison represented Young. The Supreme Court, in an opinion written by Justice Corydon Beckwith, reversed the decree. There was no fraud. The patent was proper. Then: "It is essential to the validity of a patent for a design, that it should be a new and an original one, but the law does not require that it should be useful." The record was not complete enough to judge whether the patent was novel. Any statements made by Miller about the durability and probable sales of the patented articles were mere matters of opinion.

In *Miller v. Whittaker,*[12] the decree was amended in the circuit court to add Flinchbaugh and to offer to reconvey the patent, as ordered by the Supreme Court. Herndon represented Miller on this appeal, and J. C. Conkling represented Whittaker. In this case, the decree against Miller (and Flinchbaugh) was affirmed, in contradiction of *Miller v. Young* which was appealed in the same term. In this appeal, the record was inadequate, and the court held that, since there was no error shown by the record, the decree of the court below was affirmed. When the cause below was amended (in accordance with the orders of the Supreme Court) in the previous case, by the consent of the defendant (Miller), he did not file an answer. He was not required to, but he was at liberty to do so if he chose. The record in the present case "contains a transcript of the bill, certain depositions, and the decree, but none of Miller's answer. We do not know what allegations of the bill were admitted, or what were denied, and with no knowledge of the contents of the answer, we are unable to say that the allegations of the bill were not admitted. The pleading in every case must be brought before us." This case seems to have been lost by inadequate pleading, when it should have been won. The same court had held that Miller's acts were not fraudulent. Herndon represented Miller in each, but the attorneys for the appellees were different. Perhaps one knew more law than the other, and recognized a fatal error in Herndon's presentation of the appeal in the Whittaker case, which could have also been present in the Young case. The Supreme Court obviously knew of the prior Young case, but was not allowed to consider anything other than what was presented in the record. For appeals handled by Herndon without Lincoln's presence, see chapter fourteen.

Cases of Assault

The term assult shall be used to include the various wrongful acts committed by the defendants in the suits. Assault is defined as any willful attempt to inflict injury upon the person of another. When accompanied by touching the other person, it is also a battery. The cases here that meet that category are actions for seduction, criminal conversation; and one is identified as trespass, assault, and battery. The first two cases of seduction are related in subject matter, and are of particular interest because Lincoln represented opposite sides in each of the identical cases.

Grable v. Margrave,[13] July term 1842, was a case wherein Thomas Margrave, represented by Lincoln, sued William G. Grable for damages in the Gallatin County Circuit Court, before Judge Scates, for the seduction of his daughter. Margrave's young daughter worked in the household of Grable, and during that time Grable allegedly seduced her. Based on the common law, a father is entitled to the services of his young daughter, and Grable's dastardly act impeded her capability to fulfill that duty. Also at the trial, Judge Scates permitted evidence of the pecuniary ability of each party. This was objected to, and after a judgment was rendered for Margrave for $300, Grable appealed the case saying an error had been committed in allowing such evidence to be heard by the jury. J. Shields and J. C. Conkling represented Grable on the appeal. Justice Treat wrote the opinion of the court, which affirmed the judgment. He commenced by reciting the common law basis of the action originally given to the master to recover damages for loss of services occasioned by the seduction of his servant. Loss of services is still the basis of the action, and the father was to prove that because of the seduction, his daughter was less able to perform the duties of a servant. However, Lincoln cited English common law cases that stated this rule of damages had been extended to cover more than the mere loss of services. In vindictive actions like this, juries should be permitted to give damages for the double purpose of setting an example and of punishing the wrongdoer.

Thus, to make certain a guilty party is punished, his pecuniary ability is a proper subject of evidence. "A verdict which, as against one individual, would be sufficient for all purposes, would, as against another, be scarcely felt, by reason of the difference in ability to respond in damages." Evidence of the defendant's wealth was admissible. As far as evidence of pecuniary ability of the plaintiff, Justice Treat said "This evidence does not go to the jury, as was stated in argument, for the purpose of exciting their prejudices in favor of the plaintiff, because he is a poor man, but to enable them to understand fully the effect of the injury upon him, and to give him such damages as his peculiar condition in life and circumstances entitle him to receive." This last point is not very clear, but it is clear Lincoln relied on the disparate pecuniary positions of each party to influence the jury for Margrave's victory.

The companion case is *Anderson v. Ryan*,[14] December term 1846, in which Lincoln represented the seducer in a similar situation. This case was an appeal from a judgment against Elias Anderson in an action of trespass for assault, debauchery, and carnal knowledge of the daughter of Michael Ryan, rendered in the Coles County Circuit Court before Judge Wilson. Lincoln, representing Anderson, contended there had been no loss of services proved by Ryan, as father of the girl. This had been a necessary element under common law in an action of this sort and had been necessary in *Grable v. Margrave*. It was proved that the daughter had lived with her family, and was four months advanced in pregnancy by Anderson when the action was brought. U. F. Linder and A. T. Bledsoe represented Ryan on the appeal.

The Supreme Court, with Justice Lockwood writing the opinion, affirmed the circuit court, saying that loss of services to the father was no longer a necessary element. Justice Lockwood cited *Heart v. Prince*[15] (which strongly supported Ryan's side, but was not included in the large list of authorities cited by his attorneys in the appeal) as follows: "As this question has never been discussed in this court, previous to the case at the bar, we feel authorized in extracting from that opinion, because it furnishes reasons fully justifying the doctrine, in action of seduction brought by the parent, that loss of service need no longer be proved to sustain the action." One reason given for this was: "If it were otherwise, says Littledate, justice, in *Maunder v. Venn*, no action could be sustained for this injury in the higher ranks of life, where no actual services by the daughter are usual." Also: "the views presented by Chief Justice Nelson *(Heart v. Prince)* place the ground of this action upon the elevated consideration of protecting the moral purity of female character. Such an object must meet a cordial response in every noncorrupted heart. This opinion also satisfactorily vindicates the modern doctrine, as more in accordance with the original design of the action for seduction. It has long been considered as a standing reproach to the common law, that it furnished no means to punish the seducer of female innocence and virtue, except through the fiction of supposing the daughter was a servant of her parent, and that in consequence of her seduction, the parent has lost some of her services as a menial. It is high time this reproach be wiped out." Later: "This action ought, then, no longer to be considered as a means of recovering damages for the loss of menial services, but as an instrument to punish the perpetrator of flagitious outrage upon the peace and happiness of the family circle."

Justice Koerner wrote an opinion that concurred, but stated that loss of service was still an essential element: "I consider that the loss of service in a case of seduction is still the just and only legal foundations of the actions, and that it is the rule of evidence merely which has undergone a change in the course of time, by the decisions of the courts according to a more just and refined feeling of society on this subject, at once so delicate and so painful." The law, from the seduction itself, will presume the loss of services resulted.

Lincoln was on the losing side in this, and had to insist on the only argument which could have won the case for his client, despite it being an outmoded doctrine just ripe for being overthrown in the Illinois Supreme Court. Koerner, showing his reverence for the common law, said loss of services is still an essential element, but is presumed to exist and cannot be disproved by the defendant—a rather strained compromise of tradition and the practicality of agreeing that carnal knowledge, resulting in pregnancy, should be punished.

Lincoln won the first case, proving loss of services of the daughter to the father, and was protected by the common law. He lost the second case when he represented the seducer, even though the other side did not prove the seduction caused the loss of the daughter's services for the father. Lincoln should have expected to win here because of the absence of proof of what had been an essential condition in the previous case.

There are two other sets of cases noted in this book in which Lincoln took opposite sides in similar circumstances—he won the first case and established new precedent and lost the second because of that precedent. One example, found in chapter seven,[16] involves subscribers of railroad stock breaching their obligations to pay for stock after changed conditions in railroad construction thwarted their plans for ancillary profits which had been based on the original plans of the railroad. Another example, in chapter five,[17] deals with legislative changes in the location of the seat of government in a county. In this case, the claimants had donated land when the original county seat was established for use for the county court house. They wanted the donated land returned when the new county seat was established in another community. These I have labeled the "hoisted by his own petard" cases.

The case of *McNamara v. King*,[18] December term 1845, is also a companion case to *Grable v. Margrave*. Here Lincoln represented Charles McNamara, a rich man, and the evidentiary ruling he won in the Grable case worked against him in this one. This was an appeal from an action of trespass, assault and battery brought by George King against McNamara in the Kane County Circuit Court before Judge Caton and a jury. A judgment was rendered for King in the amount of $650. During the trial, the court allowed King to prove he was a poor man with a large family, and that McNamara was a wealthy man, with no children and but a small family. Lincoln and J. B. Thomas, representing McNamara on the appeal, contended that the amount of the judgment was excessive, and the evidence about the relative economic status of the parties had been improperly admitted. I. G. Wilson represented King on the appeal.

Justice Treat, writing for the Supreme Court, affirmed the judgment. He stated, "The evidence is voluminous and will not be here particularly stated. It has been carefully examined and considered. In the opinion of the court, it shows an aggravated case of assault and battery, without any attending circumstances to justify or excuse it." He did not believe the damages high enough to draw a conclusion that they were excessive. "It must be apparent at first blush that the damages are glaringly excessive," and that is not the case here. He also stated it is proper that the jury should be influenced by the pecuniary resources of the defendant. The more affluent, the more able he is to remunerate the party he has wantonly injured. It is appropriate to punish the defendant.

This was obviously a tough case for Lincoln, with adverse factors of a wealthy assaulter of a poor man, and an aggravated case of assault and battery. Lincoln represented a poor man suing a rich man for rape of his daughter in *Grable v. Margrave,* and was successful in obtaining a higher verdict because of the "poor man injured by rich man" relationship. So he probably wasn't too surprised when the judgment here was affirmed, but he had to make the appeal to fully serve his client.

In *Roney v. Monaghan,*[19] December term 1846, Lincoln was successful in representing Owen Monaghan, who sued John Roney in the Lake County Circuit Court before Judge Hugh T. Dickey, of the Cook County Circuit Court, and a jury, in a case of criminal conversation. Evidence was presented that a criminal intercourse existed between Roney and the wife of Monaghan. The verdict was rendered for Monaghan, and he was awarded $225 for damages. Lincoln, G. Spring, and G. Goodrich represented Monaghan in the appeal brought by Roney, who contended a new trial should be awarded as the verdict was against the weight of the evidence. Roney was represented by J. Pearson.

Justice Norman H. Purple, writing for the court, stated simply that the evidence was of a character to warrant the inference which the jury had drawn. "In such cases, a court will never disturb the verdict of a jury. The judgment of the circuit court is affirmed with costs."

Cases of Malpractice

Malpractice is defined as professional misconduct or unreasonable lack of skill. Lincoln and Elliott B. Herndon (the younger brother of William H. "Billy" Herndon) unsuccessfully represented Dr. Powers Ritchey in the case of *Ritchey v. West,*[20] January term 1860. Keziah West sued Dr. Ritchey for injuries resulting from alleged malpractice of Ritchey as a physician. The facts are not presented in great detail, but West ended up with a deformity and the inability to use one of his hands, after receiving the medical services of Dr. Ritchey. Testimony was given that the splints the doctor applied were not adequate, and that Ritchey never saw his patient after the initial treatment. Judgment, in the Adams County Circuit Court before Judge Joseph S. Sibley, was entered for West. William S. Grimshow and Williams represented West.

The judgment was affirmed in an opinion written for the Supreme Court by Justice Walker. The opinion stated several errors apparently committed in the trial court by Dr. Ritchey's attorneys. Firstly, the evidence could not be reviewed since, "no question can arise on the correctness of the decisions of the court below in admitting or rejecting evidence, in this case, as no exceptions were preserved in the record. We shall therefore decline their examination." Secondly, the application for a new trial because of newly discovered evidence was faulty, because in such an application, "it is not sufficient for the party to state that he has been informed and believed that the witness will testify to the facts, but the truth of such facts must be verified by affidavit."

The principle of law in this case is that when a person assumes the profession of physician and surgeon, he must, in its exercise, be held to employ a reasonable amount of care and skill. And whether the injury results from a want of skill, or the want of its application, he will, in either case, be equally liable. Ritchey failed one or both of these tests here; failing either one was sufficient to support the judgment against him.

Cases of Slander

Slander is defined as the speaking of base and defamatory words tending to prejudice another in his reputation, office, trade, business, or means of livelihood. The essential elements are: a false and defamatory statement concerning another, an unprivileged communication; fault amounting at least to negligence on the part of the person making the statement; and either actionability of the statement, irrespective of harm, or the existence of special harm.

There were three cases involving slander tried by Lincoln and in all of them he represented the plaintiff. In *Rogers v. Hall*,[21] July term 1841, he and Logan represented George B. Rogers who believed he had been slandered. The case was tried in Schuyler County Circuit Court before Judge Peter Lott. Robert C. Hall pleaded he had told the truth in what he said about Rogers. The court believed him, and thus Hall had a valid defense since slanderous statements must be false. Possibly the case was lost because of inadequate pleadings on the part of Logan & Lincoln, but there is not enough information in the written opinion to have any conclusions on this. In this case Rogers brought an action of slander against Hall, alleging Hall had said that Rogers had attempted to assassinate and murder him. Hall pleaded the words were true, and proved that some unknown person had shot at him. To prove that Rogers had done this, Hall offered in evidence several anonymous letters and advertisements of a threatening and hostile import. Rogers objected, stating there was no evidence these had been written by him. The court overruled this objection, and found a verdict for Hall. O. H. Browning, E. D. Baker, and B. S. Edwards represented Hall on the appeal.

The Supreme Court, in an opinion written by Justice Thomas Ford, affirmed the judgment. The bill of exceptions was inadequate to justify Rogers's position that there was no evidence the threatening writings were written by him, because the bill of exceptions simply stated there was no evidence the papers were written by Rogers. Without any additional information, it could be inferred there might have been other evidence connecting Rogers with the writings submitted at the trial. The bill of exceptions is a pleading, and the one who makes it is liable for ambiguity, uncertainty or omission. Like any other pleading, it ought to be construed against the party who prepared it. Thus, there is nothing stated in the bill of exceptions to make it appear that the evidence was improperly admitted.

In *Regnier v. Cabot et al.*,[22] December term 1845, Logan and Lincoln represented Eliza Cabot and/or Elijah Taylor who won an award against T. Regnier for uttering slanderous language. Cabot and Taylor brought an action of slander against Regnier, who stated Cabot had engaged in fornication with Taylor. They both denied it. The action was originally brought in Menard County Circuit Court before Judge Lockwood, and a judgment of $12 was awarded. Cabot moved to set aside the verdict, and it was not only set aside, but the case was removed to the Mogan County Circuit Court. Here the outcome was the same, but the award was $1600. Samuel D. Lockwood was the judge. Regnier appealed based on erroneous exclusion of certain evidence he introduced concerning Cabot and Taylor being seen in her bedroom late at night, when Cabot was wearing her night clothes, and also on evidence of her bad character. S. W. Robbins represented Regnier on the appeal, and T. L. Harris and S. T. Logan represented Cabot.

The Supreme Court, in an opinion written by Justice Purple, and in which Justice Lockwood did not hear the evidence and thus did not vote, affirmed the judgment. Purple said there had been some conflict about how much evidence a defendant in a slander case can offer to cast guilt on the plaintiff. He stated the rule is now clear—he can only offer proof of the bad character of the plaintiff to mitigate damages or to show absence of malice. Neither was applicable here, so Regnier's evidence was properly excluded. The witness who offered to prove Eliza's bad character only knew of three people who believed her character to be bad. There was not enough evidence to prove a general bad reputation. Purple said: "In my judgment, character is too valuable to permit it, in a court of justice to be destroyed, or even sullied by a report derived from a majority of three persons only. It is general, and not partial reputation in the neighborhood where the party resides which, in legal contemplation, establishes character for good or evil."

The record doesn't indicate how Cabot had the first verdict for $12 overturned when it was in her favor. Giving up an award of $12 for one of $1600 was a wise gamble on her part, and the size of the award should have made anyone careful of impugning her character in public.

Lincoln and M. McConnel represented Edwards *et al.* in *Patterson et ux. v. Edwards et al.*,[23] December term 1845. The Pattersons were represented by W. A. Minshall. This was an action for slander, brought by Ambrose P. Edwards and wife, a white woman, against William Patterson and wife in the Mason County Circuit Court, before Judge Treat and a jury. The declaration stated that Mrs. Patterson said, "Mrs. Edwards has raised a family of children by a negro, and I can prove it." Judgment was rendered for the Edwardses for $220. The Pattersons' appeal was that the proof did not sustain the allegations in the declaration. The statute supporting the action of slander specified that words falsely published, which in their common application shall amount to charge any person with having been guilty of fornication or adultery, shall be actionable. The words spoken by Patterson did not necessarily imply fornication or adultery.

The Supreme Court, with Justice Koerner writing the opinion, reversed the lower court and remanded the cause with leave to the plaintiffs (Edwards *et al.*) to amend pleadings. The Supreme Court said that the pleadings on the Edwardses' behalf were inadequate to support the judgment against the Pattersons. Koerner wrote "As the pleader has it in his power to state his own case, he must negate all inferences which may reasonably be drawn, and which, according to the rule of pleadings will always be intended strongly against him." Also: "The proof did not sustain the allegations in the declaration. Though all the words used need not be proved as laid, yet so much thereof as is sufficient to sustain the cause of action must be proved, and it will not do to prove equivalent words of slander. The rule as here stated is a relaxation of the strictness once required by the courts in Great Britain, which held the slightest omission or addition to be fatal. To go further would be destroying the fundamental principles of correct pleading."

NOTES

The legal definitions in this section are all from *Black's Law Dictionary*, Fifth Edition.

1. 4 *Ill.*, 170; *LCL*, 22.
2. 13 *Ill.*, 242; *LCL*, 154.
3. 14 *Ill.*, 112; *LCL*, 162.
4. 6 *Ill.*, 269; *LCL*, 68.
5. 7 *Ill.*, 650; *LCL*, 102.
6. 16 *Ill.*, 207; *LC*, 180.
7. 16 *Ill.*, 214; *LCL*, 181.
8. 17 *Ill.*, 179; *LCL*, 187.
9. 17 *Ill.*, 184; *LCL*, 188.

10. 23 *Ill.*, 400; *LCL*, 222.
11. 33 *Ill.*, 355; *LCL*, 241.
12. 33 *Ill.*, 386; *LCL*, 241.
13. 4 *Ill.*, 372; *LCL*, 32.
14. 8 *Ill.*, 584; *LCL*, 121.
15. 21 Wend. 81.
16. *Barrett v. The Alton and Sangamon Railroad Company*, 13 *Ill.*, 504; *LCL*, 158.
    Sprague v. The Illinois River Railroad Company et al., 19 *Ill.*, 173; *LCL*, 202.
    Terre Haute and Alton RR Co. v. Earp, 21 *Ill.*, 291; *LCL*, 291.
17. *Adams et al. v. County of Logan*, 11 *Ill.*, 352; *LCL*, 132.
    Harris v. Shaw et al., 13 *Ill.*, 457; *LCL*, 157.
18. 7 *Ill.*, 432; *LCL*, 97.
19. 8 Ill., 85; *LCL*, 110.
20. 23 *Ill.*, 329; *LCL*, 220.
21. 4 *Ill.*, 5; *LCL*, 12.
22. 7 *Ill.*, 34; *LCL*, 80.
23. 7 *Ill.*, 720; *LCL*, 105.

Chapter Eleven

Wagering

LINCOLN WAS INVOLVED in three civil cases where wagering was offered as a defense. Wagering was defined as a crime in the criminal code. Under the common law, wagering was generally regarded as being against the public interest. Therefore, obligations entered into through wagering were not enforceable.

The first such case is *Abrams & Klein v. Camp*,[1] April term 1841, which involves not only wagering, but an important issue of the relative jurisdictions of courts of law and courts of equity. Courts of law were the first forums established under the English common law to adjudicate controversies between two parties, where judgments were rendered in terms of monetary damages. As the court system evolved, many types of controversies were created where the best results could not be obtained through monetary damages. An example of this might be when a party wanted to recover specific property unlawfully in the possession of another rather than to be paid its value, or when justice can only be served when a person is required to perform a promised act rather than to pay monetary damages. In an attempt to achieve justice in such situations, "courts of equity," which were empowered to compel specific actions, were created. The following case involves a judgment of a court of law, with the losing party bringing an action in a court of equity to prevent the enforcement of that judgment.

A person named Klein, whose first name is not indicated, brought an action against William Camp for $191.43 on a note made by Camp to William G. Abrams, and assigned by him to Klein. Camp contended the note was for a gambling debt, and thus he wasn't liable. Camp called Abrams as a witness to the game, but Abrams refused to testify on the grounds he would incriminate himself. He was excused from testifying, and Camp offered no other evidence. Judgment was rendered for Klein.

Camp then brought this action in a court of equity to set aside the judgment of the court of law because the note had been for a gambling debt from a card game between Camp and Abrams, and the statute to restrain gaming declared all notes given in consideration of money won at play void and of no effect, whether in the hands of a payee or an assignee. Logan & Lincoln represented Abrams and Klein, and the Honorable Samuel H. Treat rendered a decree for Camp, enjoining the award for damages of the court of law. J. Lamborn represented Camp.

The decree in this action, which was appealed to the Supreme Court by Logan & Lincoln, reversed the injunction. Justice Treat, in writing the opinion, stated that the Supreme Court would not give relief against a judgment at law on the ground of its being contrary to equity, unless the defendant in that action was ignorant of the facts constituting his defense while the suit was pending, or that those facts could not have been received as a defense at law. Neither exception was applicable here. Camp had a good defense if it were truly a gambling debt. He set up his defense in the court of law, but failed to prove it due to his own neglect or want of preparation. His only remedy was to appeal the decision. There is a well-established principle that the decision of a court of competent jurisdiction is conclusive upon all courts of concurrent powers.

Logan & Lincoln cited English cases and a reference in *Story's Equity*, which Justice Treat relied on in his opinion. The mystery is why *Justice* Treat states the decree of the Circuit Court (presided over by *Judge* Treat) "was clearly erroneous."

In *Williams v. Smith*,[2] December term 1842, Logan represented Edward O. Smith, who sued Andrew S. Williams regarding a note which Williams declined to pay because he deemed it to be a wagering note. He was proven wrong.

Williams made a promissory note to Smith, as part of a real estate transaction wherein Smith sold a house to Williams. The note was for $500, to be payable when William Henry Harrison was elected president of the United States. Harrison was elected, but Williams declared the agreement void, claiming it was a wagering agreement against public policy and good morals. The court, in an opinion written by Justice Treat, rendered judgment for Smith. Josiah Lamborn represented Williams.

The Supreme Court, in an opinion written by Justice Scates, affirmed the judgment. There were no facts to infer the contract grew out of a bet upon the presidential election.

Perhaps the court experienced revulsion when the maker of a note suddenly decided what he did was "against public policy and good morals." We all respect confession of wrongs, but respect it more when the confession is not made to relieve one of a monetary obligation.

In *Smith v. Smith et al.*,[3] January term 1859, Lincoln & Herndon represented the "wrong" Smith, who lost. Isaac Smith made a wager with George Moffitt, two days after the 1856 presidential election. Moffitt bet his buggy against $110 put up by Isaac Smith that Millard Fillmore had received the most votes in New York State. The stakeholder, J. H. Alexander, determined Isaac had won, returned his $110, and awarded him the buggy. However, in the meantime, sore-loser Moffitt had sold the buggy to John H. Smith, who brought this action in *replevin* to recover the buggy. The Bond County Circuit Court awarded the buggy to John H. Smith, who was represented by Lincoln & Herndon. J. and D. Gillespie represented Issac Smith.

The Supreme Court, in an opinion written by Justice Caton, reversed the lower court and remanded the cause. The opinion stated that the wager was not against public policy. The event had already occurred. Caton said: "Nor did the event which was to determine the wager depend upon any chance, accident, effort or skill. It was a fact irrevocably fixed as the number of grains of wheat in a measure standing on the table, or the date of a coin held in the hand. Such a contract the parties had an undoubted right to make, by the common law, and it is not forbidden by our statute." Caton further stated that a stakeholder (Alexander), unless some other mode has been provided, is the proper person to decide who has won a wager.

Thus, ownership of the buggy was properly transferred to Isaac Smith, and John H. Smith could not recover it. In remanding the cause for a new trial, if John H. wanted one, Justice Caton remarked, "and the proof satisfactorily shows that John H. Smith purchased with full knowledge of the defendant's right to the property." It seems logical to assume Lincoln & Herndon did not advise him to try again.

NOTES

1. 4 *Ill.*, 290; *LCL*, 29.
2. 4 *Ill.*, 524; *LCL*, 41.
3. 21 *Ill.*, 244; *LCL*, 215.

Chapter Twelve

One of a Kind

THE PRECEDING SECTIONS have been groupings of Lincoln cases with at least one additional important common characteristic. This leaves a large number of cases which are not related in subject matter, but are important as meaningful Lincoln cases for various reasons, and I believe they will be interesting to the reader. Lincoln had a very diversified law practice; and his appellate practice covered a wide spectrum of topics, since he not only argued appeals from his own trial cases but was also sought after by other attorneys to argue appeals of cases they had argued in the trial courts. This was especially the case as his reputation as a successful appellate lawyer grew.

1. AUCTIONS. *Webster & Huntington v. French et al.*[1] was a leading case on sealed-bid auctions. Lincoln won the case for his client, and the case was sent back to the trial court for a new trial based upon rulings on the applicable law which were favorable to Lincoln's clients, Bela C. Webster and George Huntington. The follow-up case contained a rude surprise for Lincoln and his clients.

An act of the legislature authorized the sale of Quincy House, located in Quincy, Adams County, and owned by the state. This act established procedures for an auction by sealed bids. The bids ranged from $15,250 by Jacob Bunn to a bid by Webster and Huntington for $21,000. In addition, there was a bid promising to pay $500 more than any other bid, and another by Horace F. Ash and Isaac R. Diller to pay $601 over the highest bid. The governor, Augustus C. French, sold the property to Ash and Diller for $22,101, which was the aggregate of $21,000 plus $500 plus $601. This action was a bill filed in Sangamon County Circuit Court before Judge Davis to enforce the conveyance of the property to Webster and Huntington who had the highest specific bid. It was agreed by both parties to dismiss the bill so it could be appealed. There were four lawyers on each side of the appeal, and five pages of very comprehensive briefs were submitted. Lincoln & Herndon, Logan, and M. Brayman represented Webster and Huntington, and Stuart & Edwards, W. I. Ferguson, Browning, and Bushnell represented the state of Illinois. Of special interest: Stuart & Edwards included a classic United States constitutional case in their brief, *Madison v. Marbury*,[2] holding that the acts of the governor were executive, and thus could not be restrained or directed by the United States Supreme Court. Lincoln's side argued the bid of Ash and Diller was not a specific bid, and was a total subversion of the manifest intention of the legislature.

Justice Caton, writing for the court, agreed with Lincoln, and revised the decree and remanded the case. The court had reasoned that when the terms of a sealed bid auction give one party an unfair advantage over another, it prevents fair competition. Allowing such bidding procedures would preclude all possibility of a specific bidder getting the property, and would discourage any prudent bidder from participating in future sealed bid auctions.

The case was retried in the Sangamon County Circuit Court before Judge Davis. Since the Supreme Court had ruled the two non-specific bids were not allowable, it should have been a simple matter in the new trial for Lincoln to prove his client had the highest specific bid and to have a judgment rendered in his favor. The attorneys were the same as at the previous trial except this time the governor's team included W. I. Ferguson. However an unforeseeable difficulty arose which snatched defeat from the jaws of victory. The retried case was *Webster et al. v. French et al.*, December term 1850,[3] The legislative mandate for the sale of the Quincy House specified the governor shall receive written sealed bids "until the first day of July, A.D. 1849." The bid of Webster and Huntington was received on July 2. Lincoln argued that since the sealed bids had not been opened when the Webster and Huntington bid was received, no one had been harmed. The Supreme Court did not agree with him, and in an opinion written by Justice Caton, ruled that the word "until" was used as a word of limitation and was peremptory. The act had to be done within the time specified. Thus, Webster and Huntington's bid should not have been counted at all, and the original action brought by them to have their bid accepted as the highest bid was dismissed by this second appeal.

In the first case, it was simply stated the bid had been received on June 30, since it was not an issue then. The earlier case seemed a remarkable triumph for Lincoln. It had to be a serious disappointment to win a tough case like that only to find through some inadvertence the "winning bid" was submitted a little late. July 1 was a Sunday, which is interesting, but of no importance here.

2. FENCING. The case of *Seeley v. Peters*,[4] December term 1848, is a leading case involving the application of English common law to Illinois in its early years of statehood. Herndon and O. Peters represented William Peters, who invoked the English common-law rule that an owner of animals has a duty to fence them in, so that they do not stray and cause damage to

others. The court decided that even though this was a proven common law principle, it did not apply to the Illinois frontier where conditions were different from those in England.

In this case, William Peters brought an action of trespass against Samuel Seeley, when Seeley's hogs entered Peters's land and damaged his crops. Evidence was offered that Peters's fence was in poor condition. Peters asked for and received an instruction to the jury that it was not the duty of the landowner to have an adequate fence to keep out straying animals, but the duty of the owner of the animals to keep them from straying. Judgment was rendered for Peters for damages of $4.10. Seeley objected to Judge Caton's ruling, and appealed on the grounds the instruction was improper. T. Ford represented Seeley.

The Supreme Court, in an opinion written by Justice Trumbull, reversed the judgment, and remanded the cause for further proceedings. The English common law required the owners of live stock to keep them fenced in. The Illinois legislature passed a law in 1819, which states that the English common law is the common law of Illinois, if applicable and of a general nature. But Justice Trumbull observed: "However well adapted the rule of common law may be to a densely populated country like England, it is but ill adapted to a new country like ours. . . . Perhaps there is no principle of the common law so inapplicable to the condition of our country and people as the one which is sought to be enforced now for the first time since the settlement of the State." Thus Judge Caton's ruling was improper, and the judgment was reversed.

Justice Caton dissented in a twenty-page opinion. The legislature is the proper body to define what parts of the English common law are "applicable" to Illinois, rather than the courts. He said: "By the construction given to the word applicable [by Justice Trumbull in the majority opinion], we [the Supreme Court] assume the right to disregard any other provision of the common law, which in our judgment would be inconvenient, and no one can safely advise his client relying upon the common law." He concluded, "Although this case by itself may be insignificant, yet the principles involved are important, and I have felt that I could not say less than I have, in assigning the reasons which led me to the conclusion at which I have arrived." More detail from the court's opinion in this case is included in chapter one and chapter three.

3. INNKEEPER. Lincoln represented the innkeeper in *Johnson v. Richardson et al.*,[5] December term 1855. The case revolved around the common law obligation of innkeepers to safely keep the property of their guests with an obligation resembling the absolute liability of common carriers. The opinion commented on this obligation thusly: "These rules, though seemingly hard on innkeepers, are founded on considerations of public utility, and deemed

essential to insure a high degree of security to travelers and strangers who of necessity must trust to and confide in the honesty and vigilance of the innkeeper and those in his employ."

In this case, Brush and Thompson rented a room in Joel Johnson's hotel. Thompson was carrying $3000 belonging to other parties, which he deposited in the hotel safe. He had $300 of his own money, and Brush had $434 of partnership money (Richardson and Hopkins were his partners); and each of them elected to keep those sums in his room. In the morning, the partnership's $434 had been stolen. William B. Richardson and Hopkins brought this action on the case to recover the partnership money in the Sangamon County Circuit Court, and the jury awarded them $286 (two-thirds of $434). Johnson appealed, and the only two questions considered on the appeal were the judge's refusal to give two requested instructions to the jury: (1) Plaintiffs could not maintain their action because Brush was not joined, and he was a joint owner with them of the stolen partnership money. (2) Since Brush knew there was a hotel safe, and chose to keep the money, the innkeeper was not liable for the loss. Lincoln represented Johnson, and Logan represented Richardson and Hopkins.

The Supreme Court, in an opinion written by Justice Skinner, affirmed the Sangamon County Circuit Court opinion. As to (1), the proper plaintiffs for injuries to property are all the joint owners of the property, but where the remedy is to seek the recovery of damages, and not a specific thing, the non-joinder of one or more of the joint owners can only be defeated by a plea of abatement. If this is not done, as here, the plaintiffs may recover as to their proportionate interests, as here, in the damages. Brush can still bring an action against Johnson to recover his one-third interest.

Concerning (2), innkeepers are bound to protect the property of their guests, and in case of loss, can only absolve themselves from liability by showing they were not at fault. The burden of proof is on the innkeeper. "We do not intimate an opinion that innkeepers are responsible in all cases of loss of their guests property. The guest may unnecessarily expose his money to danger, or unnecessarily carry with him large sums, which no prudent man would do in a country where exchange can readily be obtained." Neither was the case here.

4. INSURANCE. Lincoln represented an insurance company in *McConnel v. The Delaware Mutual Safety Insurance Company et al.*,[6] December term 1856. This is the only insurance case involving Lincoln before the Illinois Supreme Court. It demonstrates that attempts of insolvent owners to "sell their business property to insurance companies" was not invented in our century.

One Benjamin E. Roney was engaged in a general retail business in Beardstown, Illinois, carried on in a one-story wooden structure in which he also had living quarters. He had insured his merchandise for $5000 with

Lincoln's client, and on February 10, 1853, the merchandise was destroyed by fire that was reported at 2:00 a.m. The insurance company, upon proof of loss by Roney, paid him $4400. Roney remained in business in his repaired building, and purchased merchandise for $6029 from Goodheart and Ackerland. Upon his failure to pay for this merchandise, he was sued. Judgment was rendered against him for the whole amount of his purchases, and when execution of the judgment was attempted, the goods were not in Roney's possession. He had assigned them to the insurance company when evidence was found indicating Roney had committed arson which caused the insured loss. The company's representative, Peter Sweat, confronted Roney with this evidence, and told Roney there would be no criminal prosecution if he transferred his current inventory to the insurance company, which would sell it in order to recover its $4400. Roney agreed and the property was so transferred. Roney was then arrested for arson. Thus, Goodheart and Ackerland were unable to recover either the money or goods from Roney, and, in some unexplained fashion, their claim ended up being owned by Murray McConnel, who brought this action to compel the insurance company to return the seized merchandise or pay McConnel the amount of the judgment.

The trial court in Cass County held for the insurance company, and McConnel brought this appeal. Justice Caton, in writing the opinion for the supreme court affirming the opinion of the lower court, stated the principals of law involved were not disputed, and the only controversy was one of fact. Even though this was a civil action, the law required the same degree of proof to sustain an accusation of arson committed by Roney as would have been required to obtain a conviction for arson in a criminal case. Justice Caton stated: "In such a case every legal presumption is in favor of his innocence, and we should not, by our finding, pronounce him guilty, unless that guilt is clearly established by evidence excluding or overcoming every fair and reasonable hypothesis of his innocence." Lincoln and H. E. Dummer represented the insurance company. Murray McConnel represented himself, assisted by J. G. Grimshaw.

There were several telling indications of Roney's guilt. Part of the goods Roney swore were destroyed by fire that night were subsequently found in a Dutch chest which Roney had filled with many valuable items. The chest had been removed to a safe place by Roney just before the fire. Another indicative bit of evidence was that Roney had sent his clerk, who also lived on the premises, away on a dubious errand on the night of the fire, and another person who had always stayed with Roney when his clerk was away was not invited for a "sleep-over" on that night. Justice Caton remarked if Roney had no design in securing himself from the presence of those two persons that night it was "at least very remarkable and very unfortunate; for we can hardly resist the conclusion that he had the design of being alone that night."

Caton goes on to say:

"Now, how can we resist the conclusion that Roney set fire to this store himself, when we see that he thus deliberately prepared for it, by securing the absence of all others by a studied course of conduct, different from his usual habit, by removing the contents of the show-case, and other valuable but not bulky articles, to places where they could be saved, but not seen; by removing from his safe his most valuable papers, such as notes, etc., which is manifest, from their appearance subsequently, being unchanged and unlike those papers which were in the safe but not consumed; when we see him representing in his protest, supported by his oath, that those very articles which he thus removed and saved were consumed, and collecting, or endeavoring to collect, their value under his policy of insurance; and when we see him further magnifying his loss, by putting in his protest more goods than he had in the store at the time of the fire, and that, too, by means of a false invoice of stock previously taken?

Later in the opinion Caton wrote:

The appearance of Roney, when first seen by those who came to his relief after he gave the alarm, show that he must have been previously prepared for the fire, and was not taken by surprise when it occurred. He was first seen immediately after he gave the alarm at the door of the back room trying to get out the trunk and chest; about which he evinced extraordinary solicitude, while all else in the store seemed to be forgotten. He said the back room was so full of smoke when he discovered the fire, that he was nearly suffocated, and yet in this pressing emergency he took time to dress himself completely, for he was then dressed throughout, with his watch in his pocket and with his cane in his hand. Now we would naturally suppose, that a man with his infirmity, alone in the house, awakened out of a sound sleep by the smoke of a fire, of the extent and location of which he was ignorant, and so suffocated as to endanger his life before he could get the door open, would take but little time in making his toilet, but would rather be content to secure the artificial member as a means of locomotion, and then rush to the door out of the suffocation, and give the alarm.

Caton concluded the court could not entertain any reasonable doubt Roney set the fire himself, and thus affirmed the lower court's opinion.

5. LEGAL MALPRACTICE. Lincoln represented a partnership from Boston, Massachusetts, who had been ill served by other attorneys in *Griggs et al. v. Gear*,[7] December term 1845. He represented clients who brought an action

in a court of equity to remedy the adverse consequences of this malpractice, and was successful.

David R. Griggs and a man named Weld entered into a partnership with Hezekiah Gear, wherein they were to furnish capital to Gear to manufacture lead at Galena, Illinois, and ship it to Boston to be sold by Griggs and Weld. Griggs and Weld sued Gear for over $13,000 for goods furnished to him. Gear filed a bill to dissolve this suit, but no process was served on Griggs and Weld. The attorneys (identified as Cowles and Krum) for Griggs *et al.* took it upon themselves to seek to enjoin Gear's action, which failed, and the final result was a finding by a master in equity that Gear had suffered a loss of $50,000 because Griggs *et al.* had failed to fulfill their part of the contract. The award for Gear was $50,000 minus $13,791.98, the amount of goods furnished by Griggs *et al.,* leaving a balance due of $36,208.02. Harback, who was a partner with Griggs and Weld, but had nothing to do with this business, had been joined by Gear in his action. Griggs and Weld brought an action in Jo Daviess County Circuit Court, before Judge Thomas C. Browne, to review and reverse the former decree. Gear filed a demurrer, which was sustained, and the bill was dismissed.

Griggs *et al.* were represented by Lincoln and J. W. Chickering on the appeal. The opinion first states the attorneys' briefs, with a multitude of authorities cited, none of them Illinois cases, with a large number of references to Story's *Equity Pleadings*s. Story's book on English equity pleadings was the oft-quoted authority in Illinois cases. Chickering had a full page of statements and citations, and on the other side, J. J. Hardin and D. A. Smith had almost four pages, and on the same side was J. Butterfield, who had about one page of statements and citations. Then is stated: "A. Lincoln, for the appellants replied at length to the arguments of the counsel for the appellee (Gear)."

The Supreme Court, with Justice Caton writing the opinion, reversed the decree of the lower court, and remanded the cause for further proceeding. Caton cited one case in support of his opinion, but mostly relied on his interpretation of the rules of equity pleadings, and how the facts related. This is obviously a case where oral arguments were very influential, and Lincoln, "replying at length to the arguments" of opposing counsel, carried the day. Lincoln's clients were awarded a reversal of the unfavorable ruling in the circuit court, because Caton said they had not given their previous attorneys in the action against Gear authority to appear for them in the equity matter, and they were never personally served. Caton wrote some impressive prose on this as follows:

> It further appears, that those attorneys are irresponsible. Can it be tolerated for a moment that parties are to be bound by a decree to pay more than $36,000 which is entered up behind their backs, and without even an implied knowledge of the existence of the suit, and without their

having an adequate remedy against anyone? Can it be said, that the arm of equity is too short to reach such a flagrant case of injustice as this? Neither the law nor good conscience can tolerate such a conclusion. We cannot consent to attach such a sanctity to the character and conduct of a solution that he may bind strangers without their privity or consent in proceedings which may be utterly ruinous to them, and without their being able to respond for the damages which they may occasion, no matter how honest may be their motives. If the fortunes of all our citizens are held by so frail a tenure as this—if they may be utterly ruined without redress, either by their carelessness, the ignorance or dishonesty of every one who may get a license to practice law in a country where there are so many facilities for obtaining a license as in this, it is quite time that everyone should know it.

Immediately after this case in the reports is a related case, *Harback et al. v. Gear,*[8] December term 1845. It is a short *per curiam* report, which states that it has the same facts as *Griggs et al. v. Gear,* and thus comes to the same conclusion. Harback had not been named as a party in the earlier appeal.

6. TRUSTEES. Lincoln represented trustees in an action to require them to carry out the clear intentions of the benefactor who established the trust for specific purposes in *Gilman et al. v. Hamilton et al,*[9] December term 1854, and was unable to convince the Illinois Supreme Court to accept the substitute acts of his clients as trustees.

In 1835, Gideon Blackburn raised money from many benevolent grantees to purchase land from the government to establish a seminary. He conveyed the land to W. S. Gilman and six other trustees of the school, directing them, among other things, to erect a building on a certain portion of the land. The trustees sold some of the land at various times to pay taxes and decided that, since there was not enough money to build, they would use the trust property to establish a Blackburn Theological Professorship. Most of the land was sold to Nathaniel Coffin. The professorship was endowed under a decree of the Sangamon County Circuit Court, before Judge Davis; it was reversed by the Illinois Supreme Court and the cause remanded. Hence, this action was brought, which decreed the land could not be conveyed, and directed the trustees to carry out the wishes of Blackburn. Lincoln and D. A. Smith represented the appellants, Gilman, *et al.,* on the appeal. W. Wier, Jr. represented Hamilton, *et al.*

The Supreme Court, in an opinion written by Justice Scates, affirmed the decree. A charity must be accepted upon the terms proposed. It cannot be altered by any agreement between the heirs of the grantor and the trustees. The intention of the donor will control, unless it is impractical; and in that event it may be altered *cy-pres* (as near as may be). Granted the land itself was not valuable enough to provide funds to build, but the trustees should have sought other funds to carry out the wishes of the grantor. Secondly, the decree of the court transferring land is not a judicial sale, and anyone purchasing the land is charged with notice of the facts of the trust. Such a case as this does not allow Coffin to fall under the rule of an innocent purchaser. A trust is stamped upon the property itself, and it will follow it into the hands of those who acquire it by purchase or otherwise.

7. SPRINGFIELD BECOMES THE STATE CAPITOL. As part of the agreement to move the seat of government to Springfield in 1837, private citizens of Springfield contributed the sum of $50,000, payable in three installments, with controversy arising when the time came to pay the third. Logan and Lincoln represented Mather, who ended up having the privilege of paying the entire third installment by himself. He was generous enough to share this privilege with the other obligors, and brought this action, *Klein et al. v. Mather,*[10] December term 1845, so that they could pay a proportionate share.

The Illinois legislature passed a bill on February 25, 1837, stating the seat of government for the state would be Springfield, if the sum of $50,000 should be donated by individuals, payable as the governor should direct. Fifty-one private individuals, including Samuel Treat, Ninian W. Edwards, John Stewart, Elijah Iles, and many other names remembered by present-day Springfieldians, agreed to these terms. The money was to be paid in three installments. The first two were paid; when number three became due, some of the fifty-one had died, and others had become insolvent. Mather, one of the fifty-one, was sued by the state for the whole amount due ($16,666.66 $2/3$), and judgment was recovered against him. The legislature passed an act authorizing this debt to be discharged in state indebtedness. Mather paid the judgment in these obligations, which he bought at eighty cents on the dollar. Twenty-six of the other obligors paid Mather some proportion based on an agreement among themselves. Mather computed he was still owed $4,607.55, and brought this action to recover this amount from the eleven remaining solvent obligors in the Morgan County Circuit Court before Judge Lockwood. Judgment was entered for Mather, who was represented by Logan on the appeal. M. McConnel and T. Campbell represented Klein.

The Supreme Court, in an opinion written by Justice Purple, affirmed the judgment. Justice Purple did vary the amount each obligor owed from $351.55 found by the circuit court to $354.89, after giving a good detailed explanation as to how this sum was determined, item by item. The law was clear as to the obligation of the co-obligors. Purple said: "No doctrine is better settled, than that a co-obligor or surety, who advances money for his co-obligors or co-sureties, shall be indemnified to the extent of his advances." The court noted: "Treat, J., being a party to the suit of *Klein v. Mather,* did not sit in the case."

8. SLAVERY. The case of *Bailey v. Cromwell et al., adm. of Cromwell*,[11] July term 1841, is the only case involving this issue before the Illinois Supreme Court. David Bailey agreed to purchase a "black or negro girl or woman, named Nance" from Cromwell and gave him a note. Cromwell in turn agreed that before payment would be demanded, he would produce evidence to show the necessary papers and indenture. Cromwell died, and the girl was "in possession of Bailey for about six months, at the expiration of which time she left his service, and never since returned, she asserting and declaring all the time that she was free." Cromwell's administrators brought an action of *assumpsit* against Bailey, and recovered damages of $431.97. Lincoln represented Bailey, and Logan represented Cromwell. The case was tried in Tazewell County Circuit Court before Judge William Thomas.

Upon appeal this decision was reversed, with the opinion written by Justice Breese. The court held the note and agreement, which were made at the same time, must be taken together as forming one entire contract. Cromwell did not furnish the evidence of indenture as promised, and thus there was no consideration for the notes.

The court cited an Illinois Supreme Court case, *Kinney v. Cook*,[12] decided at the December term 1840, which decided the presumption of law was, in Illinois, that every person was free, without regard to color. There was no evidence she had been indentured to Bailey, and she asserted her freedom "in the only modes she could, by doing as she pleased, making purchases, contracting debts, and controlling her own motions." Since the sale of a free person is illegal, and that was the consideration for the note, the note was illegal as well.

This is the first Illinois Supreme Court case in which Lincoln was involved where precedent from the Illinois Supreme Court was cited as authority. In every other case, the citations have been from England, or New York, Pennsylvania, Ohio, Kentucky, and other states which had had appellate courts for a longer period of time.

9. MOST ODIOUS CLIENT. Thomas Cowls wins this award easily when compared to all of the other clients Lincoln represented before the Illinois Supreme Court—based on the Supreme Court reports at least. The case of *Cowls v. Cowls*,[13] December term 1846, in which Lincoln represented Thomas in an action brought by Ann Cowls against her husband in chancery for an increase of alimony, the custody of two infant children, and an allowance for their maintenance. The action was brought in the Edwards County Circuit Court before Judge William Wilson. In a former suit, Ann Cowls had obtained a divorce, but no provision had been made in relation to the children. The children lived with their father, who "had lived in a state of fornication with a woman, until within a few weeks of the time when this bill was filed, when he married her." He also neglected them, and "he is in the habitual use of

profane, indecent, immoral and vulgar language, as well in the presence of the children as elsewhere." The court gave custody of the children to Ann, and awarded her thirty dollars per child a year, for five years, to maintain them. Lincoln represented Thomas, on the appeal at least. A. T. Bledsoe represented Ann.

The Supreme Court, in an opinion written by Justice Caton, affirmed the decree, saying:

> The power of the court of chancery to interfere with and control, not only the estates but the persons and custody of all minors within the limits of its jurisdiction, is of very ancient origin, and can not now be questioned. This is a power which must necessarily exist somewhere, in every well regulated society, and more especially in a republican government, where each man should be reared and educated under such influences that he may be qualified to exercise the rights of a freeman and take part in the government of the country. It is a duty, then, which the country owes as well to itself, as to the infant, to see that he is not abused, defrauded or neglected, and the infant has a right to this protection. While a father conducts himself as not to violate this right, the court will not, ordinarily, interfere with his parental control. If, however, by his neglect or abuse, he shows himself devoid of that affection, which is supposed to qualify him better than any other to take charge of his own offspring, the court may interfere, and take the infant under its own charge, and remove it from the control of the parent, and place it in custody of a proper person to act as guardian, who may be a stranger.

He then referenced similar statements by Judge Story in his treatise on equity jurisprudence, and after reviewing the facts presented by Ann Cowls, he wrote: "Here we have grouped together into one disgusting and revolting picture, those features of a father's character who has become unworthy of the charge of his own offspring, and any one of which, as we have seen it laid down by Mr. Justice Story, will authorize the court in its discretion, to interfere and remove the child without the influence of such a polluted atmosphere." Also the lower court made a proper decision in awarding custody to the mother, and thirty dollars a year is not too much for the support of each child, although counsel for Thomas Cowls did not agree.

10. "BEST EVIDENCE" RULE. Lincoln and Aaron Shaw represented Benjamin F. Park in *Mason v. Park*,[14] December term 1842, which was an action of debt brought by Benjamin F. Park to recover the penalty given by "an act to prevent trespassing by cutting timber." The case had been originally brought before a justice of the peace, by Park, against George Mason. This was appealed to the Richland County Circuit Court, tried before a jury and

Judge William Wilson; a verdict was returned for Park in the amount of $48. At the trial Park called a witness to prove title to the land on which the trees were cut. The witness testified to a conversation in which Mason admitted to him that two of the trees were cut on Park's land. This was all the evidence that was presented in relation to the title. Mason appealed, on the grounds that the evidence was inadequate. The Supreme Court agreed with Mason, and Justice Treat gave the court's opinion, reversing the circuit court. O. B. Ficklin and Leir Davis represented Mason.

There is a long-standing rule in common law that the best evidence which the nature of the cause permits, should be furnished in a trial. When title to land is claimed, the best evidence would be his deeds and other documentary evidence of title. These are always presumed to be in the landowner's custody, and can be easily produced. The oral testimony of what Mason said about ownership of the two trees which were felled was the weakest kind of evidence, and far from adequate here. Lincoln argued that the admission of Mason that he knew Park owned the land precluded the necessity for Park to offer any additional evidence that he owned the land. Thus, Mason's admission, while he had the right to require Park to produce the best evidence of title, excused the necessity of application of the "best evidence" rule. Justice Treat might have said "nice try" and refused to make new law by agreeing with Lincoln's ingenious argument. Incidently, Chief Justice Wilson dissented, so Lincoln persuaded one jurist that his position was right. Wilson also had been the trial judge.

11. SURETIES. The collectors of taxes were personally responsible for the taxes they collected; to assure that the tax money would be available to the taxing authority the individual collector had to find sureties who would personally guarantee the timely payment of the tax receipts to the proper authority. The action of *Compher et al. v. The People*,[15] December term 1850, was an action brought against William Compher and his sureties, when William Compher experienced difficulties in paying Peoria County its proper share of tax collections. This was an action brought on a bond executed by Compher, as collector of Peoria County. The other defendants were his sureties. The sureties argued they should be discharged from their liabilities because the legislature changed the revenue laws after they agreed to be sureties for Compher. The Tazewell County Circuit Court, with Judge Davis presiding, held for the People and did not discharge the sureties. Lincoln & Herndon, Stuart & Edwards, D. B. Campbell, and D. L Gregg represented the People on the appeal, and submitted a brief which contained the cogent argument which the Supreme Court used in its opinion. N. H. Purple and R. S. Blackwell represented Compher *et al.*

This case is also included in chapter five.

12. QUANTUM MERUIT. In *Eldridge v. Rowe*,[16] December term 1845, Lincoln represented Nelson Rowe, who had agreed to work for Barnabas E. Eldridge on his farm for a term of eight months for the sum of $90. Rowe left after four months, without the consent and without any fault of Eldridge. Rowe brought an action before a justice of the peace of Kendall County, who awarded him $30. Eldridge appealed to the Kendall County Circuit Court before Judge Caton and a jury, who reduced the amount to $26.75. Eldridge had an offset of $3.25, which he proved. Eldridge, represented by O. Peters, appealed to the Supreme Court.

The Illinois Supreme Court reversed the decision and, with Justice Young writing the opinion, remanded the cause. Lincoln argued for the *quantum meruit* (as much as he deserves) theory, which means Rowe should be paid something because he did a lot of work which had benefit to Eldridge, and cited one New Hampshire supporting case. This was ignored by Young who held, in his opinion, that if a party promises to do a thing and abandons his work before it is finished, he shouldn't be paid anything. *Quantum meruit* applies in some special cases, but not in this situation. Justice Young wrote:

> The general rules which govern in ordinary contracts for work and labor, are simple and easily understood, but often difficult in their application to many of the cases which arise in the country, and are constantly presented in our courts for adjudication. The loose manner in which parties frequently express themselves in making verbal agreements, and not infrequently when the contracts are in writing, often obscures the intention, and necessarily involves the proper construction to be given to them by courts and juries, in much doubt and perplexity. When an agreement is fairly entered into, and upon a good and valid consideration, it should be faithfully performed, and neither party is at a liberty to disregard it, or to perform it otherwise than according to his engagement; and the rule is well established, that where one has the precedent condition in his favor, that he is not liable to an action until the other has performed. And it is our duty to discountenance any departure from this rule, which will allow a party to abandon his undertaking at pleasure and resort to a *quantum meruit*, where a part of the agreement only has been performed.

He wrote some basic truths still in fashion about the difficulty of understanding oral, and even written agreements, and about the necessity of performing a contract once one has agreed to it.

13. JUSTICE OF THE PEACE COURTS. These courts, which are creatures of municipalities, were established with limited authority in order to settle small disputes. They provided convenience, simple procedures, less necessity of attorney's involvement, and sessions not limited to the convenience of

transient judges. They filled a real need. Appeal of a decision of the justice of peace court could be made to the county circuit court, where a judgment could then be appealed to the supreme court like any other circuit court judgment. Lincoln & Herndon represented an executor of an estate in *Williams et al., exec. of Trotter v. Blankenship et al., adm. of Trailor*,[17] December term 1850. In this case, Eli C. Blankenship, administrator of Archibald Trailer, deceased, brought an action against John Williams, the executor of George Trotter, deceased, in a justice of the peace court. After a hearing, the justice of the peace awarded $43.18 to Blankenship. Williams contended that a justice of the peace court had no authority to render this judgment in his appeal to the Sangamon County Circuit Court, before Judge Davis, which affirmed this judgment.

Williams, represented by Logan, then appealed to the Supreme Court, which reversed the lower courts, in an opinion written by Justice Treat. The statute conferring powers to the justice of peace courts gives authority to handle cases when the claims do not exceed $100 when an executor is the plaintiff, but only up to $20 when an executor is the defendant. Also consent cannot confer jurisdiction, so the fact the parties appeared before the justice of the peace, and contested the merits of the case, can have no bearing on the proper decision.

14. SPECIFIC PERFORMANCE. One of the advantages of a court of equity is that it has the power to compel an obligor to transfer specific agreed-upon property instead of merely giving up the monetary value of that property. This doctrine was applied only to unique property, and every piece of real property was so deemed. Thus, if one has an obligation to convey a certain piece of land, and the grantee wants that particular land rather than its monetary value, the court of equity will decree that it shall be conveyed. Such a situation arose as the result of a promise made by John B. Broadwell which resulted in the case of *Broadwell et al. for the use of Thompson et ux. v. Broadwell*,[18] December term 1844. In this case Lincoln and E. D. Baker represented John B. Broadwell, who had executed an instrument stating he would transfer specific portions of his land to Mary Jane Sweat and William Broadwell when either of them attained lawful age. Mary Jane (Sweat) Thompson and her husband Michael brought this action for specific performance of the portion of the document giving her certain land which had been promised to her. This was given under the penalty of $1000, if Broadwell failed to carry out his promise. Mary Jane Thompson lived to a lawful age, but John B. Broadwell decided to give her $500 rather than half the land. The Sangamon County Circuit Court, with Judge Treat presiding, decreed that John B. could satisfy his obligation by giving Mary Jane $500. John B. was represented by A. K. Smedes and S. W. Robbins.

The Supreme Court reversed the Circuit Court decree. There were many authorities cited on each side, and Justice Caton wrote a very thorough opinion, commenting on most of the authorities cited. He cited a general rule of construction of written instruments:

> While the rule of law is inflexible, that a written instrument cannot be altered by *parol* proof, yet the court of chancery will never hesitate to rectify mistakes in fact, which have occurred in drawing up the paper, when a proper case is presented and clearly proved, and then carry into effect the instrument when thus corrected, as if it had been written as the parties supposed it was at the time.

However, Justice Caton said only the writing itself can be looked at to ascertain the intent of the parties, and the writing here indicated the express purpose was to convey the land. He stated:

> Whenever the courts shall establish it, as a general rule, that they will go out of the instrument, and inquire what construction each or both parties put upon it at the time it was made they will be starting upon a path which will lead to interminable labyrinths, and will present an inducement to perjury which will be alarming in its consequences.

What this meant was that if Mary Jane wanted the land rather than $500, she should have been allowed to have it.

15. INSANITY. In the following case, Lincoln was involved in the trial, and when the appeal was heard, he was in Washington otherwise occupied. The case of *Lilly v. Waggoner cons. of Waggoner*,[19] January term 1862, was the appeal from a bill in chancery brought in 1858 in the Moultrie County Circuit Court by George Waggoner, conservator of the estate of Elisha Waggoner, to set aside a conveyance of land from Elisha to Europe A. Lilly in 1851, upon the ground that Elisha was insane at the time. Elisha was declared insane in 1858. After evidence on both sides was presented, the judge entered a decree declaring the deed void, ordering a reconveyance of the land to Waggoner, and that the purchase price be returned to Lilly with interest. Herndon and H. P. H. Bromwell represented Waggoner, and Thornton and Stuart, Edwards, and Brown represented Lilly on the appeal.

The Supreme Court, in an opinion written by Justice Walker, reversed the decree, and dismissed the bill. All persons of legal age are presumed to be sane, and a deed executed several years before the maker was found to be insane has the legal presumption of validity in its favor. Walker said, "The law has never required the high order of reasoning powers that mark the gifted, or a large portion of the human family would be thus deprived of the legal capacity to transact their own business." The evidence showing the insanity of a party at the time of execution of a deed, must preponderate, or the legal presumption in favor of sanity, will sustain the act. One of the witnesses testified that Elisha, in 1851, was "about like the other Waggoners," and there wasn't enough evidence of Elisha's disability in 1851 to support George's contention. Certainly George had difficulty proving Elisha was insane in 1851, when none of the other Waggoners, especially George, were so afflicted.

16. COUNTY COURT FEES. This case, *Edgar County v. Mayo*,[20] December term 1846, involved a county circuit court clerk seeking to be reimbursed for a fee earned by him in a specific case, and he sought Lincoln's assistance to help him collect it. The case was submitted as an agreed case in the Edgar County Circuit Court, and the parties, having agreed on the facts, presented the matter to Judge Treat for his decision. Jonathan Mayo, the clerk of the Edgar County Circuit Court, issued certain documents in a case against Andrew J. Hanks. The fee for this was $7.93, payable to Mayo for his work, and to be paid through recovery of a judgment and costs from Hanks. Nothing was recovered, and Mayo wanted the county to pay him. The county resisted, and this lawsuit resulted. Justice Treat held for Mayo, who was represented by Lincoln. J. Pearson represented Edgar County.

Judge Koerner, writing for the court, reversed the lower court. Lincoln argued: "By the common law, the defendant in error [Mayo] is entitled to remuneration for his services. The county called upon him to perform those services, and he has performed them. There is no law of this state which contravenes the common law." To support his argument, he cited several cases, including one from Illinois. Koerner and the Court did not agree, stating:

> In order to settle this question, it is only necessary to refer to the 105th section of the Criminal Code, Rev. Stat. page 101, which provides that all recognizance, having any relationship to criminal matters, shall be taken to the people of this state. By virtue of this law, the people of Illinois are the plaintiffs in a suit of such a recognizance, and if any recovery is had, it inures to the benefit of the state treasury. Hence it follows that in a suit of this kind the county can under no circumstances be made responsible for the cost. It cannot be said that services have been rendered to the county for the prosecution of a suit, from the result of which it can derive no benefit. The rule, therefore, which the counsel for Mayo has insisted upon, that each party ought to pay the costs made by their request, as being one founded in natural justice and recognized in the common law, can find no application here.

Lincoln convinced Judge Treat in the circuit court, at least, but not as a justice of the Illinois Supreme Court. Also it has been written in many histories that Lincoln did not charge high enough fees. However, here's a case where Mayo sought to recover $7.93 which required a trial in the circuit court and an appeal. What is a proper fee in this situation, especially when he lost?

17. PARTNERSHIP. The case of *Lewis v. Moffett*,[21] December term 1849, turns on the issue of responsibilities of partners to each other. Thomas Lewis, Willis H. Johnson, and John R. Moffett entered into a partnership in Springfield with a firm known as Lewis, Johnson & Co. in February of 1848. Johnson and Moffett agreed to perform services, and Lewis agreed to furnish a foundry and machine shop, and to purchase stock for the firm. The firm was dissolved by mutual consent in August 1848. The partnership owned a patent on an "atmospheric churn," which it tried to sell. Lewis, when in St. Louis on personal business, sold the churn for $5047. In the distribution of the assets of the partnership, he claimed a commission for making this sale, while his partners refused him saying it was a general obligation of each partner to do what he could to promote the common good. The circuit judge, Davis, entered a decree allowing Lewis a commission of $1000 and directing the remaining assets to be divided equally. Logan and Stuart & Edwards represented Lewis; and Lincoln & Herndon and J. C. Conkling represented Moffett on the appeal.

The Supreme Court, in an opinion written by Justice Caton, reduced a portion of the decree which, if followed, would have allowed Lewis more than the $1000 he was awarded, and affirmed the rest of the ruling. Justice Caton recognized that Lewis must have done a superb job of salesmanship when "testimony shows, and all now seem to admit, that the invention is really valueless." Under the partnership agreement, Lewis did not agree to provide services. So he should be compensated for any other services he rendered. One thousand dollars was judged a proper amount for this valuable service. Lewis had claimed $12,000 originally, so Lincoln *et al.* did a good job in proving the value of Lewis's miraculous services to be much less.

18. SAVING THE FARM. Beveridge cites an example of one of Lincoln's generous acts involving a case which featured a greedy stepfather and an innocent maiden:

> Another engaging example of services rendered by Lincoln without pay is his refusal to charge anything for saving the farm of a young woman, one Rebecca Dainwood. She inherited the land from an uncle, Christopher Robinson, the administrator of whose estate was a man of the name of John Lane. It would appear that the girl had made her home with Lane who occupied the farm. Miss Dainwood married a young farmer, William M. Dorman, and claimed the land. Thereupon Lane petitioned the Court at Shawneetown for the sale of the property to satisfy his claim of a little more than a thousand dollars against Robinson's estate, which claim had

been allowed him by the Court some fifteen years earlier.

The young married couple resisted Lane's petition, but were beaten in the trial court. Their attorney, Samuel D. Marshall, took an appeal to the Supreme Court and retained Lincoln to conduct the case in that tribunal. Lane was represented by Lyman Trumbull. Argument on both sides was thorough and Lincoln supported his points by the citation of many authorities. The Court in a long opinion sustained Lincoln's principal contentions and reversed the decree of the trial court. It is interesting to find that the opinion was delivered by Justice James Shields, Lincoln's dueling antagonist of a year or two before he argued the case. When asked for the amount of his fee, Lincoln said his services were his wedding present to Rebecca and William.[22]

In a footnote, Beveridge quotes a letter from F. M. Eddy of Shawneetown to Billy Herndon, which says that "young Dorman was so grateful that, although a Democrat, he ever after voted for Lincoln."[23]

There were three Dorman cases appealed to the Illinois Supreme Court: one in 1841, one in 1844, and one in 1851. The case Beveridge references is the 1844 case; no mention is made by him of the other two.

The facts are not crystal clear in the first two cases, but the third case provided a good summary of the whole story. Christopher Robinson died in 1819 intestate, with letters of administration issued to Mary Robinson, his widow, and John Brown. They had difficulty collecting the debts due the estate, and as a consequence, debts due from the estate remained mostly unpaid. The largest such debt was in excess of $1000 owed to a bank. John Lane married Mary Robinson in 1821; Mary died in the fall of 1822. In 1826, Brown and Lane made a settlement of the estate with the probate court, with all debts paid except $1008.87 due the Bank of Illinois.

In 1827 the state legislature passed an act entitled "An act authorizing the sale of lands belonging to the estate of Christopher Robinson, deceased." Lane and Brown—at some time—paid off the bank, and sold the land under the legislative authority to reimburse themselves for paying off the bank. In 1839 the Dormans brought an action of ejectment in the Gallatin County Circuit Court to recover this land. Judge Walter B. Scates rejected the legislative act as being unconstitutional, and the jury rendered judgment for the Dormans.

Lane and Brown appealed this judgment in *Lane et al. v. Doe ex dem. Dorman et ux.*,[24] December term 1841. John A. McClernand and Jesie B. Thomas represented Lane *et al.* and William J. Gatewood represented the Dormans. The court affirmed the judgment in an opinion written by Justice Smith. The constitution provided for a separation of powers, and the act in this case was clearly a judicial matter which had to be resolved by the judicial system rather than the legislature. The justice stated: "Whenever it is clear that the legislature has transcended its authority, and that a legislative act is in conflict with the constitution, it is imperatively required of the court to maintain the paramount authority of that instrument, which it is solemly pledged to support, and to declare the act inoperative and void."

Thus the Dormans recovered the land. The next chapter of this story before the Illinois Supreme Court—comes in *Dorman et ux. v. Lane, Adminsitrator of Robinson,*[25] December term 1841. This is the case referred to by Beveridge. In this case, Lincoln represented Dorman and his wife (indicated as "ux." in the title) in the appeal of this action before Judge Scates in the Gallatin County Circuit Court. Trumbull represented Lane. Lane, as administer of the estate of Christopher Robinson, filed a petition in the circuit court for an order to sell real estate of the intestate (Robinson) to pay the sum of $1008.87 adjudged to be due Lane as an individual by order of the probate court in 1826 (fifteen years before). Lincoln argued that Dorman and his wife were the only heirs, objected because of the time delay before Lane filed this action, and also noted that Lane had lived on the land and had received the profits from it all that time. Nevertheless judgment was entered for Lane.

The Illinois Supreme Court, in an opinion written by Justice Shields, reversed the decree and remanded the cause to be reheard in the circuit court. Based on the cases cited by Lincoln that the lapse of time should bar this recovery, the court commented, "It would be extremely hazardous for this court to sanction such gross negligence, and particularly in a case where the same person was both administrator and creditor." The cases cited had different periods of time between when suit could be brought to sell assets of an estate to pay a claim, and when a claim became due. Illinois had no statutory or case authority on it, so the court stated that by analogy to the rule established in Maine and Massachusetts, the general rule of the state will be that one year would be the limit, unless there be such a peculiar case that it would be the duty of a court of equity to depart from the rule.

Justice Scates wrote a separate opinion which concurred with the decision but pointed out that it would be impractical for the circuit court to sort out whether Lane needed to sell any land to pay himself the $1008.87. The probate court would be the proper forum since it had knowledge of the total financial situation during the fifteen-year duration of the case. Scates had tried the case, and had attempted to do the impractical. Lincoln won this Supreme Court case for his clients, and strongly influenced a rule of law in Illinois to apply to comparable situations in the future.

The last chapter in this saga is the case of *Dorman et ux. v. Yost, Administrator of John Lane et al.,*[26] December term 1851. Lincoln again represented the Dormans, and D. L. Gregg and R. S. Blackwell represented Yost. Lane brought this action in Gallatin County, but upon motion of the Dormans, it was moved to the White County Circuit Court, to have the real estate sold to recover the $1008.87 he had paid the bank on behalf of the estate. The facts stated in this opinion noted that Lane had sold this land belonging to the estate by authority of the special legislative act in 1827, and had kept the proceeds to repay the amount of money he had paid the bank to discharge the debt. There is no record that any reimbursement was made to the purchasers of the land when the Dormans recovered the land in the ejectment case. The court held for Lane and ordered that the land be sold to discharge this alleged debt. Then, during the pendency of this appeal, Lane died and L. C. Yost was appointed to be his administrator. The Supreme Court, in an opinion written by Justice Treat, held the trial court had erred, and reversed the judgment of that court.

Thus, Lincoln's actions to enable the Dormans "to save the farm" were successful. William D. Beard, assistant editor of the Lincoln Legal Papers project, in an article in the Spring 1994 issue of *The Lincoln Newsletter*, provides much additional information, detailing this entire matter.[27]

19. SPIRITUOUS LIQUOR. The case of *Sullivan v. People*,[28] December term 1853, involved the alleged sale of spirituous liquor in May of 1853 by Patrick Sullivan in quantities less than a quart. He did not have a license to keep a "grocery" (a term used to mean "saloon"). Thus, Sullivan, who was represented by Lincoln, was found guilty and fined $10. Elam Rush, state's attorney, represented The People.

The Illinois Supreme Court, in an opinion written by Judge Treat, affirmed the judgment. Lincoln contended the statute of 1845, under which Sullivan was convicted, was not in force. In 1851, another statute on the same subject provided for a fine of $25. This 1851 act was expressly repealed by an act passed in February 1853. Because of another statute specifying that no act repealed by the legislature can be revived by the subsequent act being repealed, the 1845 statute was not revived.

However, on February 12, 1853, the legislature had passed an act stating that all laws in force on the subject of spirituous liquors which were in force on February 1, 1851 were thereby in full force and effect as if they had never been repealed.

Albert Beveridge commented on this case, as follows:

> Lincoln made an exhaustive argument in the Supreme Court in defence of a saloon keeper, one Patrick Sullivan, who had been indicted, convicted, and fined ten dollars in the Macon County Circuit Court, for selling liquor without a license. The case involved the construction of the liquor laws of 1845, 1851, and 1853. From the unanimous opinion of the Court, which decided every point against Lincoln's contentions, the case appears to have been uncommonly clear; but the abstract of Lincoln's argument in the report of the case indicates he did his utmost to have the

laws so construed that a person could not be fined for selling intoxicants without a license.

This case is the most curious, and seemingly, inexplicable, that Lincoln ever had. The amount was only ten dollars and the mere costs of appeal exceeded that sum. Lincoln appeared alone for Sullivan. The facts strongly indicate that the wholesale grocers of Springfield, the most profitable part of whose business was the sale of liquor to saloon keepers in Central Illinois, were back of the appeal by Sullivan to the Supreme Court. As we have seen, Jacob Bunn, Lincoln's client and personal friend, was one of these wholesale liquor dealers.[29]

20. THE DIMINUTION OF $131,480.52. Beveridge referred to this case as representing the largest dollar amount involved in any of Lincoln's cases.[30] (The smallest amount involved in a Lincoln lawsuit was $3 he sought in *Byrne v. Stout* represented in chapter six.) Lincoln, representing a creditor in a suit to recover $131,480.52, proved the debtor liable and, thus, won the case even though the amount of the judgment was only $38,361.93. Furthermore, the debtor, considering this amount exorbitant, brought action in the Sangamon County Circuit Court to further reduce the award—and was successful.

Smith & Dunlap, Assignees of State Bank v. Dunlap,[31] December term 1850, involved a note made by James Dunlap to the Bank of Illinois for $131,480.52, to be paid in State of Illinois Certificates of Indebtedness. The note became due, and was unpaid. The Bank of Illinois went into liquidation, and assigned this note to John J. Hardin and Samuel Dunlap. Samuel Dunlap died and David Smith, *et al.* were his successors. They brought this action to collect the $131,480.52. The Sangamon County Circuit Court, with Judge David Davis presiding, awarded them $38,361.93. The assignees appealed, and were represented by Lincoln & Herndon, Browning & Bushnell, and Williams & Lawrence, who appeared for the creditors of the Bank of Illinois. S. T. Logan stood alone defending James Dunlap. At the maturity of the note, State of Illinois Certificates of Indebtedness had values ranging from twenty to forty-two cents on the dollar.

The Illinois Supreme Court, in an opinion written by Justice Treat, affirmed the circuit court decision. Treat stated that in instances when a promissor undertakes to pay a certain number of dollars in specific articles—such as grain, cattle, or other commodities—he must deliver the articles on the day named, or he will be bound to pay the sum stated in money. However, when he has promised to pay in bank notes, or other evidences of indebtedness which purport on their face to represent dollars and can be counted as such, the sum is expressed to indicate the number of dollars of the notes or evidences to be paid, and not the amount of the debt. If the debtor fails to deliver them according to the terms of the contract, he is responsible only for their real, not their nominal value. Their cash value is the true amount of the debt to be discharged. Such was the case here.

Dunlap, in his natural preference to pay even less of his original obligation, made a motion in this regard in the circuit court, and was unsuccessful. However, that judgment was reversed in the Illinois Supreme Court in a short opinion which cites neither the name of the justice writing the opinion nor the names of the attorneys for the parties. Beveridge states that Lincoln was involved in both cases.[32]

The facts of the case are thus. In *Dunlap v. Smith et al., assignees of State Bank*,[33] June term 1851, James Dunlap appealed the adverse circuit court ruling. He had entered a motion in the Sangamon County Circuit Court to pay all or part of the judgment in notes and certificates of the Bank of Illinois, with face value of $28,127.35. Five days after Dunlap gave the note to the Bank of Illinois, and before it became due, the legislature passed an act putting the Bank of Illinois into liquidation. This provided, among other things, for the paying out of the liquid assets of the bank, *pro rata,* and issuing certificates for the balance due. These certificates should be received for any debt due the bank. Judge David Davis rejected Dunlap's argument and denied his motion.

The Supreme Court reversed this lower court opinion, and remanded the cause, ruling that Dunlap had the right to discharge the judgment in the notes and certificates of the bank. The anonymous justice implicitly rebuked the attorneys for Smith *et al.,* stating:

> It is to be regretted that, in so important a case as this, the parties have not thought proper to bring before the court the whole transaction out of which Dunlap's indebtedness arose. Had this been done, it is possible that the court might be called upon to pronounce a different judgment; but as the case is presented in the record, by which alone the court must be governed, Dunlap's right to discharge the judgment in notes and certificates of the bank is clear.

In the first case, Dunlap won the right to discharge his $131,480.52 by paying a lesser amount, measured by the value of State of Illinois Certificates of Indebtedness at the time the note became due. This gave him the additional benefit of being able to discharge the obligation by paying the adjudicated amount of money with indebtedness of the bankrupt bank at its face value, which probably could be bought by Dunlap at a discount.

S. T. Logan represented Dunlap in the appeal of the first case, and presumably in this second case, against an impressive array of attorneys, including Lincoln. In the first case, Logan succeeded in establishing that Dunlap could pay off the $131,480.52 with $38,361.93 in real money, and with the decision in the second case, the amount was further reduced. The records of the case do not indicate the degree of the additional savings.

21. SANCTITY OF COURT JUDGMENTS. The case of *Buckmaster et al. v. Jackson ex dem. Carlin*,[34] December term 1841, upholds the principle of protecting rights to ownership of real property which have been established by a valid judgment. Logan, William Martin, and George T. M. Davis represented Nathaniel Buckmaster and others in protecting their claim to ownership of a parcel of land. M. McConnel and A. Cowles represented Nathaniel Jackson.

The case was an action of ejectment brought in the Madison County Circuit Court before Judge Breese by William Carlin to recover possession of 320 acres of land. Carlin traced his title to an individual named Pruitt, the original patentee from the United States. Nathaniel Buckmaster *et al.* traced title from Pruitt as well. However, Pruitt had obtained a mortgage from the State Bank of Illinois; he defaulted on this mortgage and it was foreclosed, and was sold to Buckmaster's predecessors in title by judicial sale. The court refused to hear evidence of the foreclosed mortgage. Jackson's attorneys argued the mortgage was void because the State Bank did not have the necessary legal authority. The contract between the parties was void as being in violation of the Constitution of the United States, which prohibits the states from emitting bills of credit, and such bills were the consideration of that contract. Since the mortgage was thus void, judgment was rendered for Jackson.

Justice Smith wrote the Illinois Supreme Court opinion which reversed that judgment and remitted the cause, ruling the evidence should have been permitted. If a court has jurisdiction of the persons and the subject matter, as it did in the case of the foreclosure of the mortgage and sale thereunder, no errors or irregularities, which may have been committed during the progress of the cause, can render the judgment void. No question was raised as to the constitutionality of the bank's actions by the parties to the foreclosure suit, and collateral inquiry by the parties in this suit was improper. The court quoted some pertinent text from *Voorheese v. Bank of the United States*[35] (1836) in a comparable action for ejectment:

> A judgment, or executions, irreversible by a superior court, cannot be declared a nullity by an authority of law, if it has been rendered by a court of competent jurisdiction of the parties and the subject matter, with authority to use the process it has issued. It must remain the only test of the respective rights of the parties to it. That some sanctity should be given to judicial proceedings, some time limited, beyond which they should not be questioned; some protection afforded to those who purchase at sales by judicial process, and some definitive rules established, by which property thus acquired may become transmissible with security to the possessors, cannot be denied. In this country particularly, where property, which within a few years was but of little value in a wilderness, is now the site

of large and flourishing cities, its enjoyment should be at least [as] secure as in that country when its value is less progressive. It is among the elementary principles of the common law, that whoever would complain of the proceedings of a court must do it in such time as not to injure his adversary by unnessary delay in the assertion of his right.

22. RIPARIAN RIGHTS A JURY ISSUE. In *Evans v. Merriweather*,[36] December term 1842, the court held that an individual's use of water in a river, when another landowner on the same river contended too much had been used, thus depriving the normal use he could properly expect from the same source, was a matter to be decided by a jury.

Here John Evans owned a steam mill on a stream. Henry W. Merriweather also owned a steam mill on the same stream, but downstream from Evans's mill. In 1837, there was a drought, and Evans built a dam across the stream to retain sufficient water to run his mill. This prevented Merriweather from running his mill, and he sued Evans for damages. Judgment was rendered for Merriweather, who was represented, on the appeal at least, by Hardin and Logan. Evans was represented by C. Walker, R. L. Doyle, and D. H. Smith.

Justice Lockwood wrote the Illinois Supreme Court decision which affirmed the judgment. He stated:

> The language of all the authorities is, that water flows in its natural courses, and should be permitted thus to flow, so that all through whose land it naturally flows, may enjoy the privilege of using it. . . . A riparian proprietor, therefore, though he has an undoubted right to use the water for hydraulic or manufacturing purposes, must so use it as to do no injury to any other riparian proprietor. . . . Where all have a right to participate in a common benefit, and none can have an exclusive enjoyment, no rule, from the very nature of the case, can be laid down, as to how much each may use without infringing upon the rights of others. In such cases, the question must be left to the judgment of the jury, whether the party complained of has used, under all the circumstances, more that his just proportion.

The jury held that damage had been done, so the judgment of the earlier jury was affirmed.

NOTES

1. 11 *Ill.*, 254; *LCL*, 131.
2. 1 W.S Cond. Rep. 278.
3. 12 *Ill.*, 301; *LCL*, 146.

4. 10 *Ill.*, 130; *LCL*, 127.
5. 17 *Ill.*, 302; *LCL*, 193.
6. 18 *Ill.*, 229; *LCL*, 198.
7. 8 *Ill.*, 3; *LCL*, 106.
8. 8 *Ill.*, 18; *LCL*, 106.
9. 16 *Ill.*, 225; *LCL*, 182.
10. 7 *Ill.*, 318; *LCL*, 91.
11. 4 *Ill.*, 70; *LCL*, 19.
12. 4 *Ill.*, 232.
13. 8 *Ill.*, 434; *LCL*, 117.
14. 4 *Ill.*, 532; *LCL*, 42.
15. 12 *Ill.*, 289; *LCL*, 145.
16. 7 *Ill.*, 91; *LCL*, 85.
17. 12 *Ill.*, 121; *LCL*, 138.
18. 6 *Ill.*, 599; *LCL*, 77.
19. 27 *Ill.*, 395; *LCL*, 238.
20. 8 *Ill.*, 82; *LCL*, 109.
21. 11 *Ill.*, 392; *LCL*, 133.
22. Beveridge, Vol. 1, 557–58.
23. *Ibid.*, 558
24. 4 *Ill.*, 237; *LCL*, 27.
25. 6 *Ill.*, 143; *LCL*, 64
26. 13 *Ill.*, 128; *LCL*, 150.
27. *The Lincoln Newsletter*, Spring 1994, published by the Lincoln College Museum.
28. 15 *Ill.*, 233; *LCL*, 177.
29. Beveridge, Vol. 1, 548–49.
30. *Ibid.*, 573.
31. 12 *Ill.*, 183; *LCL*, 139.
32. Beveridge, Vol. 1, 573.
33. 12 *Ill.*, 399; *LCL*, 148.
34. 4 *Ill.*, 104; *LCL*, 20.
35. *10 Peters*, 474.
36. 4 *Ill.*, 491; *LCL*, 39.

Part III

Chapter Thirteen

Court Procedures

THE IMPORTANCE OF THE LARGE BODY of legal precedents, known as the English common law, has been emphasized in earlier chapters. The state of Illinois adopted this body of law in 1819 to protect the rights of its citizens. The English common law, which evolved from hundreds of years of appellate court decisions and statutes enacted by the British Parliament, gave the new state a comprehensive body of law, providing for an orderly society with recognized rules of behavior to protect individual rights. The knowledge of these rules could be used in resolving disputes between individuals, and if that failed, the same common-law rules would be applied in a court resolution.

The adoption of the common law also provided Illinois with a system of trial and appellate courts and a system to regulate court procedure that had been developed in England to support the common law. The court system could only efficiently operate with formal rules which defined as precisely as possible the issue in dispute. Guidelines also were needed to regulate court procedure including the presentation of factual evidence and the resultant decision, along with appropriate retribution.

These rules were more than mere technicalities; the system would not have worked without them. Initially, they were strictly interpreted; cases were lost when the rules were not strictly adhered to, regardless of the underlying right or wrong of the issue in question. Conflict about them in the trial courts resulted in the Illinois Supreme Court serving as the ultimate arbiter.

In fact, all the trial cases appealed to the Illinois Supreme Court are based upon the losing party's contention that some procedural error was committed during the court proceedings. The basis for every appeal is an alleged error in the trial court proceedings; otherwise, the losing party's petition for appeal is not accepted by the state's highest court. Thus, all the cases included in this volume have involved some alleged error. A point was not made of this earlier because I wanted to emphasize the presentation of the cases as depicting the development of the common law of Illinois and

Abraham Lincoln's importance in that phase of history.

I now present twenty cases in which the technical errors committed did not involve important legal precedents. These cases illustrate the great importance placed on compliance with the rules by the Supreme Court in its earliest days, and how this rigidity was modified over a period of time to better serve justice and save time and expense. Flexibility in interpretation of the rules, when no advantage was gained by either party through such flexibility, was deemed proper as the common law evolved in Illinois.

These cases also indicate the continued adherence to the common-law rules by the trial courts, with the Supreme Court providing some flexibility in overruling specific actions of strict adherence by the trial court judges. The trial court judges had a duty to follow the rules as they existed at the time of the trials. The Supreme Court had the power to change or amend procedural rules, and thus to establish new precedence when the same procedural point occurred in subsequent trials. Thus the precedence in common-law procedures evolved—with the Supreme Court introducing the flexibility required by the needs for justice.

In the next chapter I again refer to this sample of the importance of technicalities when we present eleven cases argued by the firm of Lincoln & Herndon in the Illinois Supreme Court in 1860. Ten of these were lost because the procedural rules were not followed by the lawyer representing the appealing party. I hypothesize that Herndon, rather than Lincoln, was the primary attorney in each of these instances, as Lincoln was preoccupied with his presidential campaign in 1860, a very important Illinois Central Railroad case, and federal court cases.

The first case appealed to the Illinois Supreme Court in which Lincoln was involved was *Grimsley & Levering v. Klein*,[1] June term 1837. This was a trial of the right of property brought by Joseph Klein against William Grimsley and Laurison Levering before Judge Stephen T. Logan in the Sangamon County Circuit Court. Klein, the landlord of a tenant named Bailey, seized his goods as security for overdue rent. These same goods were later taken in execution in a suit against Bailey brought by Grimsley and Levering. Klein, in order to prove Bailey's indebtedness to him, was permitted to read in evidence, without any proof of its execution, a lease signed by Bailey. Grimsley and Levering objected. Judge Logan overruled the objection and gave a judgment to Klein. John T. Stuart and M. McConnel represented Grimsley and Levering.

The Illinois Supreme Court, in an opinion written by Justice Wilson, reversed this judgment, and remanded the cause for a new trial because the judge erred in overruling the objection to the reading of the lease as evidence. Grimsley and Levering were not parties to the lease. A lease cannot be read in evidence, except as between the parties to the same, without proof of its execution.

In *Covell et al. v. Marks*,[2] December term 1837, Merrit L. Covell had a judgment by default rendered in the McLean County Circuit Court reversed by the Illinois Supreme Court with the cause remanded for a new trial. In that retrial, judgment was again rendered against them by default because of a procedural matter, and again the Supreme Court ruled judgment by default should not have been ruled against them. The lower court was reversed again and the case remanded. Here were two cases covering the same subject matter involving the same parties with the trial courts deciding against the same party on procedural matters and the supreme court reversing both trial court judgments, and remanding the causes to be tried again if the aggrieved party so wanted. There is no record in the supreme court to indicate there was a new trial.

In the first case, Jacob Marks had brought an action of *assumpsit* against Covell *et al.*, who had filed a plea of non-*assumpsit*. For some reason, not explained in the opinion, judgment by default was given against them. The Supreme Court, in an opinion written by Justice Lockwood, reversed that judgment and remanded the cause, with instructions to the circuit court to set aside the default.

The case was renewed as *Covell et al. v. Marks*,[3] December term 1838. Marks received permission from the McLean County Circuit Court to amend his declaration (the pleading by the plaintiff which states the cause of action) by adding to the description of his note: "with twelve per cent, from the date until paid." Covell *et al.* made a motion for a continuance of the cause, which was refused. Judgment was again rendered against them by default.

The Illinois Supreme Court, in an opinion written by Chief Justice Wilson, reversed the judgment and remanded the cause. In cases wherein the amendment to a pleading is a substantive one, the defendant (in this instance, Covell *et al.*) is entitled to a continuance. The addition of the interest in the declaration was substantive because it increased the defendant's liability.

Scammon v. Cline,[4] December term 1840, was the first case heard by the Illinois Supreme Court in which Lincoln was listed as counsel. It commenced in a justice of the peace court, and was appealed by Lincoln's opponent to a circuit court where the appeal was dismissed. Lincoln proved the court had no jurisdiction to hear the case. This ruling was appealed to the Supreme Court.

Jonathan Y. Scammon brought an action against Cornelius Cline before Alexander Heely, a justice of the peace in Boone County. Cline had the cause removed to Hiram Waterman, who was another justice of the peace in the same county. The brief report does not identify the issue or why it was moved. Cline may have felt he had more of a chance of success with Justice Waterman. A judgment in Cline's favor was rendered on February 21, 1839.

Scammon then appealed to the Boone County Circuit Court. His appeal bond was approved by the court clerk on March 1, 1839. The act fixing the time of holding the Boone County Circuit Court passed on March 2, 1839. Previously, the court having jurisdiction over that area was the Jo Daviess County Circuit Court. The case was continued until April, 1840, when Cline moved to dismiss the appeal because it was taken to the Circuit Court of Boone County before any court was appointed in that county. Judge Dan Stone sustained the motion and dismissed the appeal.

G. Spring and J.Y. Scammon (presumably the plaintiff listed as "Jonathan Y. Scammon") represented Scammon in the appeal. Lincoln and J. L. Loop represented Cline. Chief Justice Wilson wrote the Illinois Supreme Court opinion, claiming that the circuit-court appeal had been improperly dismissed. He concluded that Boone County Circuit Court must be considered to have been in existence when the court clerk was appointed—which was earlier than March 1, 1839. Thus, the judgment was reversed and the cause remanded for trial.

In *Duncan v. McAfee*,[5] December term 1840, Lincoln's opponent appealed a judgment because the name used by an obligor on a note was not exactly the same as that used when he was sued. The court said this discrepancy was not sufficently material to affect the court's decision. This case was an appeal of an action of debt in the Fayette County Circuit Court, before Judge Breese. James M. Duncan executed a $200 note to John S. Greathouse, who then assigned it to Isaac McAfee. When the note was due, McAfee sued Duncan. Judgment was rendered for McAfee, who was represented by O. Peters and J. S. Greathouse. Logan represented McAfee in the follow-up action. F. Forman represented Duncan..

Justice Breese wrote the Illinois Supreme Court opinion, which affirmed the previous judgment. Duncan's defense had been that he signed the note "J. M. Duncan," but was sued in the name of "James M. Duncan." Thus, he claimed the form of the written promise was not in sufficient form to be actionable. Breese had presided at the original trial to resolve the issues against Duncan, and probably had no hesitation when writing this opinion of the court.

After rendering the above-mentioned opinion, the Illinois Supreme Court demonstrated its flexibility when it allowed the judgment to be amended upon the motion of the winning party, in *Duncan v. McAfee*,[6] July term 1841. In this action, McAfee, represented by Logan, made a motion to the Supreme Court to amend the judgment rendered earlier by the circuit court by erasing "James" and inserting "Isaac" as the given name of the defendant in error (McAfee) and by adding to the judgment of the lower court the interest due on that judgment, from the time the first judgment was rendered until the time of the latest judgment. The motion was allowed, and the record was accordingly amended. The debt was $200, and the interest was increased from $6.50 to $22.50.

Leigh v. Hodges,[7] July term 1841, was another case in which the Illinois

Supreme Court held that if, in its opinion, substantial justice has been done in the trial court, irregularities of some technical points can be overlooked. This was an action of debt brought by Emmanuel J. Leigh against Seth Hodges, as surety for an individual whose surname was English in the Montgomery County Circuit Court. Leigh had sued English in an action of slander, and judgment was rendered for English. Leigh decided to appeal, but instead entered into an agreement with English, stating that if he did not appeal, English would pay the costs, including the attorneys' fees for the original trial.

Hodges agreed to be a surety to guarantee that English would carry out his promises. Testimony supporting this agreement included a statement by Leigh that he "was too good a Virginian to claim more than the costs." English paid the costs and some of the attorneys' fees, and left the state. Leigh, apparently having been away from Virginia too long, brought this action against Hodges to recover what amount, if any, English had not paid. Judgment was rendered for Hodges, who was represented by Logan and James Shields. After Leigh's motion for a new trial was denied, he brought this appeal. D. A. Smith represented Leigh.

The Supreme Court, in an opinion written by Justice Breese, affirmed the judgment. After reciting the procedural facts and certain elements of the evidence, Breese wrote: "Sitting, as the Circuit Court was, in disposing of this motion for a new trial, we are only to ascertain if, upon the whole case as presented, substantial justice has been done. It does not always follow that a new trial will be granted, even if the jury finds against the weight of evidence, against the instructions of the court, or through misdirection of the court on a point of law, provided the court is satisfied that justice is done." He went on to say that in this case, "where a surety is sued, after assurance by the plaintiff (Leigh) that the matter had been adjusted with the principal (English), who had left the country with property," justice had been done.

Wilcox v. Woods et al.,[8] July term 1841, is another example where an alleged breach of a technicality did not prevent justice being served. It also presents a special pleading, the "demurrer." A demurrer is a pleading where the party demurring says, in effect, that even if what the opposing party states in his pleading is true, he still should not win because he has failed to present adequate facts to justify a judgment in his favor. The advantage of it is that the facts then do not have to be proven by witnesses and documents—and time, energy, and attorneys' fees are saved by all concerned. If a party demurs and the demurrer is overruled, the party may still make a response, and a trial would result. In this case, Logan was so confident that his client (Wilcox) was correct, he elected to appeal the ruling on the demurrer rather than enter ano-ther defense to the suit. W. A. Minshall and C. Walker represented Woods *et al.*

In this case, Nathaniel G. Wilcox made a note to Woods, Christy & Co.

for $250.63, which was in default. James Woods, William T. Christy, and James C. Christy sued Wilcox, who demurred because they had sued as individuals rather than as a partnership. The Schuyler County Circuit Court, Judge Peter Lott presiding, overruled the demurrer, and when Wilcox made no further pleading, it awarded judgment for Woods *et al.*

The Illinois Supreme Court decision, written by Justice Treat, affirmed the judgment. Even though Woods and the two Christys sued as individuals, it was clear they were partners and had a proper cause of action. Thus, the overruling of the demurrer was proper. Secondly, Wilcox contended there had been no formal joinder of the demurrer; thus the procedure was improper. However, after judgment, the court will presume there was a joinder in the demurrer, or that it was waived by the defendant, especially, as in this case, where no objection appears on the record. Thirdly, under the practice act, a judge has the power to set the damages in the judgment when the judgment is given in default.

In *Warren v. Nexsen*,[9] July term 1841, Edward A. Nexsen *et al.* brought an action of *assumpsit* in the Hancock County Circuit Court before Judge Stephen A. Douglas against Calvin A. Warren. The facts of the case are not given in the opinion, since they were not involved in the appeal. The appeal was based entirely on procedural rulings, and the entire opinion is explanatory of those elements of the case only. As in some prior cases, the court stated that the important consideration was that justice was done despite questionable adherence to all the technicalities.

The only subject covered in this Supreme Court decision was the propriety of the judge's rulings on alleged defects in the pleading. The original judge was Stephen A. Douglas; the Supreme Court decision was written by Justice Stephen A. Douglas. Some of Judge Douglas's rulings were deemed incorrect by the Supreme Court and it, with Justice Douglas having the privilege of pointing out to Judge Douglas the errors of his ways, reversed the judgment and remanded the cause. Nexsen *et al.* were represented by Logan and C. Walker. Warren was represented by A. Williams.

The defendants responded to the complaint with an answer containing two subjects or counts. The plaintiff responded with six pleas, each of which professing to answer but part of each declaration. Since the plaintiff had not pleaded to the entire declaration of the defendants, the defendants moved for a discontinuance, which was granted. The plaintiff had moved for a judgment on the points which were not answered in the declaration, which was not granted.

The court cited common law historical precedents where, in similar situations, if one party does not answer all the parts of a pleading, the case will be discontinued. However, in some subsequent cases—in the interest of doing justice in a case, and in not allowing technical breaches to impede justice—the court said: "We think the authorities cited fully justify the following just and reasonable rule: that the plaintiff may correct his error, upon the payment of costs, at anytime before final judgment, during the term at which the plea of replication, is filed." Thus, "the court should have sustained the plaintiff's motion, upon the payment of costs, and have rendered judgment accordingly, and for not having done so, the judgment is reversed, and the cause remanded for further proceedings not inconsistent with this decision."

The common law had long-standing rules about the admissibility of oral evidence in a trial. *Palmer v. Logan*,[10] July term 1841, represents a modification of one of those rules and is indicative of the flexibility of the Supreme Court to change rules when necessary to do justice. In this case, Erastus W. Palmer sold Richard A. Logan two lots in Pittsfield, and Logan gave him two notes aggregating $1987. The notes were unpaid, and Palmer brought this action to collect. Unfortunately, he could not find the notes and contended that Logan either had them or had destroyed them. The Morgan County Circuit Court excluded oral testimony, including that of Palmer attesting to the existence of these notes, and Judge William Thomas entered a judgment for Logan. The defendant Richard A. Logan was represented by Stephen T. Logan, J. J. Hardin, and D. A. Smith. M. McConnel and J. H. McDougall represented Palmer.

The Supreme Court, in an opinion written by Justice Scates, reversed the judgment and remanded the cause. Oral evidence, including that of the plaintiff (Palmer), should be sufficient to establish the existence of lost notes, and Scates referenced the law in other states as follows:

> In New York, Pennsylvania and North Carolina, the testimony of the plaintiff is admissible as to the loss of an instrument, so as to lay the foundation for the introduction of inferior proof of its execution and contents, such testimony being addressed to the court solely. Much serious and irreparable injustice might be done to individuals should a different rule prevail. There are many circumstances which might, and most probably would, prevent any other person from knowing the fact of loss or destruction of a private writing. To deny him the benefit of his own oath would, in many cases, amount to a denial of justice. We think the rule sustained by both reason and justice.

Hinton et al. v. Husbands,[11] December term 1841, is a good example of the successful use of the demurrer. This case was an action of *assumpsit* on a promissory note brought in Sangamon County Circuit Court before Judge Treat. Moses Hinton and others had signed a blank piece of paper and delivered it to James W. Allen, who said he would have a note written on it and then discount it at a bank. Instead he discounted it with Flower Husbands, who brought this action to collect on the note. Hinton *et al.* pleaded that the note was invalid because it was used for another purpose than that for which it was intended. Husbands demurred to this plea, which was sustained and judgment was entered for Husbands in the amount of $761.40. Husbands was represented by Stephen T. Logan, and Hinton by A. T. Bledsoe and S. Strong.

This judgment was affirmed by the Illinois Supreme Court, in an opinion written by Justice Breese. The only question was whether the demurrer was properly sustained. The circuit court ruled it was, and the Supreme Court concurred. The opinion only speaks to the adequacy of the various pleas. The defendants pleaded against an action to collect on this promissory note, since they had only signed a blank piece of paper. The common law at the time stated that, in an instance when a party signs a blank note to be filled in by another party, and it is then transferred to a third party who acts in good faith, the third party prevails. That is what happened here, and the allegations of Hinton *et al.* were self-defeating. The plaintiff's demurrer admitted all the facts the defendants alleged, and the true facts they presented negated any possible defense as a matter of law.

Many of the preceding cases demonstrated the flexibility of the Illinois Supreme Court to modify the common-law rules of procedure to obtain justice. However, the court did not attempt to do this when a legislative statute specified what elements were necessary in a certain situation to constitute a cause against another person for an alleged wrong. An example of this is illustrated by the following action, which was brought to enforce a mechanic's lien.

In *Logan v. Dunlap*,[12] December term 1841, the Supreme Court commenced its opinion thusly: "This is professed by proceeding under the 'Act for the benefit of mechanics' for the purpose of acquiring a lien upon the mill of the defendant." The petition set out a note wherein Abel Logan offered to pay Dunlap $166.81 in thirty days with twelve percent interest. The note also said: "The above sum due for work on my mill." Abel Logan, represented by Stephen T. Logan and W. A. Minshall demurred. This was overruled by Judge Peter Lott in the Schuyler County Circuit Court and a judgment was entered for Dunlap. M. McConnel and W. A. Richardson represented Dunlap.

The Supreme Court, in an opinion written by Justice Wilson, reversed the judgment. The statute authorizing mechanics' liens is very specific about what must be alleged in a proceeding to enforce the lien. Most of the specified items which must be pleaded were absent here. All these omissions are fatal errors, and the demurrer to the petition should have been sustained by the circuit court.

Wells v. Reynolds,[13] December term 1841, is a case involving an action brought by an attorney to recover legal fees. Several errors were made, which gives us some indication that the common law rules of court procedure were not understood by everyone involved in the proceedings. This suit was originally brought before a justice of the peace in Rock Island County, by Harmon G. Reynolds against Joel Thompson, Lucius Wells, and John P. Judson, on an account for service as an attorney, for $66.50. Judgment of nonsuit was rendered against Reynolds, who appealed to the Rock Island County Circuit Court, Thomas C. Browne presiding. Process was served on Thompson and Wells, but not Judson. Thompson made no defense, but Wells defended, and the jury awarded $37.50 against Wells alone. Wells was represented by Stephen T. Logan. J. Lamborn represented Reynolds.

Justice Breese wrote the opinion of the Illinois Supreme Court, which reversed the judgment and remanded the cause. The jury trying the case against Wells should also have included Thompson. By making no defense, Thompson admitted a cause of action to exist against him, and he should either have been included in the judgment, or the case—as it applied to Thompson—disposed of in some way. Also, when two or more are sued in a joint undertaking, the plaintiff must prove a joint contract. If the plaintiff can't do this, the suit must be dismissed.

Reynolds, suing for payment for his services as an attorney, showed ineptitude in the lower court case. Perhaps he performed the same way for Thompson, Wells, and Judson—which could explain their reluctance to pay him.

Benedict v. Dillehunt,[14] December term 1841, was commenced in a justice of peace court, appealed to the Macon County Circuit Court, with Judge Treat presiding, and then appealed to the Illinois Supreme Court. This was an interesting case in which Lincoln's opponent in the appeal argued what seems to be a ridiculous technicality. Justice Breese, in his opinion, disposed of it in two short paragraphs. C. Emerson was associated with Lincoln in representing Benjamin Dillehunt, and L. Trumbull and J. Lamborn represented Kirby Benedict.

Benjamin Dillehunt recovered $33.53 from Kirby Benedict in a justice of the peace court in Macon County. Benedict appealed to the circuit court. The Honorable Samuel H. Treat affirmed that earlier decision but, in his written opinion, he did not state the amount of the judgment. Benedict appealed to the state's highest court on the grounds that the amount of the judgment was uncertain. However, the appeal bond he posted recited the $33.53 judgment against him.

Justice Breese said there was no uncertainty, since the reference of the amount noted in the appeal bond made the amount in the circuit court certain. He dignified it by quoting a Latin phrase found in *Blackstone's Commentaries*,[15] "*id certum est, quod certum reddi potest,*" that is certain which can be made certain.

The case of *Ward v. Owens et al.*,[16] December term 1850, involved an inadequate record of the case sent to the Illinois Supreme Court. When a case was appealed, it was the responsibility of the attorneys for the one bringing the appeal (the appellant) to give reasons for the appeal—usually alleged mistakes made by the trial judge. That record had to be complete and accurate enough to allow the justices of the Supreme Court to make a measured evaluation. If the record was inadequate, the appeal was denied—without any consideration of its possible merits. The Supreme Court, when overruling a trial court decision, could remand it (send the case back) for a new trial which would take into account the ruling of the appeal. Then the losing party could reinstate the case if there was some confidence of winning it based on the adverse (to the losing party) ruling. The matter could be compromised, retried, or just abandoned.

This case concerned a bill in chancery brought by William M. Owens *et al.* against Abraham N. Ward to set aside a conveyance in the Cumberland County Circuit Court before Judge Harlan. A degree was entered for Owens *et al.,* and Ward appealed, saying the evidence presented was not adequate to support the decree. Lincoln and Herndon represented Owens *et al.* in the appeal, and Stuart and Edwards represented Ward.

The Illinois Supreme Court opinion, written by Justice Treat, agreed with Ward and reversed the decree, remanding the cause for further proceedings. The opinion, which contains no other facts about the issue or the hearing, says: "The record fails to show that any evidence was given to sustain the averments in the bill. The statute authorizing testimony to be introduced orally at the hearing was only designed to change the mode of taking proof in chancery cases, and does not dispense with the necessity of incorporating it into the record. The evidence, or the facts proved by it, ought to be stated in the record. The court will not presume that any other proof was made than that what appears in the record." Lincoln and Herndon had a duty to their client to make sure evidence supporting his side was included in the appeal record.

Whitecraft et al. v. Vanderver,[17] December term 1850, is another case reversed and remanded. Here the attorneys for the plaintiff in the trial failed to make a case against the defendant. Common law actions like this one had certain basic conditions—all of which had to be present to have a cause of action. It was up to the plaintiff's attorney to present facts proving each element in order to win. That was not done in this case.

Here Ahijah Vanderver brought an action in debt in the Christian County Circuit Court before Judge Davis to recover the penalty for cutting trees, as specified in a statute which stipulated a penalty of eight dollars per tree for certain specific types, and three dollars per tree for others—if the trees were cut without the permission of the owner. Vanderver was awarded $476, based upon the number and type of trees that were cut. Horatio Whitecraft *et al.,* who apparently had cut down the trees in question, appealed. Vanderver was represented by Lincoln & Herndon; W. J. Ferguson represented Whitecraft.

The Supreme Court decision, written by Justice Trumbull, reversed the judgment and remanded the cause, with permission for Vanderver to amend his declaration. Trumball began the opinion, as follows: "All the facts stated in the declaration may be true, and yet the defendants below have committed no act that would subject them to this action. It is not alleged that he felled the trees without having first obtained permission so to do from the owner of the land." The want of permission from the owner is a necessary ingredient to constitute the offense, and "he who would make a party liable under the statute, must allege all the facts upon which the statute creates the penalty."

The circuit court case was tried in Christian County; there is no indication whether Lincoln & Herndon had represented Vanderver there. One would assume not, because of the fundamental fatal error of inadequate pleading when the original complaint failed to include the essential words, "without my consent."

In *Schlencker et al. v. Risley*,[18] December term 1842, Lincoln represented Joshua Risley, who brought an action of trespass for false imprisonment in the Wabash County Circuit Court before Judge William Wilson against several parties, including a person named Wallace and Gideon Schlencker, who were the only parties found guilty. The sum of $333 was assessed against them. Wallace, acting as a constable, arrested Risley with the assistance of Schlencker, who was recruited as part of a posse. Wallace and Schlencker moved for a new trial based on three points: (1) that there was newly-discovered evidence, (2) that the verdict was excessive, and (3) that the judgment was defective in form. Lincoln defeated each one of these points, and the judgment against Wallace and Schlencker was appealed. O. B. Ficklin represented Schlencker.

Schlencker said he was summoned by Wallace to aid him in arresting Risley. Schlencker objected, and offered Wallace one dollar to let him out. Wallace refused it. He also offered new evidence of a witness who confirmed what Wallace and Schlencker had said to each other. Justice Caton, who wrote the opinion, said this new evidence was on a point already established at the trial, thus did not constitute adequate grounds for a new trial. Regarding the second point, he stated that courts have always manifested a reluctance to disturb verdicts on account of excessive damages, unless it is probable the jury had acted under the influence of prejudice or passion. The damages here were not so high as to induce that belief. Also it was too late (point three) to object to the form of the verdict. If objection had been raised at the delivery of the verdict, it could easily have been adjusted then. No harm was done to anyone by the form of the verdict. The lower court opinion was affirmed. Justice Semple dissented with no formal opinion to explain his decision.

Bissell v. Ryan,[19] January term 1860, was based on trial court errors in allowing an improper juror to serve, and on an erroneous ruling on a rule of evidence. The rules were exact as to what kind of evidence was proper to establish proof of facts in a trial. Admission of improper evidence could result in a reversal of a lower-court decision. This case was an action brought by Charles Ryan against William Bissell for medical services in the Sangamon County Circuit Court. Bissell had children of his brother-in-law living with him, and one became ill. Dr. Ryan was called to render medical services, and Bissell refused to pay, contending his brother-in-law should pay. The court held for Ryan. Two of the issues involved on the appeal were:

(1) One of the jurors had served on another jury within the past year, and under a statute of 1859, this was improper. Although requested to dismiss the juror, the judge allowed him to serve.

(2) Ryan contended it was the custom and usage for the head of the family to pay medical expenses for those who lived with him, and offered proof of this with the testimony of one Dr. Helm.

Herndon and Milton Hay represented Bissell on the appeal, and Stuart and Benjamin Edwards represented Ryan.

The Supreme Court, in an opinion written by Justice Breese, reversed the judgment and remanded the cause. Justice Breese, commenting on the mistake in allowing the juror to serve and explaining the need for the regulatory statute, said:

> There had grown up in our State, a formidable corps of professional jurors; persons who having no honest means of livelihood, or resorting to them, if they had, were found, at ever term, hanging around the court-houses, importuning the sheriffs and their deputies, and seizing every occasion to be put upon juries—making their living, in fact, by jury service.

Breese felt strongly that this was wrong and should not have happened here. Also, to establish a usage, it ought to be so general, uniform, and frequent, as to warrant an inference that the party against whom the right is claimed, had knowledge of it and contracted with reference to it. It will rarely happen that one witness will sufficiently establish a usage, and Dr. Helm did not do so here.

The case of *Penny v. Graves, assignee of White*,[20] December term 1850, involves oral—also called *parol*—evidence. One of the rules governing the admissibility of *parol* evidence was a critical element in this case. Thomas Penny gave a note to George Wilson and Andrew Beard for $52.13, stating: "This being for twelve per cent interest on account of hogs bought." Wilson and Beard assigned the note to James White, who assigned it to Martin Graves. The note became due, and Graves brought an action in the Sangamon County Circuit Court to collect the amount due from Penny. Penny sought to introduce evidence from two witnesses, claiming that it was orally agreed upon between himself and Wilson and Beard that interest would not be paid, assuming that interest was not asked of Penny by the people who sold him the hogs. No interest was demanded by those sellers, so Penny believed he didn't owe the money specified in his note. Judgment was entered for Graves, when the evidence of the oral (or *parol*) agreement was disallowed. Lincoln & Herndon represented Graves, and Stuart and Edwards represented Penny.

The Supreme Court opinion, written by Justice Trumball, affirmed the judgment. The court said the law was clear: "*Parol* evidence is inadmissable to vary, contradict, or explain the terms of a written agreement, and yet it is allowable to show by *parol,* that the consideration of a promissory note has wholly or in part failed, or that it was given without consideration."

It is sometimes difficult to apply this rule, but it seems clear here. The effect of the *parol* evidence here was to show the note, although absolute in terms, was in fact conditional. If Penny had intended the note to be conditional, he should have expressed it on the terms of the note. He now wanted to change the written terms of his promise, to the detriment of innocent transferees of the note, by *parol* evidence, and the law did not permit this.

In *Kincaid v. Turner,*[21] December term 1845, Lincoln and T. L. Harris represented Starling Turner. Turner sued John K. Kincaid in the Menard County Circuit Court before Judge Treat and a jury for damages incurred when a prairie fire set by Kincaid on his own property spread to and destroyed property belonging to Turner. Turner contended that Kincaid was negligent in allowing the fire to spread.

Kincaid proved that previous to this suit, he and Turner had submitted this question to three arbitrators. They could not all agree, but reported to the parties that two of them agreed on a position (deemed favorable to Kincaid), and asked the parties what to do. Both were silent. Kincaid pleaded this award was binding because silence gives consent, and constituted a defense in this suit. The jury disagreed and awarded $150 to Turner.

The Supreme Court, with Justice Caton writing the opinion, concurred. S. W. Robbins, attorney for Kincaid, in arguing that the award of the arbitrators was binding, offered an ingenious argument, without citing any legal precedent for it: "Silence gives consent, for instance, in the marriage ceremony. If a man bawled out 'aye!' when his assent was asked for by the minister, he would be considered as caring nothing about it. It is the silence that gives consent."

Lincoln argued that the jurors are sole arbiters of the facts. When questions of fact are submitted to a jury, the decision of the jury is binding. Caton, agreeing there was evidence for the defendant, said: "Although we would have been entirely satisfied and perhaps better satisfied with the verdict, had they found the other way, yet we cannot say that the verdict is so palpably against the evidence, or acted from prejudice or partiality, which should be the case before the court would be authorized to set aside the verdict.... This silence, when this remark was made (by the arbitrators), and immediately after the award of the majority was published, we do not doubt could have been sufficient to have authorized to have found that way, but it, as clearly, did not constrain them so to find. . . . When a question is fairly and intelligently submitted to a jury, their determination ought not be set aside without the most substantial reasons."

Apparently, the facts in this case more strongly favored Kincaid. Two of the arbitrators believed this, as the earlier quoted statement from Justice Caton indicates. Apparently Lincoln was very effective in convincing the jury that the facts were in Turner's favor, in spite of the contrary opinions of everyone else involved in the case.

NOTES

1. 2 *Ill.*, 343; *LCL*, 5.
2. 2 *Ill.*, 391; *LCL*, 6.
3. 2 *Ill.*, 525; *LCL*, 6.
4. 3 *Ill.*, 456; *LCL*, 10.
5. 3 *Ill.*, 559; *LCL*, 11.
6. 4 *Ill.*, 93; *LCL*, 20.
7. 4 *Ill.*, 15; *LCL*, 13.
8. 4 *Ill.*, 51; *LCL*, 16.
9. 4 *Ill.*, 38; *LCL*, 16.
10. 4 *Ill.*, 56; *LCL*, 18.
11. 4 *Ill.*, 186; *LCL*, 23.
12. 4 *Ill.*, 188; *LCL*, 24.
13. 4 *Ill.*, 191; *LCL*, 24.
14. 4 *Ill.*, 287; *LCL*, 28.
15. 2 Fl. Comm. 143; 1 Bl. Comm. 78.
16. 12 *Ill.*, 282; *LCL*, 143.
17. 12 *Ill.*, 234; *LCL*, 141.
18. 4 *Ill.*, 483; *LCL*, 38.
19. 23 *Ill.*, 517; *LCL*, 229.
20. 12 *Ill.*, 286; *LCL*, 144.
21. 7 *Ill.*, 618; *LCL*, 101.

Chapter Fourteen

January Term 1860

THE LAW PRACTICE OF LINCOLN & HERNDON was sorely tested by the partnership's performance during the January term 1860 of the Illinois Supreme Court. In this term, the firm participated in eleven cases about which reports were written. In the eleven cases, Herndon was listed as representing one of the parties—either by himself, with Lincoln, or with another attorney. Since Lincoln was extremely busy during this particular time of his career, we may assume Herndon played the major role in these cases. It was Lincoln who had had the prominent role in appellate cases during most of the life of the partnership. The Lincoln-Herndon partnership was a very successful one—despite evidence of its performance sagging at the end. The results of these ten cases for their clients amounted to nine losses and one win.

We hesitate to measure capabilities of lawyers based on won/lost results, since there can be extraneous factors in a case beyond the control of the advocates. In appellate cases, for instance, a loss could be due to inadequate representation by other lawyers at the trial level; mistakes, which could not be overcome on appeal, might have been made, or what would be counted as a loss could have been an even more adverse judgment if quality representation had not been given. However, since there is no better objective measure with which to judge legal performance, we accept won/lost results as an indication of capability.

Lincoln Day-by-Day (1960) lists Lincoln as appearing in twenty-four United States District court cases during the month of January in 1860. It also lists his presentations to the Illinois Supreme Court in two of the eleven cases, both of which his firm (Lincoln & Herndon) lost. He also represented the Illinois Central Railroad in a very important case—for both himself and the railroad. The case, due to its nature, was originally heard by the Supreme Court. The *State of Illinois v. The Illinois Central Railroad Company*,[1] January term 1860, involved taxation by the state on the property of the railroad. The state levied a tax of five percent of gross revenues on the railroad, and then later added an additional tax on the value of its property. The subject case involved how the property should be evaluated. For the year in dispute, the five percent of revenues amounted to $108,000—which everyone agreed the railroad owed. The State then demanded an additional $132,000, based on its evaluation method; under the railroad's evaluation method only $37,600 was due. Lincoln eventually won this dispute, which obviously affected not only the tax year in question but all following years. This case certainly was one of Lincoln's top priorities during January of 1860. Additional details about this case are discussed in chapter seven.

Another of Lincoln's top priorities at this time involved his ongoing efforts to retain the support of the Republican party in Illinois. With an eye toward the 1860 presidential nomination, he made speeches, met with supporters and hoped-for supporters, and prepared for the now-famous Cooper Institute lecture in February. In *With Malice Toward None* (1977), Stephen B. Oates says:

> The trouble was he [Lincoln] had no such unified support. In truth, some Illinois Republicans considered him to be too 'liberal' or too inexperienced for the Presidency. His friend Orville Browning opposed his candidacy and favored Edward Bates of Missouri. Senator Trumbull frankly went for Judge McLean. And Herndon—loyal Billy, who usually stood by Lincoln come what may—scoffed at his chances and dropped out of his inner circle. In the state at large, there was sympathy for Bates, in southern Illinois, some for Chase and Seward in the north.[2]

So since Billy dropped out of the inner circle, he had to have had much more time to devote to these eleven cases than Lincoln.

The eleven cases, together with the outcomes and brief commentaries, follow:

Walters v. Smith,[3] January term 1860—lost. Herndon and Hay represented Green B. Walters who executed a promissory note and failed to pay it according to its terms. Walters claimed an oral agreement with the payee, which was disallowed as a defense at the trial; a judgment against Walters was affirmed on appeal. A written contract could not be changed by oral evidence in this situation.

Leonard v. Villars,[4] January term 1860—lost. Herndon represented John Villars who brought an action to foreclose a mortgage against Peter R. Leonard, who was married, but whose wife was not included in the action. The trial court awarded the foreclosure but this was reversed on appeal because Leonard's wife's dower rights had been ignored. See chapter nine for additional information about this case.

Cass v. Perkins,[5] January term 1860—lost. Ford had given a mortgage to Rodham who assigned his interest to Robert Cass. The debt became due, and Cass took possession of the property several days later. In the meantime, someone placed a lien against the property which was executed by Joseph B. Perkins, the sheriff of Sangamon County. Cass, represented by Lincoln & Herndon, sought to recover the property. The trial court ruled that Cass had taken possession of the property too late to prevail. The Supreme Court affirmed the lower court.

Ritchey v. West,[6] January term 1860—lost. West sued Dr. Ritchey, who was represented by Lincoln & Herndon, for malpractice. West was treated by Dr. Ritchey, and ended up with a deformity and inability to use one of his hands. Judgment was for West, which was approved on appeal. West's attorneys failed to raise questions about admission of evidence, and thus were not allowed to do so on the appeal. Secondly, the request for a new trial on the basis of newly discovered evidence was faulty because it was not supported by an affidavit presenting alleged new facts. (Additional facts on this case can be found in chapter ten.)

Kelleher v. Tisdale,[7] January term 1860—lost. Herndon represented Edward Tisdale who brought an action to collect for goods sold by him to Daniel and Dennis Kelleher, as partners. Dennis alone was served. Tisdale won, but it was reversed on appeal because the partnership had not been proven, and the abstract prepared for the appeal was defective.

Tomlin v. Tonica and Petersburg Railroad Company,[8] January term 1860—lost. Herndon represented the railroad which brought this action to enforce a promise of Thompson and Tomlin to buy railroad shares of stock, and the trial court held for the railroad. This was reversed by the Supreme Court saying the railroad did not adequately prove the procedure in seeking the stock subscription was proper. (Chapter seven includes additional details about this case.)

Gill et al. v. Hoblit,[9] January term 1860—lost. Samuel Hoblit, represented by Lincoln & Herndon, brought an action against Richard T. Gill and two others, and served a summons on Gill, directing the sheriff of Cook County to compel Gill to appear in Logan County at a certain time. Gill did not appear, and a default judgment was entered against him. Gill appealed, and the judgment was reversed, since the summons was faulty and imposed no obligation on Gill.

Unknown Heirs of Asabel Langworthy v. Baker,[10] January term 1860—lost. Asabel Langworthy issued a promissory note in 1828, and died in 1834. In

1855 David P. Wells presented the note to Jonathan H. Baker, the public administrator of McDonough County and demanded payment with accumulated interest which exceeded the amount of the note. Baker found no assets belonging to Langworthy other than six sections of land, and after feeble efforts to find heirs of Langworthy, sold the land for $270 to Wells. A guardian *ad litem,* representing the unknown heirs, thought this was a grossly unfair procedure, and the Supreme Court agreed since, in its opinion, it estimated the value of the six sections as being $9600 at least—calling the transaction "concocted fraud." The decree of sale was set aside. Herndon represented Baker. Additional facts on this case can be found in a supplementary report at the conclusion of this chapter.

Kinsey v. Nisley et al.,[11] January term 1860—lost. Charles Kinsey, represented by Herndon, brought an action on a note against Isaac Nisley and others, who contended the note usurious. The trial court agreed, and so did the Supreme Court, when it affirmed the judgment.

Bissell v. Ryan,[12] January term 1860—won. Dr. Charles Ryan brought an action for payment for medical services he had performed for the children of William H. Bissell's brother-in-law. A judgment was entered for Ryan. Bissell was represented by Herndon and Milton Hay, who succeeded in persuading the Supreme Court to reverse the lower court's judgment, since Bissell had no obligation to pay a bill his brother-in-law should pay. (This case is covered in more detail in chapter thirteen.)

Gregg et al. v. Sanford,[13] January term 1860—lost. Hiram Sanford contracted with M.S. and David Edmiston to buy hogs for him. They did so and gave Hiram Sanford a chattel mortgage on the animals. While the hogs were still in the possession of David Edmiston, Jacob Gregg—to whom he owed money—levied on the hogs to discharge that debt. Sanford, who had a prior lien, protested, and the court enjoined sale of the hogs. The Supreme Court reversed the lower-court decision and allowed the hogs to be sold for the benefit of Gregg because the chattel mortgage had not been recorded as required by law. Lincoln & Herndon represented Sanford.

These cases appear to reflect various degrees of incompetence. Prior to this January, 1860 term, there was no similar pattern of concentrated losses, and only a few situations where it appeared that Lincoln and Herndon had been careless or uninformed about the law. There is no way of knowing when these cases went wrong. In some instances, it was in not following proper procedures before the trial—i.e., a summons improperly issued, a chattel mortgage not filed, or failure to include a wife in a foreclosure action. In some cases, the fatal error was made at the trial—i.e., failing to except to a judge's rulings on evidence, or failure to prove a stock subscription procedure. The discrepancies found in most of these cases indicated that Herndon had failed to comprehend legal mistakes which gave the case no possibility of success on appeal.

We have no way of knowing at what level, in each instance, Herndon was involved. We have no way of knowing the contribution to the mistakes any other lawyer made, including Lincoln, and if so, at what step in each of the proceedings. Going back to the won/lost statistics, we know the aggregate results were unsatisfactory.

Lincoln was very patient and understanding in his important dealings with people, as indicated by his relationships with his cabinet members, his generals, and other political leaders. These qualities served Billy Herndon in good stead in January of 1860.

The pragmatic answer to why the partnership continued, after such a string of lost cases, could be due to Lincoln's patience and forbearance or the impracticality of picking a new partner so close to the Republican convention in May. Malpractice suits against medical doctors had been brought to courts by this time, but we found none against attorneys. In any event, the won/lost record of Lincoln & Herndon did not seem to be a factor which would influence Lincoln's nomination or election.

SUPPLEMENTARY REPORT

Supreme Court Decries "Concocted Fraud" in Herndon Case

The following case, *Unknown Heirs of Asabel Landworthy v. Baker*,[14] listed Herndon as the sole attorney. The facts of this case are simple: Asabel Langworthy gave a demand note to N. B. & H. Wells on October 14, 1828, for $618.28 plus interest. Langworthy died September 24, 1834, owning six sections of land and leaving no will. On April 4, 1855, one David P. Wells appeared at the county court of McDonough County with proof of Langworthy's death, requesting grant of letters of administration of the estate for Jonathan W. Baker, the public administrator for the county, which were issued. At the day set for submitting claims against the estate, Wells appeared and presented the promissory note for $618.28, plus a demand for $989.24 interest. The court allowed the entire claim and ordered it to be paid.

Since there were no other assets in the estate except the real property, the court ordered the land to be sold. The six sections of land (960 acres) were sold to David P. Wells for the sum of $270. A guardian *ad litem* had been appointed by the court to protect the unknown heirs of Langworthy. This guardian protested the validity of the whole procedure, and appealed the ruling to sell the land in order to have the decree ordering that sale. Herndon represented Baker, the administrator of the estate. The Supreme Court, in an opinion written by Justice Breese, set aside the decree with the concluding summary of the case as follows: "We can consider the case in no other light than as a concocted fraud—fraudulent in its inception and in its consummation, and we would be remiss in our duty did we not declare all the proceedings void. The decree ordering the sale is set aside." Justice Breese mentioned in his opinion that the land was probably worth at least $10 an acre, which would value the land at a minimum at $9600—certainly a real bargain at the $270 David Wells had paid.

We don't know at what point Herndon became involved with David Wells. The most significant date here is April 4, 1855, when Wells initiated the legal proceedings to sell the valuable property which Asahel Langworthy owned when he died in 1834. Wells presumably had a lawyer at that time, but probably not Lincoln or Herndon, for several reasons.

The proceedings were in McDonough County, whose seat of government is Macomb, which is about one hundred miles from Springfield. Macomb County is neither in the Eighth Judicial Circuit, where Lincoln did most of his work, nor in any county outside the eighth which has been identified as a county where Lincoln practiced. According to *Lincoln Day-by-Day*, Lincoln was in Logan County for the Spring term, starting April 2, and in McLean county for its Spring term, starting on April 9. Both of these counties are about as far from Macomb as Springfield. We also know Herndon didn't have Lincoln's passion for practicing in other counties. Most of Herndon's work was in Springfield, with some other legal activities concentrated in Petersburg, located about thirty miles from Springfield.

This case next surfaces at the appeal stage during the January term 1860 of the Illinois Supreme Court when it was argued and decided. According to *Lincoln Day-by-Day*, Lincoln argued two cases in the Supreme Court during this term, neither being this case. He was also involved in twenty-four appearances before the federal district court in January, plus a significant Illinois Central Railroad case noted earlier. Presumably, Herndon argued the case; if he had counsel from Macomb assisting him, it is not noted in the case report.

Lincoln was a pragmatic lawyer who did not confine his acceptance of cases to those he was certain to win. He recognized every disagreement had two sides, and that each was entitled to competent counsel. In at least three situations, Lincoln represented one side in a case when he had represented the other side in a previous case with similar facts and identical legal questions. In each of these earlier cases (which he won) the Supreme Court established precedent which was applied by the court in each later case, and he lost. We assume he apprised his client in the second cases about the applicable law, and represented them because he believed the facts could not be proven by the opposition, or that there was something unique in each case that could distinguish it from the previous precedent-setting cases.

The major difference between the subject case here and Lincoln's other cases before the Supreme Court lies in the strong language of the court which labels this case fraud. Since it was such a reprehensibly odious situation, we assume Lincoln would have turned down a chance to represent Baker on the appeal. However, Herndon did accept it and we have no clues about how the firm decided to accept cases. Presumably each partner accepted what he wanted to, and at this time in Lincoln's career, he was really busy—possibly too busy to know Herndon had been offered this case.

David Wells was the guilty party, possibly aided by Baker and even the judge—who had a special responsibility to protect minors who could be beneficiaries of a valuable estate, even if unknown at the time. Justice Breese said a delay of twenty-seven years between the death of an obligor on a demand note and its presentation for payment was too much delay, and there was a strong presumption that the note had already been paid. Breese implied that this is what Baker should have pleaded in defense of Wells's claim. Baker also could have tried harder to find an heir since there was one then, to quote the language of the case, "residing in this state, in a county not very distant from the scene of these machinations, more than ten years, and without any notice, except such notice as may be found in a newspaper published in an obscure village, and that paper of very limited circulation, that any proceedings were pending, or had been had against the lands until they were sold." About Baker, Justice Breese went on to say:

> The administrator interposes no defense to a claim he knew he could successfully defend, obtains the order to sell the land, and six quarter sections; in all, nine hundred and sixty acres are sold to D. P. Wells for the trifling sum of two hundred and seventy dollars. There is no proof of the actual value of the lands before us, but from our general knowledge of the counties in which they are located, we feel well satisfied that they would average at least ten dollars an acre. Thus by the contrivance of these parties, a valuable inheritance, in justice and right belonging to the plaintiff in error below, the only child and heir at law of the deceased Langworthy, for the merest trifle, is wrested from her if the proceedings be valid.

NOTES

1. 27 *Ill.*, 234; *Lincoln and The Common Law*, 234.
2. Oates, Stephen B., *With Malice Toward None: The Life of Abraham Lincoln.* New York: Harper & Row, (1977), 170.
3. 23 *Ill.*, 283; *LCL*, 218.
4. 23 *Ill.*, 322; *LCL*, 219.
5. 23 *Ill.*, 326; *LCL*, 219.
6. 23 *Ill.*, 329; *LCL*, 220.

7. 23 *Ill.*, 354; *LCL*, 221.
8. 23 *Ill.*, 374; *LCL*, 221.
9. 23 *Ill.*, 420; *LCL*, 225.
10. 23 *Ill.*, 430; *LCL*, 226.
11. 23 *Ill.*, 452; *LCL*, 227.
12. 23 *Ill.*, 517; *LCL*, 229.
13. 24 *Ill.*, 17; *LCL*, 229.
14. See reference number 10.

Appendices

Bibliography

The two books most used for law reference in the early nineteenth century:

Blackstone's Commentaries. Abraham Lincoln first studied law from this book; the generally accepted and most popular treatise on English common law. Edited by Sir William Blackstone (1723-1780), English jurist.

Equity Pleadings. Edited by Joseph Story (1779-1845), United States jurist and editor of treatises on common law.

* * *

American Jurisprudence 2nd. Rochester, New York: Lawyers Cooperative Publishing Company, 1950.

Baker, Jean H., *Mary Todd Lincoln: A Biography.* New York and London: W. W. Norton & Company, 1987.

Bannister, Dan W., *Lincoln and the Common Law.* Springfield, Illinois: Human Services Press, 1992.

Beveridge, Albert J., *Abraham Lincoln, 1809–1858.* 2 vols. Boston and New York: Houghton Mifflin Company, 1928. Library edition, Boston and New York: Houghton Mifflin Company, 1928. 4 vols.

Black's Law Dictionary, 5th edition. St. Paul, Minnesota: West Publishing Company, 1979.

Buck, Solon J., *Illinois in 1818.* Urbana: University of Illinois Press, 1967 (second edition, revised and reprinted on the occasion of the Sesquicentennial of the State of Illinois).

Caton, John Dean, *Early Bench and Bar of Illinois.* Chicago: Chicago Legal News Company, 1893.

Crossley, Frederic B., *Courts and Lawyers of Illinois.* Chicago: The American Historical Society, 1916.

Donald, David, *Lincoln's Herndon.* New York: Random House, 1948.

Duff, John J., *A. Lincoln, Prairie Lawyer.* New York and Toronto: Rinehart & Company, 1960.

Howard, Robert, *Illinois: A History of the Prairie State.* 1972.

Illinois Reports (sometimes abbreviated Ill. Rep.) are the official reports of the Illinois Supreme Court decisions. Volume I was published in 1831.

Lincoln Newsletter (The), Lincoln, Illinois: The Lincoln College Museum.

Linder, General Usher D., *Reminiscences.* Chicago: Chicago Legal News Company, 1879.
Lusk, D. W., *Eighty Years of Illinois: Politics and Politicans, 1809–1889.* Springfield, Illinois: printed by H. W. Roakker.
Neeley, Mark E., Jr., *The Abraham Lincoln Encyclopedia.* New York: Da Capo, 1982.
Oates, Stephen B., *With Malice Toward None: The Life of Abraham Lincoln.* New York: Harper & Row, 1984.
——, *Abraham Lincoln. The Man Behind the Myths.* New York: Harper & Row, 1984.
Palmer, John N., *The Bench and Bar of Illinois.* Chicago: The Lewis Publishing Company, 1899.
Starr, John W., Jr., *Lincoln and the Railroads.* New York: Dodd, Mead & Company, 1927.
Thomas, Benjamin P., *Abraham Lincoln, A Biography.* New York: Alfred A. Knopf, 1952.
Whitney, Henry Clay, *Life on the Circuit with Lincoln.* Boston: Estes and Lauriat, 1892. New edition, Caldwell, Idaho: The Caxton Printers, 1940.

Glossary

Circuit Court The court system of Illinois was organized by a division of contiguous counties as designated circuits. Trial courts were held in the various county seats at designated times, with a circuit court judge presiding. As developed more fully in chapter three, at times the supreme court justices served as judges, each one assigned to a specific circuit. At other periods, circuit court judges were elected to preside at the trials. Lincoln primarily practiced in the eighth judicial circuit, and his participation with lawyers in appellate work from other circuits is developed in chapter four.

Common Law forms for law suits:

Assumpsit An action to recover damages for non-performance of a contract or when money has been received which in good conscience belongs to another.

Debt An action for a sum of money due under an express agreement.

Replevin An action wherein an owner or anyone who is entitled to repossession of personal property may recover from one who wrongfully has those goods in his possession.

Trespass An action for recovery of damages for any injury to one's person, property, or relationship with another.

Trover An action against a person who has found another's personal property and wrongfully converted it to his own use.

Demurrer A formal answer to a pleading which admits the truth of the adversary's contentions, but which states even if those facts are true they do not justify the action; thus, the proceedings should be dismissed in favor of the party pleading the demurrer. The formal mode of disputing the sufficiency in law of the pleading of the other side.

Equity (or Chancery) Court A system which administers justice according to fairness as contrasted to the strictly formalized rules of common law. In Illinois it was administered in the same court system as the common law.

Ex Rel. (abbreviation for *ex relatione*) A legal proceeding instituted by an attorney general on the instigation of a person who has a private interest in the matter.

Joinder Uniting with another person in some legal step or proceeding.

Magna Carta The name of the charter granted by King John of England at Runnymede in 1215, which is justly regarded as the foundation of English constitutional liberty. It secured the personal liberties of citizens, and their rights to property.

Mandamus Latin for "we command." An order issued by a court to compel a public officer to do specific things in performance of his legal responsibilities.

Parol Expressed by speech only, not writing; used interchangeably with oral.

Per curian By the court; it is used to distinguish an opinion of the whole court from an opinion written by any one justice.

Pro rata Proportionally; according to a certain measure.

Quo warranto A claim against an incumbent office holder to inquire by what authority he supports his claim to office.

Remand the cause When an appellate court reverses a judgment of a trial court, it return the matter to the court in which it was tried, so the case can be re-tried if the party who initiated the proceedings in the original trial (the plaintiff or complainant) so desires. In the event of a retrial, the trial judge must make his rulings consistent with the appellate court's decision.

Term A designated time for scheduled court proceedings in a particular court, both in the circuit trial courts and in the supreme court. The schedule was identified by the month in which the proceedings were to be commenced, such as January term 1860.

Index of Illinois Supreme Court Opinions

Below is a list of cases that Lincoln participated in before the Illinois Supreme Court—listed as the names appear in the court records.

Abrams & Klein v. Camp   121
Adams et al. v. County of Logan   54
Alton & Sangamon RR Co. v. Baugh   89
Alton & Sangamon Railroad Company v. Carpenter   88
Anderson v. Ryan   114
Bailey v. Cromwell et al., adm. of Cromwell   132
Barret v. The Alton & Sangamon Railroad Company   74
Benedict v. Dillehunt   159
Bissell v. Ryan   161, 168
Broadwell et al. for the use of Thompson et ux. v. Broadwell   137
Browning v. City of Springfield   56
Brundage v. Camp   67
Bryan v. Bates   58
Byrne v. Stout   68, 144
Buckmaster et al. v. Jackson, ex dem. Carlin   146
Cannon v. Kenney   65
Casey v. Casey   105
Cass v. Perkins   167
Chase v. DeBolt   95
Chicago, Burlington & Quincy RR Co. v. Wilson   89
Compher et al. v. The People   63, 135
Covell et al. v. Marks   153
Cowgill, (W. Y.) & Co. v. Long   60
Cowls v. Cowls   133

Crabtree v. Kile & Nichols   69
Cunningham v. Fithian et al.   107
Davis, adm. of Hains v. Harkness   102
Dorman et ux. v. Lane, Administration of Robinson   142
Dorman et ux. v. Yost, Administrator of John Lane et al.   143
Duncan v. McAfee   154
Dunlap v. Smith et al., assignees of State Bank   145
Edgar County v. Mayo   139
Edmunds v. Hildreth et al.   109
Edmunds v. Myers et al.   108, 110
Eldridge v. Rowe   136
England v. Clark   66
Evans v. Merriweather   147
Favor et al. v. Marlett   26
Field et al. v. Rawlings   48
Field v. The People ex rel. McClernand   20, 46
Gill et al. v. Hoblit   167
Gilman et al. v. Hamilton et al.   131
Grable v. Margrave   113, 116
Gregg et al. v. Sanford   168
Griggs et al. v. Gear   129, 131
Grimsley & Levering v. Klein   152
Harbach et al. v. Gear   131
Harris v. Shaw et al.   54
Hildreth v. Turner   110
Hinton et al. v. Husbands   157

Illinois Central RR Co. v. Allen 90
Illinois Central RR Co. v. Hayes et al. 83
Illinois Central RR Co. v. McLean County et al. 61, 84
Illinois Central RR Co. v. Morrison and Crabtree 81
Johnson v. Richardson et al. 126
Johnson v. Weedman 68
Jones v. The People 53
Kelleher v. Tisdale 167
Kimball v. Cook 27, 28, 29
Kincaid v. Turner 163
Kinsey v. Nisley et al. 168
Klein et al. v. Mather 132
Klein v. The Alton & Sangamon Railroad Company 75
Lane et al. v. Doe ex dem. Dorman et ux. 142
Langworthy, (Unknown Heirs of Asabel) v. Baker 167, 169
Laswell v. Hickox & Hickox 55
Leigh v. Hodges 154
Leonard v. Villars 98, 166
Lewis v. Moffett 140
Lilly v. Waggoner, cons. of Waggoner 138
Logan v. Dunlap 158
Martin & Warfield v. Dryden et al. 96
Mason v. Park 134
Maus v. Worthing 5
McAtee v. Enyart 105
McConnel v. Delaware Mutual Safety Fire Insurance Company et al. 127
McDonald v. Fithian et al. 106
McKinley v. Watkins 69
McNamara v. King 115
Miller v. Whittaker 111, 112
Miller v. Young 112
Myers v. Turner, ante 110
Myers et al. v. Turner 110
Paine & Alexander v. Frazier et al. 87
Palmer v. Logan 157
Patterson et ux. v. Edwards et al. 119
Penny v. Graves, assignee of White 162
People ex rel. Ballou v. Dubois 53
People ex rel. Billings v. Bissell 49
People ex rel. Davenport v. Brown et al. 59

People ex rel. Koerner & Yates v. State Bank of Ridgley et al. 51
People ex rel. Lanphier & Walker v. Hatch 50
People ex rel. City of Springfield v. Power 57
People ex rel. Stephenson v. Marshall 51
People ex rel. Stevenson et al. v. Higgins 61
Petersburg, President & Trustees v. Mappin et al. 58
Petersburg, (President & Trustees of) v. Metzker 59
Reed v. Johnson 70
Regnier v. Cabot et al. 118
Rhinehart v. Schuyler et al. 62
Ritchey v. West 116, 167
Rogers v. Hall 117
Roney v. Monaghan 116
Rusk v. Newell 95
Ryder v. Alton & Sangamon RR Co. 75
St. Louis, Alton & Chicago Railroad Company v. Dalby 9, 90
Scammon v. Cline 153
Schlencker et al. v. Risley 161
Seeley v. Peters 6, 26, 28, 125
Shillinger v. Shillinger 100
Smith & Dunlap, Assignees of State Bank v. Dunlap 144
Smith v. Smith et al. 122
Sprague v. Illinois River Railroad Co. et al. 77
Springfield v. Hickox et al. 56
State of Illinois v. Illinois Central Railroad Company (The) 86, 165
Stewartson v. Stewartson 100
Sullivan v. People 143
Taylor et al. v. Whitney 87
Terre Haute & Alton RR Co. v. Earp 78
Tomlin v. Tonica & Petersburg Railroad Company 79, 167
Tonica & Petersburg Railroad Company v. McNeely 76
Tonica & Petersburg Railroad Company v. Stein 76
Trumbull v. Campbell 49
Trustees of Schools v. Allen et al. 60

Turley et al. v. County of Logan 52
Walters v. Smith 166
Ward v. Owens et al. 159
Warren v. Nexsen 156
Watkins v. White 66
Weatherford v. Fishback 104
Webster & Huntington v. French et al. 124
Webster et al. v. French et al. 125
Wells v. Reynolds 158

Whitecraft et al. v. Vandiver 160
Wilcox v. Woods et al. 155
Williams v. Smith 122
Williams et al., exec. of Trotter v. Blankenship et al., adm. of Trailor 137
Wren v. Moss et al. 99
Wright v. Bennett et al. 103
Young et al. v. Ward 101
Young v. Miller 111, 112

Index of State Officials, Jurists, Judges, and Attorneys

Baker, Edward D. 36, 38, 62, 66, 102, 106, 108, 118, 137
Baker, Jonathan 168, 169, 171
Ballou, Martin 53
Bangs, Mark 53
Beaumont, George Anson Oliver 41
Beckwith, Corydon 16, 112
Billings, George M. 49
Billings, H. W. 76
Bissell, William H. 49
Black, W. J. 57, 58
Blackburn (only surname noted) 70
Blackwell, R. S. 39, 50, 63, 135, 143
Bledsoe, A. T. 36, 49, 66, 114, 134, 158
Bond, Shadrack 45
Brayman, T. Mason 10, 37, 84, 124
Breese, Sidney 4, 5, 6, 10, 16, 21, 24. 25. 26, 31. 46, 47, 50, 51, 57, 59, 60, 62, 67, 73, 82, 83, 86, 95, 105, 133, 146, 154, 155, 158, 159, 162, 171
Bromwell, H. P. H. 138
Broadwell, N. M. 57
Brown, George T. 51
Brown, J. J. 107, 108
Brown, Welcome B. 59, 61. 70
Brown, William W. 38, 95, 139
Browne, Thomas C. 16, 18, 20, 130, 159
Browning, Orville W. 36, 56, 62, 85, 97, 118, 124, 144, 166
Bryan, William F. 40, 96

Bushnell, N. 36, 97, 124, 144
Butterfield, Justin 40, 46, 130
Caldwell, A. G. 51
Calhoun, John 51
Campbell, D. B. 63, 100, 135
Campbell, Thomas 42, 49, 132
Carlin, Thomas 10, 17, 46, 48
Caton, John Dean 7, 8, 9, 10, 16, 17, 22, 23, 24, 25, 26, 27, 28, 50, 52, 53, 54, 61, 69, 76, 77, 78, 89, 90, 92, 95, 99, 101, 102, 106, 110, 111, 115, 125, 126, 128, 129, 130, 134, 136, 138, 140, 161, 163, 164
Chickering, J. W. 39, 42, 130
Colton, W. 102
Conkling, James C. 36, 140
Conkling, W. J. 36, 112, 113
Constable, C. H. 41, 81, 94
Cooper, J. T. 40
Coulton, Wells 68
Cowan, Thomas P. 59, 77, 79
Cowles, A. 130, 146
Davis, David 52, 54, 56, 58, 59, 63, 75, 98, 105, 109, 110, 125, 131, 135, 137, 144, 145, 160
Davis, George T. M. 146
Davis, Leit 40, 135
Davis, Levi 46, 76, 78
Davis, O. L. 38
Denning, William A. 16, 13
Dickey, Hugh T. 116
Dickey, Theophilus Lyle 27, 41, 88, 89

Doremus, J. C. 55
Douglas, J. M. 86
Douglas, Stephen Arnold 16, 21, 33, 46, 48, 156
Doyle, R. L. 147
Du Bois, Jesse K. 53
Dummer, Henry E. 39, 77, 128
Eddy, Henry 40, 48
Edwards, Benjamin 36, 37, 50, 54, 55, 57, 58, 60, 61, 63, 66, 77, 84, 95, 105, 108, 110, 111, 118, 124, 125, 135, 138, 140, 160, 162, 163
Edwards, Cyrus 48
Edwards, Ninian Wert 21, 36, 132
Emerson, Charles 36, 37, 70, 90, 100, 159
Ferguson, William I. 36, 105, 125
Fickland, O. B. 38, 81, 88, 135, 161
Field, Alexander P. 17, 48
Field, H. P. 40
Ford, Thomas 16, 17. 20, 22, 118, 126
Forman, F. 154
Foster, William P. 16, 18, 19
Fridley, B. F. 41
Gatewood, William J. 142
Gillespie, D. 69, 123
Gillespie, Joseph 39, 69, 78, 123
Goodrich, Grant 41, 85, 89, 116
Goudy, W. C. 50, 79
Greathouse, J. S. 154
Green, A. 70, 81, 90
Greene, Henry S. 90
Gregg, D. L. 63, 135, 143
Grimshaw, J. 50, 117, 128
Hardin, John J. 38, 39, 42, 104, 130, 147, 157
Hall, Junius 39, 97
Harlan, Justin 160
Harriot, (only surname noted) 59, 76, 77
Harman, D. E. 38
Harris, T. L. 37, 38, 58, 60, 69, 70, 103, 118, 163
Heely, Alexander 153
Herndon, Elliot B. 39, 75, 116
Herndon, William Henry 3, 5, 50, 54, 56, 57, 58, 59, 60, 63, 67, 69, 70, 76, 77, 78, 79, 88, 89, 91, 100, 101, 105, 108, 110, 111, 112, 122, 123, 124, 125, 135, 138, 140, 144, 160, 161, 162, 163, 165, 166, 167, 168, 169, 170
Joy, F. 37, 84, 89
Johnson, M. Y. 42
Judd, Norman B. 79, 85
Kane, Elias Kent 45
Kitchel, A. 95
Kitchel, Wickliffe 46
Koerner, Gustavus P. 16, 22, 23, 51, 108, 114, 115, 119, 139
Krum, J. M. 39, 96, 97, 130
Lacey, Lyman 79, 110
Lamborn, Josiah 87, 122, 159
Lamon, Ward Hill 35
Lawrence, Charles B. 16, 39, 109, 144
Leonard, W. H. 37
Linder, M. F. 38, 114
Lockwood, Samuel D. 16, 20, 46, 47, 108, 114, 118, 132, 153
Logan, Stephen Trigg 33, 35, 36, 37, 49, 51, 54, 62, 65, 67, 75, 77, 84, 86, 87, 88, 89, 98, 102, 104, 105, 106, 108, 111, 117, 118, 122, 124, 132, 133, 137, 140, 144, 146, 147, 152, 154, 155, 156, 157, 158, 159
Loop, J. L. 42, 154
Lott, Peter 117, 156, 158
McClernand, John A. 46, 48, 50, 51, 142
McConnel, Murray 38, 53, 66, 119, 128, 132, 146, 152, 157, 158
McDougall, J. A. 48, 56, 157
McNeeley (only surname noted) 76
McRoberts, J. 107
Manly, Uri 51
Martin, William 76, 146
Marshall, Samuel Davis 40, 51, 141
Marshall, W. 39
Matteson, Joel A. 94
Menard, Pierre 45
Merriman, Halsey C. 37, 39, 96, 99
Minshall, W. A. 119, 155, 158

INDEX OF STATE OFFICIALS, JURISTS, JUDGES, AND ATTORNEYS   185

Montgomery, H. B. 51
Morris, B. C. 41
Morrison, C. M. 112
Moulton, Samuel W. 37, 78, 101
Nelson, R. S. 106
Parks, C. 101
Parks, Samuel C. 36, 37, 101
Pearson, J. 116, 139
Pierson, G. T. 98
Peters, O. 27, 59, 125, 136, 154
Phillips, Joseph 16, 18
Powell, Elihu 39, 40, 96, 99
Power, William D. 57
Purple, Norman H. 16, 22, 23, 55, 56, 59, 62, 63, 99, 103, 116, 118, 132, 135
Rawlings, Moses M. 48
Reed (only surname noted) 70
Reeves, O. T. 60
Reynolds, John 16, 18, 20, 21
Reynolds, Thomas 16, 19
Richardson, W. A. 158
Ridgley, Nicholas 51
Robbins, S. W. 100, 118, 130, 137, 163
Robinson, John M. 16, 22
Rush, Elam 143
Scammon, Jonathan Y. 153
Scates, Walter B. 16, 21, 24, 25, 40, 48, 52, 57, 68, 84, 96, 97, 99, 107, 109, 110, 113, 122, 141, 142, 157
Semple, James 16, 22, 96, 161
Shaw, A. 41
Shields, James 16, 22, 24, 46, 48, 107, 108, 113, 141, 155
Sibley, Joseph S. 117
Skinner, Mark 41
Skinner, Onias C. 16, 24, 25, 52, 84, 90, 127
Smedes, A. K. 138
Smith, David A. 36, 38, 39, 42, 61, 76, 77, 130, 131, 147, 155, 157
Smith, Theophilius W. 16, 20, 46, 47, 76, 146
Spring, G. 41, 116, 154
Steele, James 83
Stone, Dan 154
Strong, N. D. 39, 97
Strong, S. 36, 55, 158
Stuart, John Todd 17, 33, 36, 37, 50, 52, 54, 56, 58, 60, 61, 63, 77, 84, 95, 105, 108, 110, 111, 124, 125, 132, 135, 140, 152, 160, 162, 163
Summers, Charles 83
Thomas, Jesse B. 16, 22, 37, 39, 41, 46, 62, 99, 107, 108, 115, 142,
Thomas, William 36, 38. 39, 105, 133, 157
Thornton, A. 101, 138
Treat, Samuel H. 16, 20, 23, 24, 25, 49, 55, 56, 58, 59, 60, 65, 66, 67, 68, 70, 87, 102, 103, 105, 107, 108, 113, 116, 119, 122, 132, 135, 139, 140, 143, 144, 156, 157, 159, 160, 163
Trumbull, Lyman 6, 16, 23, 24, 39, 48, 49, 53, 63, 69, 70, 87, 88, 89, 100, 126, 141, 142, 159, 160, 161, 163, 166
Underwood, William H. 68
Urquart, J. D. 37, 66
Walker, Cyrus 40, 46, 147, 155, 156
Walker, Pinckney H. 16, 24, 70, 76, 98, 101, 139
Watterman, Hiram 153
Webb, J. H. 41
Weir, W., Jr., 131
White, J. B. 36, 51, 53, 86
Whitney, Henry Clay 37, 38, 81, 83
Williams, Archibald 39, 62, 85, 109, 117, 144, 156
Wilson, I. G. 41, 89, 116
Wilson, William 4, 16, 19, 20, 46, 47, 67, 107, 114, 133, 134, 135, 152, 153, 154, 158, 161
Wingate, R. 40, 51
Woodson, David M. 16, 53, 58, 60, 61, 70, 100
Yates, Richard 51
Young, Richard M. 16, 22, 29, 62, 63, 99
Young, W. H. 40, 101, 111
Zane, C. Z. 57

Dan W. Bannister did his undergraduate work at Indiana University before serving as a cryptographer with the United States Army in World War II. After the war, he earned a J.D. degree (*cum laude*) at Albany Law School and was admitted to the bar in the state of New York. He spent thirty-five years in the insurance management business, including thirteen years as CEO of the Horace Mann Companies, whose home office in Springfield, Illinois, is only three blocks from the home of Abraham Lincoln. He has served as an officer of a number of community organizations, and was named the Copley Citizen of the year in 1971 by the Copley Newspapers in Springfield.

Bannister became involved in the study of Abraham Lincoln's experiences as a lawyer in 1989, when he began his association with the Lincoln Legal Papers project, based in Springfield. As a volunteer legal researcher for the project, he briefed Lincoln's cases before the Illinois Supreme Court. He is a member of the board of directors of the national Abraham Lincoln Association, and is currently president of the Lincoln Group of Florida, where he and his wife Audrey have their winter home. His first Lincoln publication was *Lincoln and the Common Law,* published in 1992.

COLOPHON

Lincoln and the Illinois Supreme Court was designed and typeset by Muriel Underwood on a Macintosh desktop system. The typeface is Monotype Columbus and is printed, from a laser printout, on acid-free 60 lb. Lakewood Natural. It is bound in Holliston Roxite bookcloth. Printing and binding was by Bookcrafters, Chelsea, Michigan.

This first edition is limited to 1000 copies.